LET US BLESS THE LORD

THE LORD YEAR ONE

LET US BLESS THE LORD YEAR ONE

Meditations on the Daily Office

EASTER THROUGH PENTECOST

Volume 2

Barbara Cawthorne Crafton

MOREHOUSE PUBLISHING
A Continuum imprint
HARRISBURG • LONDON • NEW YORK

Morehouse Publishing, P.O. Box 1321, Harrisburg, PA 17105

Morehouse Publishing, The Tower Building, 11 York Road, London SE1 7NX

Morehouse Publishing is a Continuum imprint.

Unless otherwise indicated, biblical quotations are from the New Revised Standard Version Bible, copyright 1989, Division of Christian Education of the National Council of the Churches of Christ in the United States of America. Used by permission. All rights reserved.

Cover art: Mark Cassino/SuperStock

Cover design: Laurie Westhafer

Library of Congress Cataloging-in-Publication Data

Crafton, Barbara Cawthorne.
    Let us bless the Lord. Year one : meditations on the Daily Office / Barbara Cawthorne Crafton.
        p.   cm.
    ISBN 0-8192-1982-7 (hardcover)
    1. Devotional calendars—Episcopal Church. 2. Bible—Meditations.
3. Divine office. 4. Episcopal Church—Prayer-books and devotions—English.
I. Title.
BV4812.C73   2004
242'.3—dc22

                                                        2004006016

Printed in the United States of America

05 06 07 08 09 10   10 9 8 7 6 5 4 3 2 1

CONTENTS

FOREWORD

Any time after four in the morning and anytime after four in the afternoon. That's my rule for Morning and Evening Prayer. Any earlier, and it isn't really morning. Or evening.

Among the best places to say the Office is on a train. Though not quiet, a train is anonymous. No one is likely to bother me. And there are always plenty of people for whom to pray.

Some places and times are more intercessory than others. Cheek by jowl with all manner of fellow humans in a subway car, you experience them with an intimacy upon which you did not plan and may not even desire. You have a choice about how you will respond to such closeness: you can resent them, or you can consider loving them. Prayer is a way of loving them.

They all come from somewhere. Often you can tell where: from work, from school, from shopping. Some of them are old: you imagine the years they must have spent riding the trains, the wooden seats and floors on the trains when they were young, the way New York must have been. Some of them are children: you ponder how hard a world it is into which they have come, the temptations they face that you did not have when you were young. They are different from the way you were. You remember old people saying that when you were a kid.

Some of your fellow passengers belong to a race other than yours. You realize for the thousandth time how much an accident of birth determines: some people come into the world with an advantage, before they've even done anything. Some of them grew up learning to fear or suspect people with skin the color of yours. Maybe you grew up learning something like that, too.

Some of them are cops. You can't tell which ones. They carry pistols. You pray that they will not have to use them today. You pray that they will never have to use them.

And some of them are thieves. They're keeping a sharp eye out for the cops, and for you, too, looking to see if you're careless with your bag or carry your wallet in the wrong place. You wonder how long they've been on the wrong side of the law. You remember that a thief was the first person Christ welcomed into paradise. The next stop is yours.

Let us bless the Lord.

Easter

EASTER DAY

Pss 148, 149, 150 * 113, 114, or 118
Exodus 12:1–14 * Isaiah 51:9–11
John 1:1–18 * Luke 24:13–35

Was it not necessary that the Messiah should suffer
these things and then enter into his glory?
LUKE 24:26

When Jesus says this to his friends, it's before they have realized who he is. As far as they're concerned, he's just another Jew walking along the same road they're walking along.

Later on, they tell each other that they were convinced by his argument. "Did not our hearts burn within us while he was talking to us on the road?" Well, apparently they didn't. Not enough so that they understood who it was with whom they spoke.

Once you know who has won, you strive earnestly to establish yourself as always having been in his corner. As soon as they know Jesus has risen, they pretend they've always believed it. That they've always had faith. But we know they didn't. They were depressed and fearful, completely at loose ends. They were a mess. They didn't know what to believe in any more.

And Jesus wasn't exactly as he had been. That much is clear. Something was different—we don't know what, but more than one person encountered him and didn't get it. My own imagination utterly fails me in this regard: I can dream up a lot of things, but I can't imagine what the encounter with the Risen Christ was like.

Unless. Unless. Unless it was like my encounter with him. And the more I think about it, the more I think it must have been. The senses don't produce its evidences. The mind certainly doesn't—it makes no sense for someone to have been raised from death. The experience they had is the same one I have—and they, like me, had to come to terms with it on their own, each in his or her own way.

Did not our hearts burn? Nope. Not right away. Maybe not for a while. For some people, it takes years.

MONDAY IN EASTER WEEK

Pss 93, 98 * 66
Jonah 2:1–9
Acts 2:14, 22–32
John 14:1–14

In my Fathers' house there are many dwelling places...
JOHN 14:2

Besides the numerical generosity of heaven's welcome, the "many rooms" speak of a diversity that begins here on earth and does not end in the kingdom of God. Renaissance paintings of the Last Judgment usually homogenize the righteous, dressing them identically in white robes, posing them identically in orderly rows, shaping their mouths in identical round Os, as they sing their endless song of praise.

I almost wrote "interminable." Because heaven sounds awfully boring, if that's what it's like.

Would the God who made such a riot of color and shape and sound and smell down here really want such dread symmetry up there? That birds and fish and spaniels should all have been intended to be different, but people were intended to be the same? Isn't it more likely that variety and complexity is contained in heaven, rather than refined away?

It is probably a mistake to attribute our own unease with difference to our creator. We like the familiar: people like us, food we know, our own music, or own styles. From this affinity, we step easily into the heresy that God, too, really prefers our kind.

Are you different from first-century Christians? Of course you are. From African Christians? Yes. From your identical twin, even? Yes. We each have a journey and a destination and they shape each of us. All that we are here is also there, recognizable but redeemed.

This is enough. Not everything is resolved in heaven. Our dissonances remain. The great difference between here and there is that they are no longer ugly. They have become lovely. In glory.

TUESDAY IN EASTER WEEK

Pss 103 * 111, 114
Isaiah 30:18–21
Acts 2:36–41 (42–47)
John 14:15–31

All who believed were together and had all things in common . . .
ACTS 2:44

So the sanctity of private property isn't part of Christianity. The earliest Christians were communists: from each according to his ability and to each according to his need.

Or were they? The writer of Acts reports this as if it were already a thing of the past. *They held everything in common then,* he writes, to a community in which that is no longer the case. Maybe it didn't work any better in first-century Palestine than it does today. People probably needed personal incentive to work; one more pointed than the general good, even then.

But that is not to say that private ownership of the world's resources represents a religious tenet, either, as many apologists for vast private wealth have believed. It's not necessarily true that I am rich because God favors me. I may be rich because I'm willing to overlook the needs of poor people who live far away, people I don't have to behold on a daily basis. Like any other gift, wealth is morally neutral: it can be put to good or evil use, it can be attained by good or evil means. No sanctity inheres in it. Rich or poor, our sanctity or lack of it is an open issue for each of us.

Rather than a socialist recipe for the ages, this description of economic life among the earliest Christians is intended to show us that they were profoundly changed. Nothing in their lives was untouched by their new life in Christ. The most mundane aspect of human life was subject to redemption.

As it is today. Maybe you won't quit your job or give away all your CDs. But your attitude toward those things can and will be redeemed, as you grow closer to God through a life with Christ as its constant friend. We come to resemble those with whom we associate. Live with Christ, and nothing you touch will be as it was before.

WEDNESDAY IN EASTER WEEK

Pss 97, 99 * 115
Micah 7:7–15
Acts 3:1–10
John 15:1–11

"I have no silver or gold, but what I have I give you . . ."
ACTS 3:6

The other trustees look so much richer than I am. *Why am I here?* The development committee chair is giving his report, and the board gifts line item is, as always, not what it should be. One hundred percent board participation is what every organization needs. Don't serve on a board if you're not able to contribute to it.

My own donations are small change compared to those of my colleagues, even now that I have tripled it. My gift of myself is small, too: many of them bring decades of crackerjack business experience to their work. I'm a terrible business person. There are so many aspects of it I don't grasp. And so many things that require nerves of steel, not the nerves of oatmeal I possess.

But Peter and John didn't have any money, either. And their nerves were of something other than steel, too, judging by their conduct on Good Friday. They are two very ordinary men, called to extraordinary things.

The gift they bring in this story is the gift of healing. But they seem also to have brought the lame man another gift before giving that one: the gift of honesty. Look at us, Peter said to the man, who had been sitting on the same patch of the same pavement for decades. Pay attention. Something new can happen, if you pay attention. Something completely unexpected. Do you want it as much as you say you do?

THURSDAY IN EASTER WEEK

Pss 146, 147 * 148, 149
Ezekiel 37:1–14
Acts 3:11–26
John 15:12–27

"Mortal, can these bones live?"
EZEKIEL 37:3

Some setbacks in life are so profound that they feel like death. I called him as soon as I heard. He was in disgrace, incredibly so: stripped of his position, perhaps even of his orders. Everyone was talking about it. The misdeed that brought about his humiliation was a grave one, too grave to overlook. He was finished.

The day of our date arrived, and there was an unsurprising message on my answering machine. He wouldn't be able to make it today. I called him back. *Let's wait a while,* he said. *Okay.* I knew we would never have lunch. And we never did.

His life and career were dry bones. A gifted ministry dead, dry as dust. I hope there was some other friend, one whose overtures he could accept. But I think there may not have been. I think he may have chosen to be alone. I think the isolation of death may have been what he craved. Life was such a mess. Don't bother me. I'm dead now.

But he is the same gifted man he was before his sin was revealed. Every good thing he ever did is still good, no matter what bad things he may also have done. This is true of every one of us. None of us can be understood solely in terms of the worst things we've ever done. Death may end our lives, but it doesn't cancel them.

And he yet may rise again. He isn't really dead yet. In the rubble of his repentance may lie his resurrection, waiting to reveal itself.

FRIDAY IN EASTER WEEK

Pss 136 * 118
Daniel 12:1–4, 13
Acts 4:1–12
John 16:1–15

There shall be a time of anguish, such as has never occurred since nations first came into existence.
DANIEL 12:1

O*h, beautiful for spacious skies,* we sing on the anniversary of the bombing. *For amber waves of grain. . . .* A song about the land, and about the dream of America. About the grace of God, spread over us as gently as a coverlet over a sleeping baby.

We think of our country by thinking of ourselves: our parents, our children, our towns. The natural beauty of the landscape. But the nations in scripture aren't so much about geography and people as they are about political and religious divisions. The nations are entities of partition, ways in which people group themselves: toward their *confreres,* to be sure, but also away from those who are outside their experience.

So a nation is, almost by definition, artificial.

Affinity for the familiar is natural. People who look and act and dress like me—that makes me comfortable. We savor the us-ness of us. It's a short step, and one often taken, to the shadow side of this delightful us-ness. If it is good to be us, it must be bad to be someone else.

How childish.

SATURDAY IN EASTER WEEK

Pss 145 * 104
Isaiah 25:1–9
Acts 4:13–21 (22–31)
John 16:16–33

*Now when they saw the boldness of Peter and John and realized
that they were uneducated and ordinary men, they were
amazed and recognized them as companions of Jesus.*
ACTS 4:13

The ordination process in the Episcopal Church is rigorous—many discernment committees, many individual interviews, background checks, psychological tests, many examinations, three years of seminary after four years of university. We want only the best.

The first people who did this work, of course, were illiterate fishermen who had no diplomas, had never taken a test and had never been to school. Awestruck by credentials and strings of initials after people's names, we have a hard time wrapping our minds around this fact.

And we don't apply it to today, either. We are apt to think that God can't raise up someone who has not been through our certification process. That was okay then, we say, but now is different. You can't function today without credentials.

Maybe not in the institution. But God's hands aren't tied by the same things that tie our hands. God can call whomever he wants to, to whatever he wishes, and we're not in charge of that. All the credentials we have developed are valuable only because they represent a certain kind of experience: you've studied, you've interned, you've put in the time. A person may have done all those things and carried nothing away from the experience besides the ability to take tests and interview well. It happens now and then, with disastrous results: this is no line of work for those not called to it.

In the end, call is about call. The qualifications for the response to call—the schooling, the hospital work, the tests—come afterward. The first thing that happens is the voice of the Savior: *Follow me.*

EASTER II

Psalms 146, 147 * 111, 112, 113
Isaiah 43:8–13
1 Peter 2:2–10
John 14:1–7

"I am the way, and the truth, and the life. No one
comes to the Father except through me."
JOHN 14:6

Beloved of some Christians, troublesome for others, this passage. When we read this, are we saying that people who aren't Christians aren't going to heaven? Gloating over their exclusion? Some people are so uncomfortable with it that they stop midway through it in a public reading: *I am the way and the truth and the life*, they read. *Thanks be to God.* Then they sit down.

But maybe we can look at it in a different way. We might begin, for example, by gently closing the door on the idea of heaven as a place you go for good behavior during the fourscore-and-ten you enjoy here on earth. It's not a place. There is no *there*. God is spirit, and needs no place to live: people with bodies need places, and God is spirit. No body. That's why the Incarnation had to happen, why God had to *put on* flesh—God doesn't have a body. That we call God a king is a legacy of our past, from the composition of scriptures in societies that had kings. Kingship and reign are half-steps to the truth about God, and they do not reach God. They are human approximations. *We* may have crowned Christ with many crowns, but the only crown *he* wore on earth was a crown of thorns.

And it is that crown with which this passage is concerned. Jesus comes close to us by living our lives. He seeks out those who do not care any more, those who do clear wrong, those whom society shuns, and he sits with them. He dies the death some of them deserve, by the standards of their time. He dies our death. Many early heresies in the Church tried to make the case for his death having been not real somehow, his humiliation not complete. Nope. It was real. It was complete. Utter humiliation.

So that we will know that not our humiliation, not our weakness, not anything that can beat us down can separate from us Christ. That God remains steadfast through a Jesus who never leaves us. That this is true of absolutely everybody. You don't believe in Christ? That doesn't stop him from believing in you.

No one comes to God without leaving behind the life of this world, however beautiful or however savage it may be—and it is both. We awaken in this life to its sanctity, amid all its sorrow and squalor, or we do not. If we do not see it here, we see it there—in that *there* that is not a place, or a time, or anything like our life here.

How strange. But it is true. We either know it now or we don't. Some of us are on our way to knowing it. And one day, we all will.

MONDAY IN EASTER II

Pss 1, 2, 3 * 4, 7
Daniel 1:1–21
1 John 1:1–10
John 17:1–11

*If we say that we have no sin, we deceive
ourselves, and the truth is not in us.*
1 JOHN 1:8

Imagine what the world would be like if people just came out and admitted it when they did something wrong. It would be a very different place.

For one thing, we'd suddenly all know a lot about forgiveness. We'd be granting it—or not granting it—dozens of times each day. We'd probably learn very quickly that granting forgiveness is the wiser course, since you never know when you might stand in need of some yourself.

We hardly ever do admit it, though. Every crooked politician, every embezzling CEO, every common murderer dumb enough to get caught looks us straight in the camera and tells us he's deeply hurt and angry at being so unjustly accused, that he's completely confident that the facts will quickly exonerate him. Or he doesn't say anything, and his lawyer does all the talking, shocked—*shocked!*—that anybody could so misunderstand his client as to intimate that he is anything but a second Francis of Assisi. Their protestations have made us cynical: we assume every accused must be guilty, and that it is only matter of time until we find out precisely how. We think every politician is crooked, and that the ones who appear not to be are just great actors. And the grieving spouse of a murder victim who is found at home is always, always, always the prime suspect.

Think of it: the truth, immediately. Never an ounce of energy spent in covering up anything. Knowing immediately where we stand with one another. Having all the facts out before us, so we could make up our minds about how we want to live.

God has all the facts. Knows all the secrets. God knows whodunit, and God also knows why. Of all the people we may think we have to hide the truth from, the one we cannot avoid is God. God already knows. And loves us anyway.

TUESDAY IN EASTER II

Pss 5, 6 * 10, 11
Daniel 2:1–16
1 John 2:1–11
John 17:12–19

The king answered the Chaldeans, "This is a public decree: if you do not tell me both the dream and its interpretation, you shall be torn limb from limb, and your houses shall be laid in ruins. But if you do tell me the dream and its interpretation, you shall receive from me gifts and rewards and great honor."

DANIEL 2:5–6

The Daily Office prescribes what amounts to biblical soap operas for many of the morning readings. It's a way of easing us into what we are apt to consider an ungodly hour of the day—not a good frame of mind in which to begin prayer—and help us stay awake, not mind too much having had to get out of bed. We want to see what will happen. Usually, we're left with some kind of cliff-hanger, like today's: the king has just ordered every wise man in the realm executed because a few unfortunate Chaldean seers were not able both to tell him what his dream was *and* to interpret it. We tune out for the day just as Daniel says *he'll* do it, and we're left to wonder how he will do it until tomorrow.

Folk tales are full of heroes performing impossible tasks. Impossible tasks kings set them, usually, or else a capricious witch or god. They solve it and they get a reward: a princess, maybe, or a prestigious job, like Pharaoh gave Joseph.

To have your hero victorious, though, you must have other characters who fail. Otherwise, there's no story. The Bible is full of them. Nobody seems able to kill Goliath until David comes along with his slingshot. The priests of Baal can't summon fire from heaven, as Elisha can. Nobody can defeat Holofernes until Judith hammers a peg into his temple as he sleeps; I imagine that would about do it for anybody. Those of us who can't accomplish things in the normal way and don't know any *other* way are the also-rans: we're *in* the stories, but only as foils for the superhero. Our role is to make him look good.

In our imagination of the superman, he performs his feats in our stead. We love stories about people going outside the system and overturning it. We dream, all of us, of being super in some way, of living a life unbound by the things that bind us all. Dream of flying. Dream of impossible and even improper loves, dream that they're somehow all right—dreams so real we awaken embarrassed. These ancient tales upend all our limitations.

People who do not believe think that our faith in Christ is just like this: a tale about a superhero who overturns the rules while everyone else must abide by them. That the most important thing about Jesus is that he rose from the dead. But that's not the most important thing. The superhero may use his power for the good of others, but he doesn't share it. He remains *super*, worlds apart from those he serves and from those he defeats.

Our Lord is different. God became mortal, St. Athanasius said, so that mortals might become God. Jesus is about *our* deliverance from death, not just his own, and about *our* availability to heal, not just his. It isn't the feat that makes us believe. It's the gift.

WEDNESDAY IN EASTER II

Pss 119:1–24 * 12, 13, 14
Daniel 2:17–30
1 John 2:12–17
John 17:20–26

*. . . so that the love with which you
have loved me may be in them . . .*
JOHN 17:26

I can't wait to get home from church so I can crawl into bed. Odd—I went to bed early last night and slept well. Nevertheless, I fall instantly into a three-hour nap.

I am so cold. I have clothes and a sweater and a down comforter and I'm still cold. I take my temperature. It's below normal—how can that be? And another thing—I ache in every bone of my body.

All this whining signifies the flu or one of its cousins, I suppose. It is a fairly light week ahead, and today is an extraordinarily light Sunday. So I can rest and drink plenty of liquids, as they say one should with the flu.

There was a time when I would have prided myself on my ability to soldier on in spite of it. When I wouldn't have yielded to my longing for a nap. I would have presented my drained self at my own door after a fourteen-hour day and been impatient with myself because I didn't feel well. I would not have thought about the effect on others of my being out and about in the company of a contagious disease.

I don't know what happened to that woman. Haven't seen her in several years. Good riddance, I say.

I was an obligation junkie in those days. Accumulated duties and buried myself in them. I still have that tendency, and it needs to be monitored carefully. But the obligation to keep one's germs away from other people seemed to escape me. This was an important clue: my dutifulness was not only about being a fine human being. It was also about being an addict. I wasn't just in it for them. I was in it for me. The egocentric image I had of myself as a heroine—one that I never would have acknowledged as mine, not in a million years—was at least as important to me as any good I was doing other people.

"Secondary gains" is what they call this in the psychology biz. The secret other reasons why we do what we say we're doing from unimpeachable motives. Few human actions are pure. Almost all of them are mixed. It takes guts to look honestly at our motives—all of them, I mean, not just the pretty ones. We conceal them from ourselves, as well as from others.

But we don't conceal them from God. *Give yourself a break*, God says. *Do you think I can't see you from here? Come on and let's start again.*

THURSDAY IN EASTER II

Pss 18:1–20 * 18:21–50
Daniel 2:31–49
1 John 2:18–29
Luke 3:1–14

In the fifteenth year of the reign of Emperor Tiberius . . .
LUKE 3:1

It was the day after President Reagan died. Poor man—his end was a sad one, the famous wit and charm snuffed out by Alzheimer's disease long before his body was ready to call it quits.

We sat in a beautiful open-air chapel in the mountain country of Arkansas and thought about mortality. The mountains are so old. Life on earth is so old, so much older than any of us; we are just a moment in the life of the earth, our bloom so brief. Look at the leaves everywhere, so beautiful and green. Their green changes throughout their lives: it is a piercing, light green when they are new, startling against the black of the trees upon which they grow. And it deepens as they mature: their tops become a different color from their undersides, and a different texture, too: tougher, with a thicker skin, able to withstand the impact of wind and rain. The underside remains paler, more delicate, more fragile. The veins of the leaf, invisible to our eyes when it was tiny, begin to be more defined, so that we can see the circulatory system of the leaf. In late summer, the leaf is broad and dark green, the darkest green of its life, its veins gnarly like the veins of our hands as we get older. And then, right before it is time to die, a brilliant farewell: *Good-bye!* they sing, *Good-bye!* It was wonderful being alive. We loved being here. Here is some red fire, the brilliant fire of our dying, so that you will never forget. But the fire of them fades, and they turn brown and small, wrinkled, and they lie in layers on the ground. Maybe we rake them up. Maybe we're smarter and we don't, just let them nourish the next year's growth of trees coming up from the rich earth.

They don't last long. We last a little longer—but not much, in the scheme of things. We mark our brief times here with the events in them. Let's see, I will say, when I try to remember writing these words, it must have been right when President Reagan died, because I mention it in the essay. Let's see, we say, thinking back, it must have been before my mother died, because she was there. Let's see, we say, it must have been during the war, because we still had those dark green shades up in all the windows.

Let's see, when was that? We mark the spiritual with the temporal. But the spiritual isn't trapped by anything temporal: God goes on and on, and we go on with God. Does it make us sad, this ephemerality? A little. For a while. But then we remember what else is true: this earth is indeed passing away, but this earth isn't all there is. Not at all. We are just at the beginning of our adventure.

FRIDAY IN EASTER II

Pss 16, 17 * 134, 135
Daniel 3:1–18
1 John 3:1–10
Luke 3:15–22

*Whoever does not fall down and worship shall
immediately be thrown into a furnace of blazing fire.*
DANIEL 3:6

It had been a long time since I was at a campfire with other girls.
The girls I was with, of course, weren't really girls any more: the
oldest among us was certainly close to eighty, and most of us were
in our fifties.

We sang songs. Some of them were the songs I remembered from
years ago, but others were new. Somebody roasted a marshmallow
and made a s'more for me: a toasted marshmallow oozing between
two graham crackers, topping a square of chocolate. Unbearably
sweet—there was a time when I couldn't have conceived of anything
being too sweet, but now I had a hard time finishing the s'more.

People told stories, stories about their mothers, about when they
came to this camp as young girls. I told a funny story about a friend
of mine from New Jersey, and taught them a funny song about New
Jersey that I sometimes teach audiences when I travel.

All the while, the fire blazed in the center of our circle. We loved
it as the woods around us grew dark, felt the fire as if it were love,
protecting us from evil: people have sat around these fires ever since
there have been people, gathering warmth and courage, telling stories, singing. The tales we have in scripture were first told around
fires such as these, most of them—only later were they written down
in books. They were campfire tales first.

The flames licked the logs and destroyed them. But we were not
destroyed by the fire; we managed its power that night, and it was not
deadly. We put on more logs, gazed at the fire, and sang in the dark.

SATURDAY IN EASTER II

Pss 20, 21:1–7 (8–14) * 110:1–5 (6–7), 116, 117
Daniel 3:19–30
1 John 3:11–18
Luke 4:1–13

*Then Nebuchadnezzar was so filled with rage against Shadrach,
Meshach, and Abednego that his face was distorted.*
DANIEL 3:19

An anger so bitter that it is akin to murder—we know more about such an anger than we wish we did. An anger so bitter it cuts off prayer—not just prayer about the person in question, but any prayer at all. It is like cancer, metastasizing throughout the soul like a tumor metastasizes throughout the body, claiming more and more precious space, until there isn't enough room for life itself. Too serious for surgery, this anger. You can't get rid of it by yourself; it's too entwined with who you are. You'd bleed to death.

So you turn to a very specific kind of prayer. A prayer that does not descend into the pit of your anger, but calls it up out of you, a little bit at a time. A prayer that steadfastly refuses to be sucked into its venom: just the name, please, of the one with whom you are angry. Just the name, every time you pray, no matter what the occasion: from "Now I lay me down to sleep" to the prayers of the Holy Eucharist to grace before meals to "Oh, God, I hope I get it." Always, always, without fail: add the name of the one with whom you are bitterly angry, and then nothing more. Not a word. No false blessings, no attempts at a Christian charity you do not yet possess. Just the name.

Do this for a while, and you build up your soul's immune system. You have had an allergic reaction to your foe, all this time. He has functioned within your soul as an allergen, taking everything over. But letting him in little by little in this way, carefully limiting the damage he can do within you, brings him down to his actual size, shows you who he really is. He's not a monster. He's not just his offense against you. His whole life is not about what he did to you. He's a person. That's all.

This kind of prayer will change you. It will also change him, in ways you can't begin to guess, and neither can I. And who knows what else it will change? Though usually quite subtle, prayer is mighty. So get ready: pray this way and your life is sure to change.

EASTER III

Pss 148, 149, 150 * 114, 115
Daniel 4:1–18
1 Peter 4:7–11
John 21:15–25

But there are also many other things that Jesus did; if every one of them were written down, I suppose that the world itself could not contain the books that would be written.
JOHN 21:25

There is something touching about the last hyperbolic lines of this fourth and most mysterious of the gospels. Words fail the writer, in the end: he is all written out, empty of any power to write more. And yet there is much more. More than anyone can say. More than there is time and strength to write. *You're just going to have to take my word for it.*

Here is the order in which the Church recorded the life of Christ: the Passion narratives were written first. The very earliest of them did not include material about the Resurrection. Collections of sayings and ethical teachings were added next. The beloved birth narratives and miracle stories were the last to appear, together with expanded explanations of some of the parables.

Each of these different kinds of writings brings us a different Jesus—just as the various people who know you, if they were all called together in a room to write the story of your life, would each bring a different version of you to the project. No single version would suffice. We would need them all to get a complete picture. And even then, it would not be complete.

Your own version of yourself would be missing. We do not have Jesus' version of himself in any of these four books. Nothing he wrote is here. We are not aware of his having written anything.

The Jesus we have from scripture came from the community. *Take our word for it.* They themselves, perhaps, are his version. And we are, too. Christ continues to show himself, and our community of faith is one of the ways of his showing. For better or worse, people see him when they see us.

So we should be careful how we treat each other. How we look. What people see when they see us. We are not alone.

MONDAY IN EASTER III

Pss 25 * 9, 15
Daniel 4:19–27
1 John 3:19–4:6
Luke 4:14–30

Daniel . . . was severely distressed for a while.
His thoughts terrified him.
DANIEL 4:19

Daniel has the ill fortune of being the possessor of bad news for a powerful person. And this is very bad news indeed: the king is about to go crazy for a spell, wandering around outside like a wild animal. How does a communications professional *put* this, exactly? People have been killed for less.

Somehow, though, everybody gets through it. The king survives his wilderness experience and is even the better for it: more humble, less apt to mistake himself for God. What he refused to do in response to an invitation he manages to do when he has no other choice. One way or another, he gets the point.

You don't know things will work out well in advance of something like this, though. Not if you're Daniel. All you know is that you have bad news for your boss, and that your boss hates bad news.

Will you tell a truth even if it's dangerous? Can you pay the price candor sometimes exacts? Serving a superior well sometimes means telling him what he doesn't want to hear. Bringing her some bad news.

And so we try to cushion the blow. We begin to second-guess our news. To package it, try to find ways of making it easier and more palatable. But it's a big mistake to stop short of relaying the entire truth. Truth has power. Ignore it and it might come back to bite you later on.

TUESDAY IN EASTER III

Pss 26, 28 * 36, 39
Daniel 4:28–37
1 John 4:7–21
Luke 4:31–37

In this is love, not that we loved God but that he loved us . . .
1 JOHN 4:10

Is the love of God our love for God? Or it is God's love for us? Do you love God? Do you love God more than you love your children, your wife? *No*, you say to yourself. *I can't say that I do. I didn't know we had to choose.*

We don't have to choose. God doesn't send beloved people into our lives as some kind of test or trap, to rip them away from us later if we grow too attached to them.

I know a man who thought that's what God did. He lost his only child, a grown son, to a sudden and devastating viral illness. He and his son were best friends. His son had been the answer to prayer. Bob and his wife had even gone to Lourdes in their longing to conceive, and then there he was. A beautiful boy, who grew to be a fine young man. He was the light of their lives.

Bob believed that his boy died because Bob loved him too much. Loved him more than he loved God. That God became jealous of this, I guess, and took him away.

That may be where "the love of God" leads, if it means my love for God. Maybe we're better off focusing on God's love for us.

God's love causes us to be. It sustains us. It teaches us, comforts us, invites love to kindle in us, too, love that reflects it, love that isn't crazy or possessive or jealous. Love through which we see everything we have, beautiful and full of light and a gift of God, for however long we have it.

WEDNESDAY IN EASTER III

Pss 38 * 119:25–48
Daniel 5:1–12
1 John 5:1–12
Luke 4:38–44

Under the influence of the wine, Belshazzar commanded that they bring in the vessels of gold and silver that his father Nebuchadnezzar had taken out of the temple in Jerusalem, so that the king and his lords, his wives, and his concubines might drink from them.

DANIEL 5:2

I *got that at a flea market. Sometimes you'll see one sold by an antique dealer as a "Victorian candy dish,"* Lloyd said, as I admired a gleaming silver baptismal shell. *They don't know what they really are.*

The little dish with a shell handle could hold candy: mints, maybe, or little chocolates. Jelly beans at Easter. Mixed nuts, maybe, for somebody's bridge party.

A censer hangs from its chain in a secondhand shop: heavy brass, in need of a polish. You could put a tea light in it, I guess, and the light would shine through the holes in the side from which fragrant smoke used to escape the hot coals. Hang it in a window, maybe. That would be pretty.

"Embroidered handkerchiefs, 2 for $1" read a sign at a rummage sale. Some of the scraps of white linen were ladies' handkerchiefs. But two of them were purificators, with white crosses embroidered on one end. They didn't know what they were. Just handkerchiefs with crosses on them, they thought. Why not? I bought them, a rescue.

I saw an oak wall tablet in a bar once. It listed the monetary gifts of families to a building project in an English church. It hung on the wall in the bar, as it had once hung on the wall in the church to which all those faithful people went each Sunday. They had old wooden oars, hanging on the wall, too, and an old bicycle, and lots of old photographs of sports teams from a hundred years ago. You could use a paten as a little tray for calling cards, I suppose. Or, if it were more bowl-shaped, for forcing bulbs. If you didn't know what it was.

But if you did know, you never would.

THURSDAY IN EASTER III

Pss 37:1–18 * 37:19–42
Daniel 5:13–30
1 John 5:13–20 (21)
Luke 5:1–11

"Put out into the deep water and let down your nets for a catch."

LUKE 5:4

To begin with, Jesus is not a fisherman. As far as we know, he is probably a carpenter, like his dad. So his friends might not immediately be disposed to take his word for it in matters relating to fish.

Peter and his colleagues *are* fishermen, and they've been fishing all night with nothing to show for it. Giving up is beginning to look like a good idea, especially since they've taken a break already while Jesus preached a sermon from one of their boats. Tomorrow is another day. But they do what he says, and their catch is so sudden and so huge that it almost overwhelms their preparedness.

You think you're ready for what God does, but sometimes you're not. You think you can handle what you pray for, but sometimes you're unprepared. Sometimes you've gotten used to not having it and stop expecting it. Then success ambushes you, and you almost wish it hadn't.

Lots of fish come closer to the shore in the evening: the water temperature is lower then, and there's always more food nearer the shore anyway. Then in the morning, they head back out to the relative safety of the deeper waters: larger predators, perhaps, but then there is more room to get away from them.

People are more catchable in the deeper waters, too. Keep things light enough and none of us experience our need of God. It's when the going gets tough that we remember, that we feel our weakness and long for strength. Every life puts out for the deeper waters sooner or later, whether we want to or not. We don't stay in the shallows.

FRIDAY IN EASTER III

Pss 105:1–22 * 105:23–45
Daniel 6:1–15
2 John 1–13
Luke 5:12–26

"Know, O king, that it is a law of the Medes and Persians that no interdict or ordinance that the king establishes can be changed."
DANIEL 6:15

Not even, apparently, by the king himself. The Pont du Gard in the south of France is an engineering marvel: miles of aqueduct, tilted just enough to keep water running through it to supply a city far away from the water's source. Its golden stone is the ground note in the color feast of Provence, a stone that warms the heart. It is enormous, the aqueduct, and amazing: most amazing of all because it was built so long ago. Such skill those people possessed.

On the sides of its pylons, certain stones jut out at intervals. They are not the same length as their neighbors. A mistake? An error? *Well, let's use this one anyway, even if it is the wrong length. We're behind schedule already, and we can't afford to waste a stone.*

No, those stones of a different length are not mistakes. They are steps. They were placed there so that workmen in the future would be able to climb easily up the sides and repair the Pont du Gard. Alter its incline perhaps, or even adjust its route. These ancient engineers didn't think their work should stand immutable for all time. They expected it to need adjusting and repair.

Plan for things to change. Don't think that something that works in one era must be imported unchanged into another. Don't think it's disloyal to the past to build upon it. The past is tough. It expects to be the basis for history, and history only moves forward.

SATURDAY IN EASTER III

Pss 30, 32 * 42, 43
Daniel 6:16–28
3 John 1–15
Luke 5:27–39

Then Levi gave a great banquet for him in his house;
and there was a large crowd of tax collectors
and others sitting at the table with them.
LUKE 5:29

Luke calls him Levi; Matthew calls him Matthew. Most people assume it's the same tax collector, since the description of the party that follows the call is the same.

Almost the same. Luke tells us that Levi *threw* the party, that it was a great banquet. One pictures a corporate dinner of some kind. That he was thrilled, as we can imagine, by being tapped by a celebrity, and wanted to introduce Jesus to his world of the power people in Jerusalem. That Levi was flattered to think of himself as the "go to" guy.

In Matthew's account, people just dropped over while Jesus was having dinner with the tax collector. It wasn't a banquet in his honor. It may have been a crowd, before the night was over, but it wasn't a power occasion.

We know that the position of tax collector was an ambiguous one in Israel. A collaborator with the occupying government. A prosperous person, as a result of that collaboration, more than able to put on a good party. That's the problem with evangelizing the rich—they give such good parties. It can turn a person's head. Spend enough time at a person's fine dinner table, and it becomes harder and harder to tell him the truth.

Levi/Matthew thought he was introducing Jesus to Jerusalem society. But soon he was living a very different life himself, a disciple of the Lord, wandering with him throughout the countryside. Not collecting taxes. Not collecting much of anything. And soon he would be in big trouble with the government he used to serve. And eventually, like all the rest of them, he would be killed.

Open your life to God and your life will be changed. You don't always get to say how.

It seems, initially, as if everything is your idea. Later on, you're not so sure. Maybe you didn't find God. Maybe God found you.

EASTER IV

Pss 63:1–8 (9–11), 98 * 103
Wisdom 1:1–15
1 Peter 5:1–11
Matthew 7:15–29

*Do not invite death by the error of your life, or bring on destruction
by the works of your hands; because God did not make death, and
he does not delight in the death of the living. For he created all
things that they might exist; the generative forces of the world are
wholesome, and there is no destructive poison in them . . .*
WISDOM 1:12–14

Now the generative power of the earth is in glorious evidence:
flowers, leaves, the beginnings of fruit in some places.

Now the smell of the earth's bloom is upon us, even in the city.
Pass a flower stand, and the hyacinths pluck at your sleeve with their
sweet scent. Then the lilacs, even sweeter. And daffodils wind in and
out among the trees in the big parks, stand bravely up in wooden
box planters in the small ones—part of the enormous donation of
daffodils to New York City parks that the Netherlands made in
memory of the bombing. Every spring, more and more beauty. To
remember and honor the lost.

Life returns again and again, even returns to help us remember
the time when death came much too close to many of us, when it
reached out a bony hand and took some of us away. Seeing life
makes us glad to be alive. Makes us want to live. Live well.

But seeing death sometimes makes us want to die. Makes us cling
to things that deal death to us. Amid the verdant smells of the garden and the flower stand, pockets of forlorn people stand outside
the doors of office buildings. Plumes of smoke emanate from them.
Tarry death snakes down their throats and into their lungs, blacken-
ing everything in its path. They can't smell food, or flowers, or even
themselves. They don't know that their houses and apartments are
sepia-colored, just a little bit, everything in them. They remove a

picture from the wall and look at the rectangle of clean original paint where it was, framed by the brown of something that they have also taken into themselves. I've got to stop, they think. But I can't.

But you can. You can start this minute. It is spring. It is the time of life, not the time of death. Go outside and breathe deeply. Don't take your cigarettes with you. Search the sky, look at the ground bringing forth its store of life. You can find Someone to help you.

MONDAY IN EASTER IV

Pss 41, 52 * 44
Wisdom 1:16–2:11, 21–24
Colossians 1:1–14
Luke 6:1–11

"Come and stand here."
LUKE 6:8

The fiction was that Jesus did not respect the Sabbath and that he was, therefore, a dangerous person. And there was some truth to the charge—Sabbath observance wasn't high on his list. If you were hungry, you needed to eat. If you didn't have any food, it was perfectly all right to get some. Let common sense prevail, for heaven's sake.

He knew that the scribes and Pharisees were watching him closely to see what he would do when he encountered a man with a withered hand. And so the healing he performed was a careful one. No Sabbath law was broken. "Come and stand here." No law against walking a few steps and standing still. Then a few words directed at the onlookers, some teaching words. Then "Stretch out your hand." No law against that, either. Nobody did any work here but God.

It didn't matter, though; his enemies were angry anyway. Angier than before, even, because they'd been tricked and made to look foolish. Angry, also, because they were frightened at Jesus' power to heal. Some people respond to fear with aggression. You feel a sense of control if you can feel your own aggression. Stronger. Maybe not able to heal, but more than able to destroy.

Did a casual attitude toward Sabbath observance make Jesus dangerous? No. But other things did. Power doesn't want to hear about its own ephemeral nature. It prefers the illusion of its own permanence. It arranges and rearranges the furniture of its authority in a hundred different ways—anything to hide from the fact that everything is passing away. Those in power want to keep it, and Jesus represents a significant threat to every power on earth, just by telling the truth about it. *It is disappearing*, he reminds us. *Don't count on it. Everything else will fail you. You can only count on God.*

TUESDAY IN EASTER IV

Pss 45 * 47, 48
Wisdom 3:1–9
Colossians 1:15–23
Luke 6:12–26

The souls of the righteous are in the hand of God,
and no torment will ever touch them.
WISDOM 3:1

This is one of the funeral readings. I don't use it much, though; it begins well enough, but then we get to the part about those who suffer "seeming to be punished." I have enough trouble with people thinking their illnesses are their own fault to want to open up this subject at their funerals.

What did I do wrong? Why is this happening to me? Everyone asks this question: young people struck down in the prime of life, to be sure, but also old people, sometimes—old people, for whom the answer to "What did I do to deserve this?" can only be "Nothing. You're just old. Things happen to the body when we get old. That's all."

Ah, but they don't feel old. Not always, anyway, not inside. They feel like the same person they were at twenty, or at forty, or at seventy. Hey, it's still me in here, you know, they say, when people talk past them as if they weren't there. I'm not an old person. I'm just me.

The body gets old. And the mind. But the spirit is ageless. I think that's what people mean when they say they feel just the same as they did when they were young: their strong spirits live in their old bodies just as they always have, strong, young, curious spirits that observe the whole of life from their perch within the experience of an individual. Our spirits are old, older than we are. But they are also young. Young as tomorrow. They have no age.

And God doesn't punish them by making their bodies ill. The immediate relation between good deeds and prosperity and bad behavior and illness simply is not borne out by human experience. Good people suffer terribly, sometimes, and bad people do just fine, and there's no way to predict which will happen beforehand.

Here is what I think happens: we're in the hand of God, no matter what. In sickness and in health, we are there. The people this passage called "the righteous" live in expectation of more and better life as the body weakens and becomes unable to contain the strong spirit. They are more than just good people who did good deeds when they were alive. They might be people who made a lot of mistakes, too. But the ones whose souls turn to God to heal are healed, whether in this life or in the next, made righteous there, if they lacked something here.

WEDNESDAY IN EASTER IV

Pss 119:49–72 * 49, (53)
Wisdom 4:16–5:8
Colossians 1:24–2:7
Luke 6:27–38

I am now rejoicing in my sufferings for your sake, and in my flesh I am completing what is lacking in Christ's afflictions . . .
COLOSSIANS 1:24

In the end, what troubled many people about Mel Gibson's *The Passion of the Christ* was its goriness. Even more than the worries about whether or not it was anti-Semitic. For Gibson, the most important thing about Jesus was his death. He is not alone in that belief. Many Christians jealously guard the primacy of Jesus' suffering. Nobody else's death can be said to have been as terrible as his—it's not allowed. As if it were the horror of his death—much, much worse than ours—that makes him Messiah.

Maybe. But maybe not, too. I can think of a number of deaths as terrible as crucifixion, and so can you. When Paul talks about what is lacking in Christ's afflictions, he doesn't mean that Jesus left some stone of suffering unturned. What makes Jesus Savior is not the horror of his death, but his participation in our life—all of it, right up to and including that moment when his spirit left his body, as all of ours will someday leave ours.

And what makes him my messiah is my participation in his life. We participate in each other, Jesus and I.

And so Paul preached and argued and scolded his way through the ancient Mediterranean world telling people about it. He doesn't add to the event of the crucifixion, or to the mysterious events that came after. He just lets us all know.

THURSDAY IN EASTER IV

Pss 50 * (59, 60) or 114, 115
Wisdom 5:9–23
Colossians 2:8–23
Luke 6:39–49

"Can a blind person guide a blind person?
Will not both fall into a pit?"
LUKE 6:39

Annie Sullivan was blind—not as blind as her student, Helen Keller, who was completely blind, and deaf, as well. But Annie herself was profoundly disabled, legally blind and then some.

In her case, the answer to Jesus' question was a resounding YES. She led her young pupil out of her lonely darkness into a new life, one of the more famous lives of the twentieth century. For as long as she was alive, Helen Keller was on every list of most admired women anybody ever published.

There are some blind people who can only be led by another blind person. Addicts are blind—not blind like Helen Keller, but unsighted in another way. They can stare disaster right in the face and not recognize it. They can be near death, divorce, unemployment or homelessness—or even all of these at once—and still think everything's perfectly fine.

A person who's never been blind like that can't help them. *Pull yourself together, for God's sake!* you might plead. *Think of your family, if not of yourself,* and you might as well be talking to the wall. It is the person who has been there herself who can point the way.

In teaching, it is important to remember what it is not to know. What may be obvious to you is frustratingly unclear to one who hasn't yet found his way, and patience is the name of the game.

I once was blind, but now I see. That's true, sometimes. And sometimes I may still be blind. Maybe I can't see, maybe not yet. But if someone who knows the way will lead me, maybe I can still follow.

FRIDAY IN EASTER IV

Ps 40, 54 * 51
Wisdom 6:12–23
Colossians 3:1–11
Luke 7:1–17

One who rises early to seek her will have no difficulty,
for she will be found sitting at the gate.
WISDOM 6:14

By now, surely, you know whether you're a morning or an evening person. Wisdom is, apparently, an early riser, but wise human beings come in both varieties: some are early birds and some are night owls.

In beginning to pray, it's best to lead with your strengths. Maybe later you can tackle that discipline for which you are manifestly unsuited, as a kind of spiritual challenge; for now, start with something that's likely to work. The best time of day to pray with focus is the time when you are relaxed and alert, able to concentrate, when things are easy for you. Don't try to start something new at the time when you're apt to bite someone's head off.

Of course, get up early enough and there's nobody to bite. Nobody else is awake. The phone doesn't ring. There is a hush in the wee hours, a silent gathering of strength to meet the sun when it arrives. But that's hours from now. You awaken in the dark, and creep from your bed into your prayer place. You light a candle. It is as if you had the whole world to yourself.

Or maybe that's the way you feel about midnight. That you have the whole world to yourself.

Prayer at your time of least strength is a very different animal. Your alert sense of competence is gone. You fear drifting into sleep, fear being unable to focus on God or on anything at all. Speech is out of the question.

Fortunately, God doesn't give us grades on the quality of our prayer. It is enough that we turn to God at all, in whatever condition we find ourselves. It's pretty darned brave to stumble through a prayer when you're wishing you were asleep. When you're tired, keep it short and simple. Save the challenging stuff for the good times.

SATURDAY IN EASTER IV

Pss 55 * 138, 139:1–17 (18–23)
Wisdom 7:1–14
Colossians 3:12–17
Luke 7:18–28 (29–30) 31–35

. . . my first sound was a cry, as is true of all.
WISDOM 7:3

And a thin little cry it is, too. Foreign, a new voice. All the other voices in the room are deep, even the women, but this one is high-pitched and new. Never used.

And the first glimpse of the new little friend is strange, too. Round, a light purple in color, no matter what skin tone will eventually come to predominate. Round eyes, peering from beneath a furrowed little brow, as if unable quite to believe the evidence of them. So inscrutable a face that people argue for months about what the baby knows: *Do you think she can see us? There, did you see that? He smiled! Honest! I saw him.*

It is hard, being born. Small children don't like having turtlenecks pulled over their heads—perhaps they remember what it was like and it reminds them of that terrible moment when escape seemed impossible. Still, they all made it here.

Most growth comes from struggle. We start out that way and it doesn't stop until we leave. *When will it ever end?* we groan sometimes, when everything just seems too heavy to carry any more. *Never*, a voice from somewhere reminds us, and we shoulder our burdens and keep on walking.

As difficult as life is, though, we love it. Almost all of us want to stay here. We pay its price, over and over, and we don't want to leave. And when someone does leave, we weep and wish them back.

Life is hard, but life is good. Worth what you pay for it, even when you must pay over and over again.

EASTER V

Pss 24, 29 * 8, 84
Wisdom 7:22–8:1
2 Thessalonians 2:13–17
Matthew 7:7–14

"Ask, and it will be given to you; search, and you will find . . ."
MATTHEW 7:7

Do they like begging for money? Of course not. They're journalists. It must feel terrible to have to sell public radio, and themselves, on the air three or four times a year.

Or maybe they do like it, sort of—maybe they find it unexpectedly exhilarating, an activity utterly unlike what they usually do. Maybe they compete with each other to see whose show raises more. Maybe they discover within themselves a flair for marketing they never knew existed.

I remember hating to ask for anything when I was little. I would see something in a store I wanted and couldn't bring myself to inquire if we might buy it. It seemed selfish, a bother, a burden to my mother. And it showcased the power imbalance between us— she was an adult and I was a dependent child. She had money and I didn't. I was the one who had to ask, she was the one who could decide yes or no. I have carried this dislike of fundraising into adulthood. People who are good at it point out that what we're really doing is giving people an opportunity to be part of something they value. Don't feel reluctant to ask; you're giving them a gift by asking, a chance to do something important. Right. I do believe that.

But I am scarred. I write fundraising letters and feel sorry for the people to whom I send them, afraid that they'll resent me for asking. That's funny, since I don't resent them for asking. I must restrain myself from penciling in an apology, in the manner of fundraising letters: usually, you cross out the name in the typed salutation of the form letter and write, "Fred" where it says "Mr. Smithers." Sometimes you put another little personal scrawl down at the bottom of the letter: "Hope you can help!" or, if it is an event "Would love to see you there!" You're not supposed to write, "Listen, I feel just terrible about this, but they made me send it."

So I imagine that, in Hell, I'll have to be the development director. Little demons with pitchforks will force me to send out billions of letters to our donor base, which by then will be very large: "If by some chance you did find a way to take it with you, won't you consider making a gift to make it possible for your loved ones to go to Hell, too?" I'll invite people to the annual Disco Madness Gala, which will feature only one song, "Turn the Beat Around," over and over and over. We'll have a fundraising drive on the radio every other week, and we will pre-empt the season finale of "The West Wing" for our Gingivitis Telethon. This could happen. We do not know what lies beyond this life. Better be very, very good from now on.

MONDAY IN EASTER V

Pss 56, 57, (58) * 64, 65
Wisdom 9:1, 7–18
Colossians (3:18–4:1) 2–18
Luke 7:36–50

Wives, be subject to your husbands, as is fitting in the Lord.
COLOSSIANS 3:18

What's *it about?* my husband wants to know. I am haunting the Internet, looking at pictures, copying them into e-mails I send to myself. I want to stud my text with artwork. I have a deadline: the Quiet Hour meeting this afternoon, at which the fruits of my labor must be presented. *It's about Frida Kahlo and Diego Rivera,* I tell him. This is my Quiet Hour paper. The Quiet Hour Club has existed in Metuchen since 1895. Its members each present a paper to the group once a year; a program committee chooses the broad topics. This year it's "America's Neighbors: Canada and Mexico." Frida and

Diego seemed a more interesting choice than, say, Toronto, so I chose them.

Tortured, promiscuous, communist, alcoholic, brilliant. Joined irrevocably together—they married each other twice—in order that they might tear each other apart. Diego is not anybody's husband and never will be, she told someone once. But he is a great comrade.

And Frida? The overwrought anatomical correctness of her self-portraits, the brooding focus on the physical pain that never left her—she was grievously injured in a bus accident as a teenager, her spine pierced by a metal rod that entered her body through her abdomen, and she endured more than thirty surgeries. The frank use of her own biography as a subject for her work. People some-times think artists "work things out" in their creations. They don't work things out. They report. This is what it is, they say. I don't know what to do about it, but this is what it is.

She died first. It might have been suicide; no autopsy was per-formed, but she told friends she wanted to die, didn't want to be saved again, as doctors had saved her so many times before. And as her corpse was carried toward the flames of the crematorium on a conveyor belt, it sat straight up. She went into the fire like that, straight ahead, sitting up straight.

He thought she was the best painter Mexico had ever produced, better than anyone, including himself. He survived her by three years.

A tumultuous life together. But then, all life together is tumul-tuous, a never-to-be-repeated-in-just-the-same-way cycle of disap-pointment and gratitude, love and frustration, loyalty and betrayal. Maybe it is not always so dramatic. But no paired life is seamless.

TUESDAY IN EASTER V

Pss.61, 62 * 68:1–20 (21–23) 24–36
Wisdom 10:1–4 (5–12) 13–21
Romans 12:1–21
Luke 8:1–15

*Wisdom protected the first-formed father of the
world, when he alone had been created . . .*
WISDOM 10:1

In an essentially futile effort to control the uncontrollable, the bishop set forth what would be considered acceptable ways in which worshippers could reference the Trinity in language more gender-neutral than the traditional Father-Son-Holy Spirit trio: we could refer to the Holy Spirit as "she" if we wished.

He did this because he wanted something standardized: people had been fooling around with expressions of the Trinity for a long time, and it troubled him that different people were doing different things.

Some people smirked and others were delighted. Some thought it too little, too late and some thought the whole thing a trendy waste of time and energy.

But here is the ancient Book of Wisdom, giving us a "She" who has led and protected humanity from the beginning. Wisdom offers alternatives to dumb violence, relief from the wounds inflicted upon the innocent. She gets righteous Noah into his ark, Joseph into the catbird seat in Egypt, the children of Israel across the Red Sea on dry land. And, in all this hard work, all this undoing of human folly, Wisdom is feminine. And so, the Church reasons, if she's been around from the get-go, she must be the Third Person of the Trinity. The Holy Spirit is a girl.

Well, good. It's time for those who find this thought utterly distressing to turn their attention to things of a more pressing nature, like peace in the Middle East. And it's time for those who find it an answer to prayer to consider praying for larger things and refrain from correcting other people's grammar. And, perhaps, for all of us to remember that all religious language is metaphor. We don't know anything about God, and anything we might say falls far short of the truth before we have said it.

Language is about our reality. It seeks to capture and describe it. It also creates it, in a way: the way we speak about something forms pictures in our minds, and we hand them down to each other as the truth. But it is, at best, a partial truth, and our circling it endlessly seems never to make it clearer. The most we can do is agree not to get in one another's way as we peer through a glass, darkly.

WEDNESDAY IN EASTER V

Pss 72 * 119:73–96
Wisdom 13:1–9
Romans 13:1–14
Luke 8:16–25

If through delight in the beauty of these things people assumed them to be gods, let them know how much better than these is their Lord, for the author of beauty created them.
WISDOM 13:3

A longstanding tension between two loves: love of the creator and love of the created. The Judeo-Christian tradition had long regarded the exuberance of other ancient faiths with suspicion: it seemed that the potent tree stumps, opinionated sunsets, and wise stars of the nature religions could lead only to anarchy, to each of us grabbing our own rock or block of wood and wandering off alone with it to worship. Local deities might be all very well for wandering folk, but Israel's first cities needed some conformity, and God seemed a good place to start.

They weren't content to allow people to come to a sense of God's oneness and centrality on their own. It had to be imposed, and the devotion to household gods suppressed. How much of our faith is rooted in the sociological changes of the ancient near East is lost to us now, but it was significant.

Still, we would have gotten there eventually. Local customs may vary, but those who have devoted many years of their lives to contemplation—in many traditions besides our own—have been unanimous in their deepening sense of the oneness of things, the dissolving of boundaries between God and matter, the distillation of everything that is to one still point of divine being.

The Wisdom literature is late by Old Testament standards. Israel's worship had been centered in Jerusalem for a long time. Not much danger any more of people running off to worship their ancestors' fertility gods and sacred stones. Now it seemed safe to rely on the indwelling instruction of Wisdom, the teacher who lives with us and teaches us as we go long.

They could relax. We can, too. Rely on your common sense. Listen more than you talk. Sit tight and keep alert. The truth is not hiding. God wants to be found.

THURSDAY IN EASTER V

Pss [70], 71 * 74
Wisdom 14:27–15:3
Romans 14:1–12
Luke 8:26–39

Some believe in eating anything,
while the weak eat only vegetables.
ROMANS 14:2

Yes, the portion of the Letter to the Romans appointed for today really *is* about eating your vegetables. About being a vegetarian, or not being one. About which day to keep as Sabbath, and how to regard other people who keep a different one.

There are people who can make your heart sink just by entering the parish hall: you know they're going to crusade at you about something you're doing wrong. Eating wrong, sitting wrong, wearing the wrong color. Somehow they have decided that their mission in life is to correct others, and they don't notice how seldom anyone welcomes their advice. Churches attract such people, and every congregation has some.

If we all respected the practices of others as regards religious observance, the world would be a quieter and more peaceful place. But sometimes something in us hangs back: we want our way to be acknowledged as the best way. As if our rightness depends on the wrongness of someone else.

Early Christians were frequently divided about such things: whether or not to abstain from meat, from wine, from marriage—almost from life itself. We are on our way to heaven, the argument went, and we should detach from earthly things now. So we'll be ready.

Exactly, Paul said. We're on our way to heaven, and that's why it doesn't much matter whether you're a vegetarian or not. Or married or not. Love what God has given you. And then leave each other alone. Live your life as if you didn't have much time—you may not. Look for the kingdom of God, and leave the details to smaller minds. Don't get your undies in a twist about what you consider other people's sins to be. You have better things to do.

FRIDAY IN EASTER V

Pss 106:1–18 * 106:19–48
Wisdom 16:15–17:1
Romans 14:13–23
Luke 8:40–56

"Someone touched me; for I noticed that
power had gone out from me."
LUKE 8:46

In the gospel reading for today, Jesus' response to the well-known and important Jairus is interrupted by a powerless stranger. Jairus himself comes to ask, and falls at the feet of the itinerant wonder-worker. Certainly Jesus will come and help, but before he can set out, he feels power come out of him: the woman with a chronic hemorrhage has touched the hem of his garment and he feels it at once.

Was Jesus depleted when he used his power to heal? If he was, he was like us: we're easily tired, too, whether we know it or not. Adrenalin carries us for a while, if we're passionate about what we're doing, but eventually we feel how much energy we've spent.

But wait a minute. Jesus couldn't have lost energy, could he? He was God. How could that be?

God he was, yes, but human as well. He modeled them equally, divine strength and human weakness. And, if you don't understand precisely how it could be that the divine and the human could meet in Jesus of Nazareth, you have lots of company. House infinite power in a sack of bone and flesh? Join my narrowness to the breadth of God? Find God in a dusty Palestinian village? How?

We keep trying to get out of it: Jesus was human, we say, but not human like us. No pettiness, no selfishness, no crying he makes. Not like us, we say.

Wrong. That's a cheap way out of the mystery of Christ. The mystery is less powerful if Jesus were a perfect human, not more so. He must carry our weakness within him on earth, if he is to carry it with him to heaven.

And the "how" of it is for another life.

SATURDAY IN EASTER V

Pss 75, 76 * 23, 27
Wisdom 19:1–8, 18–22
Romans 15:1–13
Luke 9:1–17

*. . . an unhindered way out of the Red Sea, and a grassy
plain out of the raging waves, where those protected by
your hand passed through as one nation.*

WISDOM 19:7

A recitation, in this portion of the Book of Wisdom, of a story we
have heard before: the deliverance of Israel at the Red Sea. A
few extra miracles, things we don't remember from Exodus: land
animals living in the water, fire burning there, burning everywhere,
but consuming nothing.

So entranced is the writer with all the special effects that we've
pretty much lost track of the figure of Wisdom as we progress
through the book named for her. That's all right: the writer's purpose
is to connect the powerful mythology of Israel's past with the lofty
vision of Wisdom's inward-looking guidance of human spirit and
behavior. Perhaps the rocks don't gush forth water anymore; perhaps
the sea is no longer divided in two. No matter: we have that same
Spirit within us. It animates and informs our small doings as surely
as it split the heavens with fire. No miracles in your life? Then content
yourself with reasonable behavior, righteousness, common sense.

It is interesting to watch the rich, earthy legends of ancient times
yield to the refinements of a more philosophical age. Interesting,
but we do not behold it without a certain wistfulness, a slight sense
of loss. For the Israel of the Exodus, life was simple: we knew our
chosen-ness by our good fortune, the speedy vanquishing of our
enemies. By the time of Wisdom, though, there was too much water
under the bridge for such a ready correspondence between divine
favor and temporal prosperity. The writer of Wisdom is more like
us than is the writer of Exodus. More reasonable. More modern.
But less optimistic.

But still: very, very old. Still in place is the certainty of what right-eousness *is*. The writer of Wisdom is not adrift in a relativistic moral sea, as we are. Time has muddied the waters of every decision we make. We are Freud's grandchildren, too thoroughly his legatees to take our-selves at face value any more, ever. That train has left the station.

Will the household of heaven be different? Will it be simple again, as in ancient times? Or will it instead—does it right now, for that matter, and we just don't see it—render our complexities endurable at last, and even lovely? Do all our ambiguities and com-promises melt at last into something good and pure?

I look at the mixed motives of even my most selfless act, and pray that it is so.

EASTER VI

Pss 93, 96 * 34
Ecclesiasticus 43:1–12, 27–32
1 Timothy 3:14–4:5
Matthew 13:24–34a

Let both of them grow together until the harvest . . .
MATTHEW 13:30

A gardening parable today, one of many: an enemy has come and sown weeds in among a farmer's wheat. Pulling up the weeds now, while the plants are tiny, is a perilous business: they all look too much alike. Just leave them alone—we'll see soon enough who's really out there.

You often *don't* know who's who. Plants, like people, look alike in infancy: a pair of bright green leaves, called cotyledons, way smaller than your smallest finger nail. They stay that way for a little while. Then they get their secondary leaves, but you can't always tell much from them, either. By the time the plants have finally shown themselves as individuals, you may have forgotten who you planted. So you have to wait and see.

Sometimes, too, the same species function as weeds against each other, crowding each other at the dinner table, so that nobody ends up getting enough.

Then draconian measures are called for: you must choose who will stay and who will go, choosing the largest and healthiest of the tiny plants, the ones most likely to make it. If you do this with your hands, picking out your victims between thumb and forefinger, you might miss and pull both little ones out of the soil by mistake—your fingers are too large. Use a pair of tweezers.

In a perfect garden, there would be no weeds. Each plant would be just where you wanted it, with no competitor. In a real garden, though, it's never like that: it's rife with uncertainty, full of risk, the good and the bad mixed together so thoroughly that you can't tell which is which. Sometimes you must just decide, ruthlessly and without benefit of the big picture. Sometimes you get it wrong.

And sometimes you just have to wait and see. Life is just like that. If you can wait for more wisdom, wait. But if you must act before you get it, take a deep breath and choose. There are other plants in the garden. God never has only one way of doing things. There is always a plan B—and a C and a D.

MONDAY IN EASTER VI

Pss 80 * 77, (79)
Deuteronomy 8:1–10
James 1:1–15
Luke 9:18–27

"But truly I tell you, there are some standing here who will not taste death before they see the kingdom of God."
LUKE 9:27

I don't know when I first realized that there is no such thing as time, but I do know why. I came to know it because I needed it to be true: I needed to stop the tragic march to oblivion that had claimed, or would claim, everything dear to me. I needed to dig beneath the finality of death and find a way to express resurrection.

So, do you just make stuff up? Just because you can't stand the thought of death?

But it is time that is made up. We take the periodicity of the natural world and project it onto the universe, as if we knew for sure it applied there. But we do not know that. And we apply it, also, to the spiritual realm of God—even as we affirm that it cannot be a "realm," that it is not a place at all. It is spirit, not earth. It is not the same.

Scripture refers to this at every turn. A day is not a day—it's the same as a thousand years. All will be in Christ, and Christ will be all in all: the living and the dead are part of "all." Everything is part of all. All means all.

I think God experiences everything right now. We are the ones who stretch reality out on a line, with a beginning and an end—God doesn't need to do that. I think that this life is like a basket sitting in a larger basket: we can see out, a little, to the larger one that contains the one we're on, but mostly we forget there is a larger one.

Can I prove any of this? No—proof is a matter for this world, not the next. But for God to be God, it must be true. God either contains all things—and all times—or God is not God.

TUESDAY IN EASTER VI

Pss 78:1–39 * 78:40–72
Deuteronomy 8:11–20
James 1:16–27
Luke 11:1–13

*Every generous act of giving, with every perfect gift, is from
above, coming down from the Father of lights, with whom
there is no variation or shadow due to change.*

JAMES 1:17

A slight tightness in my chest as I walk across the concourse to
Track 4. Not pain. But the tightness and my awareness that I am
tired suggest that a nitro under the tongue might not hurt. I open my
purse and fish out the bottle: it's a bottle-within-a-bottle, actually.
Nitroglycerin is unstable: I don't *think* it would explode in my purse,
but its tiny bottle is dispensed in a larger plastic one, just in case.

Actually, your head does explode, sort of, when you take one.
Nitroglycerin dilates every blood vessel in the body, not just the
ones in the heart. It dilates every capillary in your head, too. You
feel as if the top of your head were coming off. You get used to it.

My grandmother had the little bottle of pills, too, although she
was much sicker than I am. She was forbidden by her doctor to listen
to the baseball game, as it made her too excited, giving her chest pain.
Nobody could come between her and baseball, though: my brother
would smuggle the radio up to her room so she could listen. She
would put one of the little pills under her tongue and enjoy the game.

Both my grandmothers died at home. My mother took care of
them, with help from a cousin who was a nurse, and a practical nurse
who came several days a week. It must have been hard on her, but to
a child it all seemed fairly normal: sometimes you have an invalid in
the house and sometimes you don't. Everybody has to pitch in and
help out, and sometimes things that you might like to do will have to
wait for a better time. It strikes me that this was very good training

for life: Help out. Be patient. Squeamishness is a luxury. There is no such thing as a menial task. We're all going to die someday.

And a big one: if nothing is beneath you, nothing will be beyond you.

WEDNESDAY IN EASTER VI— THE EVE OF THE ASCENSION

Pss 119:97–120 * 68:1–20
Baruch 3:24–37 * 2 Kings 2:1–15
James 5:13–18 * Revelation 5:1–14
Luke 12:22–31

Consider the ravens: they neither sow nor reap,
. . . and yet God feeds them.
LUKE 12:24

The birds need a drink. We have a birdbath in front and another in back, so they can always find water. Even in the winter: people don't really think of that in the dead of winter, when snow covers everything and everything is frozen, but they still have to drink, like all the rest of us, so we have a little heater for the birdbath. Although it is electric, the birds don't electrocute themselves with it. I don't know why. And they flock to it when the temperature plummets and water everywhere is frozen solid.

God takes care of the birds, Jesus says. In our case, he takes care of them by allowing us to fall in love with them and feed them. But they would manage just fine, even if we were not here.

It is not the brevity of life that God's attention repairs. Life is brief. But God repairs the anonymity of life. The pointlessness of our short span on the earth. Creatures like us, capable of reflection, aware of our own finitude and the endlessness of our universe: we would succumb to our own absurdity if we didn't think there was a context larger than ourselves. If Someone didn't see us fall.

ASCENSION DAY

Pss 8, 47 * 24, 96
Ezekiel 1:1–14, 24–28b
Hebrews 2:5–18
Matthew 28:16–20

And remember, I am with you always, to the end of the age.
MATTHEW 28:20

No alternate-side-of-the-street parking restrictions today in New York: it is Ascension Day. Or, as the radio is more apt to say now, "a religious holiday," so as not to privilege any of us over any of the rest of us. This vagueness is a good early morning exercise, because alternate-side-of-the-street parking is suspended frequently in New York for "a religious holiday"—almost once a week, it seems—causing us to think hard while brushing our teeth, struggling to remember what day it is. Are we in Ramadan? Is this an obscure Jewish feast? Is alternate-side parking suspended for Hindu feasts now?

But this is one of ours. The feast of the simultaneous presence and absence of Christ. In the account in the book of Acts, the disciples gaze openmouthed into the sky and would have stood there like that all afternoon, had their attention not been directed back to earth by two well-dressed angels who happen to be nearby. You saw Jesus go, they say, and you will see him come. You're staying here, for now.

Alleluia, Christ is risen. The Lord is risen indeed, Alleluia. This is the antiphon at Morning Prayer these days, and has been since Easter. You say it before the invitatory, and again after it. Here is a confession: in the last couple of weeks, I've grown tired of saying it every day. I want to move on into ordinary time, into those long green weeks of prayer and work and rest, stretching into the summer and into the fall, seeing the changes of the seasons. I've wanted to move on from Easter into the rest of life.

The Risen Christ cannot remain with us and we can't remain at the empty tomb, on the way to Emmaus, in the upper room. We can't stay at the party forever, not here. We can't stand gazing into the sky, wondering where he went. Here there is work to be done and life to be lived, and it is all ordinary. In every Eucharist we bring the resurrection back to our experience, its shocking soak of joy— no matter what time of year it is—but in the rest of life we are on the road again, applying what we have learned and who we have become. Who we are becoming. Learning Christ, and teaching him.

And receiving the Holy Spirit. As mysterious as Easter is, Pentecost will be more so. The spirit of God is present in us in exactly the same way as it was when Jesus walked the earth. How can that possibly be? Where is the evidence of it?

This funny feast prepares us to begin our answer. No need to rush toward false certainties about him—you've got the rest of your life. Up he goes—some ancient pictures show just his feet, disappearing into a cloud, and others show his footprints, with no one in them, the disciples gaping at the sight. Where did he go? Where is he? Here. And not here. Now, and not yet.

FRIDAY IN EASTER VI

Pss 85, 86 * 91, 92
Ezekiel 1:28–3:3
Hebrews 4:14–5:6
Luke 9:28–36

*For we do not have a high priest who is unable
to sympathize with our weaknesses...*
HEBREWS 4:15

I *didn't do my fifteen minutes,* my friend says grimly. *I was going to clean in the basement for fifteen minutes every day and I'm about four hours behind.*

But you did do a lot of cleaning in the living room, I point out. *Cleaning is cleaning. It all counts.*

My friend has a major case of perfectionism. This makes her a valuable worker in any number of causes—believe me, if you ask her to do it, it'll be done right. But there's a terrible cost: she's never satisfied with anything she does. Never. Never at peace. Nothing is ever good enough.

We've had this talk many times. We have it about the fifteen minutes in the basement, about her routine of daily prayer, going to the gym. It's the mistakes she remembers: the times she didn't get there, the times she didn't pray. She remembers the misses. I want her to rejoice in the hits.

It's not good for the soul to be perfect, I say. *God doesn't ask that of us. If we could be perfect, we would have no need of God. We'd be gods ourselves.*

She looks at me dubiously. Unhappily. *I hear you, but I'm not sure I believe you. How can it be okay just to accept that you're not going to be perfect?* It feels to her like I am asking her to surrender to chaos.

I know, I say. Just sit with it for a while and think about it. Ask yourself if demanding perfection of yourself has ever once made you perfect. Even once.

I see a war on her face: the demon of perfectionism locked in a death grip with the God of Grace. God always wins that one if you can just keep the fight going long enough. My job is to stay in there and keep the discussion going for however long it takes. It can take a long time.

And it always takes some kind of collapse: we have to experience the fact that we're not perfect and that God is with us in our imperfection. It's not enough to be told. We have to experience it. And we usually experience it with a painful thump.

You don't have to come up with everything on your own. We don't make all of our own history. Some of it is made for us, and every good gift in it comes from God. *Just ask,* I say, *just ask God for the gift of prayer that's best for you to have, for the gift of housekeeping, even, that's best for you to have. Ask for balance and enough rest. Just ask. You're really not alone in all this. God is really real.*

SATURDAY IN EASTER VI

Pss 87, 90 * 136
Ezekiel 3:4–17
Hebrews 5:7–14
Luke 9:37–50

. . . you shall give them a warning from me.
EZEKIEL 3:17

A flurry of kind notes about an eMo expressing some strong opinions about a political hot button—I usually try to be more gentle—balanced out the angry ones I received from a couple of readers, who do not come to me for political analysis and are not interested in my take on the headlines. I am a poor activist—like most clergy, I have a strong desire to be liked and hate to be criticized. That being the case, I take the hate mail to heart more than I should.

But sometimes you have to take a stand. Faith has a moral component, and it works in the world, where all the hard issues live. The only sure way not to be attacked is to avoid any engagement with ethics other than personal ones. And God wants more from us than that. Faith strikes a balance between the personal and public. We can't live in the world God created, among the people God loves, and take no notice of what happens to them.

To enter into public life assures controversy. Controversy is not a sign that something is wrong with our faith. It's a sign that something is right. Scripture is full of controversy. People of faith can honestly disagree about how the world's ills should be healed.

So is my particular take on an issue prophetic? Do I know for sure that my words are God's words? I don't think we ever know that. We study a situation and pray. Perhaps we're moved to speak or write. We may be wrong or right: time will tell and history will judge.

But we ought not to remain silent. Just in case.

EASTER VII

Pss 66, 67 * 19, 46
Ezekiel 3:16–27
Ephesians 2:1–10
Matthew 10:24–33, 40–42

So do not be afraid . . .
MATTHEW 10:31

*S*he's *so little!* the technician said, sliding Kate out of her arms and onto the pan of the scale. Five pounds and change. Down a whole pound from last year. That's not good.

Little. Bony. Cats shrink when they get old, just as we do, and Kate is seventeen. But she's pretty active at the doctor's office, stretching on tiptoe to look out the window, jumping from the examining table into Q's lap. She's in good shape, the vet tells us. She should live to a good old age. She already has.

Just a few things: she needs some special food for her kidneys and a thyroid pill, and she needs to have her teeth cleaned. Kate doesn't floss.

Sometimes she cries out, a long wail, a wail with more than one syllable, a wail with a couple of diphthongs in the middle of it. It is eloquent, full of despair. Does something hurt her? Did she have a bad dream? I hear her wail and go in search of her. When I find her, she betrays nothing of what distressed her so. I am at a loss to understand.

Someone tells me that her elderly cat did that, too, cried out for no apparent reasons. She says that her vet told her that the cat became momentarily confused and forgot where she was. Maybe Kate forgets where she is, here in this house where she has lived for all but one of her seventeen years. Maybe she sits in the corner between the wall and the old dentist's chest, where she always sits for a little while after breakfast, and suddenly everything looks strange to her, unfamiliar, frightening. Maybe for a moment she has no family, no one around her, no sense of ever having been here.

We have to belong somewhere. There has to be a place where they would notice if we disappeared, where they know us. We need a family of some kind—either one into which we were born or a family that we collect around ourselves, later on. It is frightening to think of being a person whose disappearance would leave no wrinkle in the world, would make no difference to anyone. Perhaps that is Kate's frightening vision.

Here I am, I call to her when she cries, and come down the stairs to find her sitting in her corner. She feigns indifference—or maybe her indifference is genuine. But then she arches her back and pushes her head into my hand for a nice scratch. *It was just a bad dream, Kate. You're safe at home.*

MONDAY IN EASTER VII

Pss 89:1–18 * 89:19–52
Ezekiel 4:1–17
Hebrews 6:1–12
Luke 9:51–62

"Foxes have holes, and birds of the air have nests;
but the Son of Man has nowhere to lay his head."
LUKE 9:58

There's no such thing as social responsibility, the senator is telling the interviewer on the radio. Just personal responsibility, that's all he believes in. Society doesn't have a responsibility to people, and people don't have a responsibility to other people. People are responsible for themselves.

Oh? Children? *Their parents are responsible for them.*

But what happens if their parents die? Or leave? Or just fail in their duty? *Well, they shouldn't do that.*

No, they sure shouldn't. But what if they do? How about addicts? *Well, they shouldn't be addicts.*

No, they shouldn't. But what if the demon has them and won't let go? Or what if they did get free, finally, but found themselves in a wilderness of employment and responsibility for which their years of substance abuse did not prepare them?

I suppose all this preaching about independence comes down to not wanting to pay taxes, so there will be more money for shopping—you'd be amazed at how many things you can buy if you stop caring for the poor.

Two points of view that cannot, I think, be reconciled: one holds that each of us single-mindedly pursuing his own interest will somehow end up producing the general good. The other is the biblical one: we need to provide for the general good, not just for our own. And we need to do it first, before taking care of ourselves.

My personal experience is only with the second of these two approaches, and my experience is that it works: if you make early provision for the needs of those so much less fortunate than you are that there's no point in even comparing the two ways of life, you yourself will end up doing just fine.

TUESDAY IN EASTER VII

Pss 97, 99, (100) * 94, (95)
Ezekiel 7:10–15, 23b–27
Hebrews 6:13–20
Luke 10:1–17

See, the day! See, it comes! Your doom has gone out.
EZEKIEL 7:10

Is doom real? Are there really dark clouds of misfortune that follow certain people through life because of something they've done? Or maybe because of something someone else did, years before they were even born?

There are moments in life in which it seems that way. Things go from bad to worse to even worse. Everything you touch turns to dust. Nothing is right. Somebody up there hates me, you tell someone. It's a joke, of course. But it's not a very funny one.

Some of the bad things that have happened to me were my fault. Some weren't. Repeated bad decisions have, in my life, produced repeated bad results, but there have been runs of what could only be called bad luck. How do I know it wasn't a curse?

Because God has been present in them. Comfort has appeared—maybe not the cessation of pain for which I prayed, but comfort in the midst of it. Comfort all the more profound because the pain has been so great.

Fate is not a Christian concept. It comes from earlier times. We understand the love of God to surround the world. People who are beloved of God are not, at the same time, cursed by God. Life is hard, but its hardness is not ordained—it just happens. And blessedness grows right alongside it.

WEDNESDAY IN EASTER VII

Pss 101, 109:1–4 (5–19) 20–30 * 119:121–144
Ezekiel 11:14–25
Hebrews 7:1–17
Luke 10:17–24

*I will remove the heart of stone from their
flesh and give them a heart of flesh . . .*
EZEKIEL 11:19

Insert an emotion, it says when I move the mouse. *Hmmmn.* My emotions have never come when called like that. I don't *insert* mine.

I scroll down the emotional offerings. There is a little stick figure with his head on his desk. He is banging his fists on the desktop and weeping. Poor fellow. If I were still in parish ministry, I could have used him for my parochial report. At least he would have had work.

All of the emotions available for insertion are negative ones. There are several of people telling each other off, one of a woman gossiping with another woman, one of an annoyed-looking man, one of several little stick people being much too busy. Not a single happy face among them. I guess the designer doesn't envision communication being much fun, at least not at work.

How's retirement? I ask my friend. She's just out, after thirty-five years. She is glad to be free, eager for the next chapter of her life. But she spent her first free weekend in bed. *I didn't even go to church*, she said. *I was so depressed.*

How about that? Longing for retirement for years and finally retired, and BOOM! Who am I? What do I do? This was not a person who didn't plan for retirement. She has a plan. But leaving work is hard. Even if you're ready. Even if, like my friend, you didn't really like your job that much anyhow.

We're not machines. It takes time to make a change. Your feelings lag behind. You don't feel like yourself. *Insert an emotion*, says your computer, and you scan the stick figures for one that looks like you.

THURSDAY IN EASTER VII

Pss 105:1–22 * 105:23–45
Ezekiel 18:1–4, 19–32
Hebrews 7:18–28
Luke 10:25–37

For I have no pleasure in the death of anyone, says the Lord GOD.
EZEKIEL 18:32

Waiting for our mutual friend outside her hospital room, a young woman and I face each other across the narrow corridor. Death lurks everywhere in hospitals: death, or the fear of death. He lurks here, although I think he will not win today. Our friend faces surgery. Her mother just died. The young woman to whom I am speaking lost her dad some years ago.

"Religions all make no sense!" she said. "They never tell you the main thing you want to know: why do bad things happen to good people? Why?"

Nope. Religions don't tell you why bad things happen to good people, not in any way that would satisfy any of us. They don't even tell us why bad things happen to *bad* people, in case any of us wondered. Not in any way that holds water.

But I suspect that *why* isn't really what we want to know. No reason for the suffering humanity must endure would seem good enough to me to justify it. A balance could never be struck.

So here's the situation: there *is* no justification. Things happen to people. Their being good or bad has nothing to do with it. People often seem surprised to hear that from a religious figure, although I can't for the life of me understand why: I would think a five-minute look around at the way things are would make it obvious.

Can we live with such a thing? Can we handle the idea that God is not up in the sky, dispensing illness or prosperity to humankind as reward or punishment for our behavior? How badly do we need that kind of God in our imagination, so like a strict teacher or parent? Some of us seem to need it pretty badly—it's hard to give it up, and many people are offended by the thought that there is no way to earn or worship or pray your way into a guarantee of safety from the sorrows of life.

The narrow calculus of punishment for sins, of retribution in some weirdly karmic manner through ages of ages, the cursing of one generation for the actions of a previous one—these are not part of Christian faith. God the scorekeeper has proven an inadequate image for us, one too much like us to be God at all.

Besides, what would we do with our new knowledge of why things happen if we had it? Would knowing why he had to die bring back my dead son? Make me miss him less? Ease my pain in any way?

Forget why. We can't know and it doesn't matter. Instead, ask what. What can happen, now and in the future, now that this has taken place? What could be wrung from my sorrow that might, one day, grow into a joy?

FRIDAY IN EASTER VII

Pss 102 * 107:1–32
Ezekiel 34:17–31
Hebrews 8:1–13
Luke 10:38–42

And they shall not teach one another or say to each other,
"Know the Lord," for they shall all know me . . .
HEBREWS 8:11

To continue the implications of yesterday's train of thought, a question: does this mean that prayer is irrelevant? If there is no stern schoolmaster in the sky, dispensing reward and punishment, to be placated, is prayer a cruel farce? If we're not going to find a way to talk God out of letting us get sick and die?

Only if the only relevance possible were an essentially consumerist one. Only if prayer were really like shopping, getting what we wanted because we prayed the right way. Only if what happens to us is the sole measure of the love of God. But it is not.

The measure of God's love is limitless. God loves us into being and accompanies us with love throughout our walk here. God loves us as we die and loves us afterward. Nobody is ever outside the love of God. Prayer is the process of coming into contact with the reality of that love. That's all it is.

And that's enough. You have to live into it in order to feel that way, of course, let it grow in your life by practicing prayer frequently, by being extremely honest in prayer—not telling God what you think God wants to hear. By allowing yourself to wonder freely about God, by listening to what comes up within you in response to your wondering. And you have to do this before you're even sure it's worth doing. That's what faith is. It takes a long time to learn to pray in this wondering way, and it takes some encouragement from others along the way. It's not inevitable, nor is it easy—many, many people never progress beyond the shopping stage.

But everybody can. And God stands ready to begin teaching us whenever we are ready to begin learning.

THE DAY OF PENTECOST

Pss 118 * 145
Isaiah 11:1–9
1 Corinthians 2:1–13
John 14:21–29

None of the rulers of this age understood this; for if they
had, they would not have crucified the Lord of glory.
1 CORINTHIANS 2:8

We think that we'd have abundant faith if only we could have lived when Jesus lived. Seen him, and heard him speak. We'd know so much more. We wouldn't be plagued with the doubts that assail us now, two thousand years later.

But wait a minute: many people saw Jesus and heard him and didn't believe. Enough people didn't that it was possible to kill him without touching off an insurrection. For the most part, nobody cared. Barabbas had more public support.

And if the common people, who needed his message of love and freedom, didn't believe, certainly the rulers didn't. There was not a thing Jesus was selling that they wanted to buy. The great inversion he preached, about the last being first and the first last? That prostitutes and tax collectors might be more blessed than civic and religious leaders? Forget it. Paul was alive during the life of Jesus, but he didn't believe. Not then. He didn't believe until long after the crucifixion and resurrection. He didn't believe until he had an experience of the Risen Christ.

And that's the one we can have. We can't experience the earthly Jesus, the one who lived in the first several decades of the first century. That was then. This is now: the Risen Christ is the only one we can encounter, and the Risen Christ is the only one we need. We have missed nothing by our late birth.

The Season
after Pentecost

TRINITY SUNDAY

Pss 146, 147 * 111, 112, 113
Ecclesiasticus 43:1–12 (27–33)
Ephesians 4:1–16
John 1:1–18

We could say more but could never say enough;
let the final word be: "He is the all."
ECCLESIASTICUS 43:27

Before and after the birth of Christ, much the same language: nothing was made apart from him, nothing lives apart from him. In him all things live and move and have their being. We can't think about this accurately, because we have no room in our minds to conceive of anything else beyond God. We have no place to put God. We simply cannot encompass the presence of God. It is too mysterious and too immense.

We know something about awe just from being alive. The natural world teaches it to us, and nobody is completely immune. You stop and look in amazement at stars that seem close enough to pluck from the sky. You drive through mountains and gasp at the view. The trees change color and you simply cannot look away. We have known this kind of awe.

And from it, you step backwards. Away from what you see. Behind it. Where did it come from? The Big Bang, maybe? Back another step, even behind the Big Bang. Now where? The mysterious domain of God comes into view and then disappears again: you can't hold onto it—you are too small.

Now we see why it is that people in the Bible are filled with fear when they encounter God. They are too small. They will be crushed by all that power. The universe will crush them. More than the universe.

Sometimes we say that Jesus saves us from the fires of Hell. Perhaps. But he also saves us from our fear of the immensity of the mysterious God. He speaks and, by the grace of all this mystery, you can understand what he is saying. He takes your hand in his hand, his hand that is so like your hand. He knows the same things you know, and knows them in the same way—from experience.

MONDAY IN PROPER 1

Pss 106:1–18 * 106:19–48
Isaiah 63:7–14
2 Timothy 1:1–14
Luke 11:24–36

*I am reminded of your sincere faith, a faith that
lived first in your grandmother Lois and your
mother Eunice and now, I am sure, lives in you.*
2 TIMOTHY 1:5

Here is a reading that gives us some clues about what Paul's churches were like. Lois and Eunice were old friends of Paul. The fact that they were both women seems to have been unimportant, either to him or to them. They were leaders. That's a change from what was usual in first-century Judaism. It wouldn't have been something Paul was used to.

He assumes that Timothy has been raised in the faith and has absorbed it well. That he inherited it from his mom and his grandma. Paul himself had a dramatic conversion to Christianity. Most people back then came to it as adults. But Timothy had been raised in it. Unusual.

And another thing: as cranky as we know Paul to have been at times, one person genuinely loved him. Timothy cried when Paul left him. That Paul remembered this may mean that it didn't happen all that often. Who knows?

Paul writes from prison. Now, that's not unusual. But recent scholarship has suggested that persecution of Christians by the Romans may have been overstated in Christian histories. It is not confirmed as extensive in non-Christian Roman records.

Hmmn. What would it mean if we were to find out that our fore-bears were not all thrown to the lions? We base so much of our self-understanding on it. What if the ancient persecutions weren't real?

I think they were plenty real enough, even if it does someday turn out that they might not have been universal. The ones today certainly are, and a person sometimes has to look hard in secular sources of news about them to understand what is happening. That the victims are Christians is really important only to other Christians. Was then, and still is.

The century just past saw many more Christian martyrs than the centuries we think of automatically as the centuries of martyr-dom, and hardly anybody batted an eye. Even other Christians, the ones who weren't face to face with it. Most of us didn't know or care. Indifference to one's sacrifice on the part of those for whom one is making it: maybe that's the cruelest martyrdom of all.

TUESDAY IN PROPER 1

Pss (120), 121, 122, 123 * 124, 125, 126, (127)
Isaiah 63:15–64:9
2 Timothy 1:15–2:13
Luke 11:37–52

Woe to you lawyers!
LUKE 11:52

Q. A teacher and a doctor and a lawyer are swimming in the sea. A shark comes along, and eats the doctor and the teacher. Why didn't the shark eat the lawyer?

A. Professional courtesy.

So many lawyer jokes make the rounds that there has been more than one book published containing nothing but lawyer jokes. But why are lawyers funny?

They symbolize the desire in all of us to go as far in the direction of our selfish interests as we can, stopped only by our desire not to get into trouble. They symbolize self-interest and self-serving analysis. If you're smart enough, you can make a convincing case for just about anything you want to do. Lawyers remind us of that.

And they frighten us. They make us fear that our rights will be trampled by someone with a smooth argument. They make us afraid that there is no steady moral compass, that anything and everything is on the table.

Maybe they do symbolize all these fearsome possibilities, but they are also the ones charged with making sure they don't happen. Regardless of what they symbolize, what they actually do is trust the battleground of the legal system, and they sally forth into it every day, armed only with the law and their own wits. Their job is to go to the mat for us, if we need them to do that.

In scripture sometimes, Jesus is referred to as our "Advocate." Our lawyer. The one who will go to the mat for us. We often think of him as our judge, but he is also our lawyer. You are on trial and enter the courtroom. The bailiff says "All rise!" and everyone stands up. You look up at the judge's bench and there is your lawyer.

Justice may be blind, but Jesus is our lawyer. He is biased toward us. Even when we are wrong, he does not desert us. Not ever. We can't commit a crime into which he cannot enter with redemption, regardless of the consequences we may have to face for the things we have done amiss. Defeating his mercy is beyond our power.

WEDNESDAY IN PROPER 1

Pss 119:145–176 * 128, 129, 130
Isaiah 65:1–12
2 Timothy 2:14–26
Luke 11:53–12:12

Avoid profane chatter . . .
2 TIMOTHY 2:16

I don't know why I did it. A young woman and her young male friend were seated across the aisle from me on the train. They were enjoying each other: laughing, joking, having a great time. It was fun to see their pleasure in each other's company. Except for one thing.

Every other word the young woman said was the f-word. Not "friend." The other one. I am not squeamish about swearing. I swear myself—I didn't spend eleven years on the New York waterfront and not learn to swear. But those potent four-letter words have a place in life: they're for expressing strong emotion, sudden pain, deep anger. They're not a substitute for a vocabulary.

After twenty minutes or so of this, I spoke up. I had overheard them refer to New York University, and so I asked her if that's where she went to school. She nodded in a friendly way. I tried to be friendly too, as I made my next remark.

"Then you must be very bright," or you wouldn't have gotten into such a fine school. Surely you have other words in your vocabulary besides that one. It makes you sound silly.

She was nonplussed. She argued with me a little, about her right to use that word, a right she certainly had. About how she didn't mean anything by it. I knew that. About how it didn't really make her sound stupid. I disagreed.

"And I know you can't be stupid. You and your parents worked hard for your fine education. I hate to hear you talk that way."

It was a fool's errand. It was none of my business. I did not convince her to clean up her language, at least not right then and there. She and her friend got off before me.

But maybe she did hear me. Maybe she realized that she, a college graduate now, was just too old to behave that way. Maybe I functioned as an angel of the Lord for her, bringing her a message she needed to hear. You never know.

THURSDAY IN PROPER 1

Pss 131, 132, (133) * 134, 135
Isaiah 65:17–25
2 Timothy 3:1–17
Luke 12:13–31

"Teacher, tell my brother to divide the family inheritance with me."
LUKE 12:13

The parents are the bond—the bond, and also the buffer between the sisters and brothers. While they live, they rule. At the very end, though, their rule falters: they cannot decide any more. The seams in the family begin to show: differences of opinion about care at the end, about life-prolonging measures, about which hospital, when hospice, how much medicine.

And when they are gone, the house. The furniture, the linens, the Christmas ornaments, the favorite chair, the books, the treasured ring. Two sisters cannot wear one ring. One antique bed cannot reside in two different states. One painting cannot grace two different walls.

On the division of these things ride rivalries unspoken since childhood. Unacknowledged, perhaps, even then, because Mother and Father did not permit them to flare. We were always such a close family—what has happened to us?

It's not really the money, they say—one sign that maybe it really *is* the money. Or is it? Is it the ancient feeling of being second best, the old jockeying for position, the outrage of displacement in favor of the new baby, you and that new baby both middle-aged now, and Mother gone now, but the sting still there. You had not known it was still there until now.

What to do? The man who questioned Jesus wants him to decide. But this is something the family must do. The weak must stand up to the strong; we are not children any more. We are adults. We can say what we want. We can give and take. We can compromise.

We hope, in the pain of fresh bereavement, that there will be someone who can read our minds, who will give us what we want without our having to ask. Someone magic, like our parents. But there is no one like that. There has never been anyone like that. They were not like that: our parents were not magic. They were just two people with a home and children, strong and weak, wise and foolish by turn. And they are gone now.

We must decide.

FRIDAY IN PROPER 1

Pss 140, 142 * 141, 143:1–11 (12)
Isaiah 66:1–6
2 Timothy 4:1–8
Luke 12:32–48

*"From everyone to whom much has been given,
much will be required; and from the one to whom much
has been entrusted, even more will be demanded."*
LUKE 12:48

You want the big job, the one that comes with a corner office and a hefty salary. You want to be a doctor. You want to be a bishop, to be president.

But these things carry obligations equal in weight to their power and prestige. Years of education, hour upon hour of work, frightening amounts of courage in making decisions that could cost other people their livelihoods or even their lives. We think people in power can do anything they wish. The fact is that what they wish is often the very thing they cannot do. *I have a lot of power, but I have very little freedom,* a high-powered CEO once told me, and it was true.

And we hold them to standards they usually cannot meet, repose hopes in them beyond the power of human beings to reward. We have modeled our image of God after the important human beings among us: King of Kings, we say, and Lord of Lords, as if God were an ancient ruler or nobleman. And so we expect our own kings and lords to be gods.

We peer over their shoulders, uninvited, at their lives, their marriages, their children. We are angry at their divorces and affairs. A man in his position , we sniff, certainly ought to know better than to act like that. And he certainly should. But some of them do not, as some of us do not.

The worst thing that can happen to a powerful person is to forget the source of his power. Power comes from God, all of it, and power is neither bad nor good: it is neutral. We decide which ours will be.

SATURDAY IN PROPER 1

Pss 137:1–6 (7–9), 144 * 104
Isaiah 66:7–14
2 Timothy 4:9–22
Luke 12:49–59

Do your best to come to me soon.
. . . Do your best to come before winter.
2 TIMOTHY 4:9, 21

I was looking forward to our friends' visit, but I cannot say that I am disappointed to learn that they're not coming after all: in my daily battle for private time, I just won some. A couple of hours I wouldn't have had. One of the hardest things about being an adult is accepting limits, choosing between two good things because I can only do one of them. Do I take time for a visit, or do I keep chipping away with my never-ending pile of work? It is always a treat when someone else chooses for me.

Friendship is a choice. We choose to make the time for a friend or we do not, and the relationship can't sustain itself forever if we consistently chose against it.

But what about the ones with people we don't see frequently? People who live far away, to whom we must travel long distances— or they must? Years can go by without a sighting. Your own busy life where you live every day takes over, its demands nearby and insistent. Maybe next year, you think as another chance to get together folds under the pressure of your work schedule.

But when it does all work out, when you do find the time to get together, Why don't we do this more often? you ask yourself. The richness of old friendship, the memories from years ago, the amazing fact that we really haven't changed a bit, as different as we are from what we used to be. Let's not wait so long next time, you say when it is time to part, and you mean it. It may be a while, longer than it should be. But don't let it be forever.

MONDAY IN PROPER 2

Pss 1, 2, 3 * 4, 7
Ruth 1:1–18
1 Timothy 1:1–17
Luke 13:1–9

*"Sir, let it alone for one more year,
until I dig around it and put manure on it."*
LUKE 13:8

You either like the smell of horse manure or you don't. I adore it. I can go down to the horse farm and pick up a few bags of it any time I want to—Leo and his colleagues produce a fair amount. It's about time to do that, in fact: we're running low.

The elegance of the garden economy attracts me powerfully. A leaf falls to the ground and rots, becoming nourishment for the next season's plants. A bird passes overhead; next year, a seed from a berry she ate in Connecticut takes root in Metuchen, and there's a raspberry bush where I didn't plant one. And plants multiply all by themselves, too, sending their emissaries under the ground to establish new plants a few feet away, so that the three plants you put into the ground two years ago are twelve plants now and twenty plants next year. Elegant.

The natural vector of life is production. Not just being: growing. Our natural state is not just to consume, but to produce. We are unhappy if we are not producing—even if we don't know it.

The chronically homeless usually lose the capacity for production. They have no job and no home to clean and they hate it that this is so, but the longer they remain in this situation, the less able they become do the things one must do in order to live in a normal setting: they become unable to make and keep appointments, to arrive places on time, unable to work for any extended period, unable to tolerate the bureaucratic intricacies of modern life, the interpersonal tensions that arise in any work setting. So few choices are available to them that they become unable to make any choices at all. They cannot bloom.

Probably most of them can, if somebody can spend the time and energy it takes to re-nourish them. Retrain them in the art of living. Usually they resist wanting this: a body at rest tends to remain at rest. And you can't force them to change.

Sometimes I thin out a group of plants, so that those that remain have access to a greater share of what the soil has for them. And sometimes I transplant the ones I have removed from their midst, take them to another part of the garden and plant them there. It is a shock: they hate it at first. They wilt, drop leaves. Some of them die.

But some of them survive the move, dig into the new soil on their own, and make it.

TUESDAY IN PROPER 2

Pss 5, 6 * 10, 11
Ruth 1:19–2:13
1 Timothy 1:18–2:8
Luke 13:10–17

So the two of them [Naomi and Ruth] went on until they came to Bethlehem. When they came to Bethlehem, the whole town was stirred because of them; and the women said, "Is this Naomi?"

RUTH 1:19

So Naomi is from Bethlehem. So is Jesus, of course. Centuries later, at the beginning of the gospel of Matthew, we are treated to three lists of Jesus' forebears. Ruth is in one of them, a foreign-born ancestress of the messiah, a woman with an interesting story of triumph over the devastating effects of loss. Her husband is dead and she and her mother-in-law are refugees. She is intelligent and shrewd, positioning herself to attract the attention of her husband's powerful relative and regain what she has lost.

The story of Ruth and Naomi is very old. Scripture contains a number of such stories, stories of people triumphing over great adversity, stories of the weak overcoming the strong by outsmarting them. Humanity has always loved such tales: we see ourselves in the resourceful hero who bursts through the limits life has set upon him. Or her.

What you don't find in these stories is much attention to conventional morality. We think it very important that people behave themselves sexually, and talk about the biblical principles governing marriage and sexuality, but Ruth *seduces* Boaz—or, at least, she lets him seduce her—and the writer who tells us this story offers no moral condemnation of this act. She uses her beauty, one of the few resources she was left with, to care for herself and her mother-in-law.

I remember my father telling me about occupied Japan after the Second World War. There were women there who would sell their bodies for a small amount of food, a chocolate bar, an American dollar or two. My father was extremely modest, straight-laced, but he offered no condemnation or disapproval of their actions, either. They had nothing else to sell, those women.

Conventional morality is conventional. Some circumstances are extreme, and call for new duties we might never entertain under normal conditions. Usually this is sad, in some way, like the situation with the Japanese women, or like Ruth's desperate flirtation with Boaz. But sometimes it is necessary.

WEDNESDAY IN PROPER 2

Pss 119:1–24 * 12, 13, 14
Ruth 2:14–23
1 Timothy 3:1–16
Luke 13:18–30

*He must manage his own household well, keeping his
children submissive and respectful in every way . . .*
1 TIMOTHY 3:4

Submissive and respectful? Oh, dear. It's not easy being the child of a religious leader. People expect things that you sometimes fail to deliver. Your faults seem to surprise people, as if you weren't supposed to have any.

But the worst thing is the extent to which you have to share your mom or dad. Both of them, sometimes. Everyone wants their attention. They have to work on Christmas Eve and Christmas Day. Sometimes they have to run out in the middle of the night because someone is injured, or has died. Everyone wants to talk to them, and be understood by them. Sometimes it seems as if there's nothing left over for you: you'd like to talk, too, and you, too, want very much to be understood.

Probably the best thing you can do is remain demanding of what you know you need. Your mom or dad also needs to be close to you. They need to stop working sometimes, and play, and that is something you can offer them. With you, they're not up in front of a crowd. They're at home.

And, if you're not the child of a pastor? If you're one of the people who looks to one? Remember that the things he or she needs at the end of a long day are probably very like the ones you need, and respect the need. Remember that you can't get blood from a stone. And that nobody is perfect.

THURSDAY IN PROPER 2

Pss 18:1–20 * 18:21–50
Ruth 3:1–18
1 Timothy 4:1–16
Luke 13:31–35

"Herod wants to kill you."
LUKE 13:31

Jesus knew he would die, it seems certain. He went anyway. Dr. Martin Luther King was like that: he seems to have known that his public life would one day result in his death—he said so in public, many times—and he was willing to continue living it. Mohandas Gandhi knew, too: as he died, he blessed his assassin in the name of God.

We've all got to go sometime. Everybody dies. Some people's lives stretch far beyond their temporal limits, and we remember them forever. Other people are quickly forgotten.

Most Christians would say that the great souls of the world are animated by the Holy Spirit, showing in their lives the way to live in the world. We easily see Christ in someone like Gandhi, who was not Christian.

Some would say, though, that those who do not die as confessing believers in Jesus Christ as the Son of God cannot be exemplary to us. That, in fact, they are damned. This seems so sad to me, and so impoverished, narrowing the scope of God's power far below the might I know God wields. Throughout the course of human history, God has worked in every time and place, both before and after the edifice of Christian theology existed. God didn't need that edifice. It is a way of our understanding God. It is not a prison for God. God is free.

Free to create life. And sometimes, free to lay it down out of love of the world so immense it is beyond the comprehension of almost all of us. Except for a few. Humankind doesn't stretch that far.

FRIDAY IN PROPER 2

Pss 16, 17 * 22
Ruth 4:1–17
1 Timothy 5:17–22 (23–25)
Luke 14:1–11

Let the elders who rule well be considered worthy of double honor, especially those who labor in preaching and teaching . . .
1 TIMOTHY 5:17

Don't preach more than one sermon at a time. You'll get another chance.

Don't use Greek or Hebrew words gratuitously in sermons. If you need people to know you went to school, hang your diplomas on the wall of your office. Use foreign words only if they enlarge your meaning.

Don't allude to people currently in the parish, or to members from the recent past. Not even in a complimentary manner. Unless, of course, you're preaching at their funeral. Such things can come back and bite you in ways you can't imagine.

Don't preach on topics you can't discuss without crying. Everyone mists up now and then, but you can't break down crying in front of a paying audience. Until you can talk about it with composure, don't preach about it.

Don't be afraid to talk about yourself, but never use yourself as an example of good behavior. You're of much more use to people as a sinner than you ever will be as a saint. Most of the saints were serious, anyway.

Don't quote too much. You're the one in the pulpit—give them your ideas, not someone else's.

And don't worry. God didn't bring all those people together on a Sunday morning so you could put them to sleep. Ask God to use you as a channel of the divine grace and then trust that this will happen. It's God's will that they hear and grow as a result of what they hear. Do your best to prepare and then trust God for the rest. Never fails.

SATURDAY IN PROPER 2

Pss 20, 21:1–7 (8–14) * 110:1–5 (6–7), 116, 117
Deuteronomy 1:1–8
1 Timothy 6:6–21
Luke 14:12–24

There is great gain in godliness combined with contentment . . .
1 TIMOTHY 6:6

You can be rich and good at the same time; it's just harder—you have more temptations actually available to you, available as more than daydreams, which is what most material temptations are to poor people.

The things that tempt you aren't illegal. They're just excessive: enormous cars that block the view of everyone else on the road and guzzle gas that everyone else needs, too. Three or four of them in a family, because nobody ever wants to wait and nobody ever wants to share because, well, I'd have to *wait*. Enormous houses where a family farm used to be, or where wildfires are frequent—if I decide to live where it's not really safe to build a house, because I can afford to live anywhere I damned well please, I can cost a firefighter his or her life. To say nothing of my own life, and that of my family. Dozens and dozens of outfits, scores of shoes. Things get out of hand easily when it's no big deal to buy them.

And a great deal of your time and energy must go toward maintaining all these things. You need all that space, to store all those shoes. Your insurance has to be expensive—you have so many cars.

You have to work a lot—it seems you're never in that beautiful house, must fight to get to your summer home—which also takes money and energy to run.

Sometimes you step back and ask yourself who's in charge here. How much time do you have for quiet and meditative moments alone? To read? Is it hard for you even to *want* such a thing: has the easy availability of all our distractions drowned out the gentle voice of God, inviting you to turn aside from the busy highway of life and rest awhile? Does the cost of maintaining all your possessions make it hard for you to give money away, and hard to take pleasure in doing so?

It doesn't look like a grave situation. The pickpocket, in jail overnight or the prostitute picked up yet again—they look like they're in trouble. Sure.

But we look just fine.

SUNDAY, PROPER 3

Pss 148, 149, 150 * 114, 115
Deuteronomy 4:1–9
Revelation 7:1–4, 9–17
Matthew 12:33–45

". . . and the last state of that person is worse than the first."
MATTHEW 12:45

The demons Jesus means are familiar to me: I have more experience with depression than I wish I had. All will be well, for quite a while, and then too many stressors pile up on my plate, and I feel the demons begin to nibble. Trouble sleeping, a short temper, a feeling of hopelessness, of worthlessness, a pervasive guilt. Sometimes I even wish I were dead in an idle, passive kind of way—just too dispirited to lift life itself.

The really diabolical part is that it is worse each time they visit. They really do bring their friends with them, the jerks. It is a blessing that we live in a time when much more is known about their ways than was known in Jesus' time: I treat the first glimpse of the first demon as a serious medical event, as serious as a sudden fever would be in the physical realm, and I get to my doctor. Just making the call makes me feel better. There is hope. This will end. I don't have to feel this way forever.

Of course, nobody wants to admit to being possessed by a demon. It's embarrassing. Other chronic things—diabetes, heart disease—these don't embarrass us. But the demons do. It's part of their charm. They want us to dismiss them, to scold ourselves. *Oh, pull yourself together,* one of them sneers into my left ear. *Shut up, you jerk,* I reply. *Do you think I don't know who you are?*

They will not prevail against me. They may be stronger than I am, sometimes, but Jesus is stronger than they are. And I'm with him.

MONDAY IN PROPER 3

Pss 25 * 9, 15
Deuteronomy 4:9–14
2 Corinthians 1:1–11
Luke 14:25–35

"For which of you, intending to build a tower,
does not first sit down and estimate the cost,
to see whether he has enough to complete it?"
LUKE 14:28

Just show me where you want 'em, the man in the dump truck said, and I pointed to a spot over by the garden. He turned the back of his truck up toward the sky and discharged two pallets of heavy rocks. They bounced into the garden, into the lawn; miraculously, only one eggplant was hit, and I think it's going to be all right, with some rest.

We're not building a tower. We're building a wall. The cost? $352.93—in money, that is. The cost in labor remains to be seen. I am sure that it will be a bigger job than we anticipate—everything in a garden is. But the stones are beautiful, and the wall will be wonderful.

There's a fine line between a leap of faith and plain foolishness. The first is essential if there is to be any vision: otherwise, we would only do the things we've already done, the things we're sure of. There needs to be that little uncertainty, that mighty stretch, and risk attends these things. But you need, at the very least, to be able to say how you will accomplish what you say you will, and it needs not to be crazy. It can't have winning the lottery as a given. Because you just don't know.

We may need more stones. Other people might have counted and measured better ahead of time; we will just begin with the part you see first, and go from there.

TUESDAY IN PROPER 3

Pss 26, 28 * 36, 39
Deuteronomy 4:15–24
2 Corinthians 1:12–22
Luke 15:1–10

For we write to you nothing other than what
you can read and also understand . . .
2 CORINTHIANS 1:13

Isn't there a manual? Q wants to know. Did I tell you that I call my husband Q? I am cursing over the computer. *Yes, there is,* I say shortly. *For all the good it does,* I add to myself. Manuals and operating instructions never make any sense to me. The little drawings techies make to clarify the things they do—they muddy them hopelessly for me. I don't understand their terms and their jargon, and their instructions seem ambiguous.

The key to all teaching is to remember what it was like not to know, a seminary professor used to say to us tutors. Exactly. Almost everyone who is enthusiastic about a subject assumes a like interest and experience in it on the part of others: how can anyone *not* know about something so fascinating?

Easy.

Understanding things of the spirit is even harder than understanding how to take the battery out of a cell phone; I know, I know, it's really easy, but it's hard for me. The spirit's knowledge isn't communicated in words: it's not *information*. It soaks into us in another way of knowing, a way impossible to describe to others—sort of like a computer manual, although I suppose there is somebody, somewhere who actually *does* understand those. But you have to be on board already, *prepared* to know, in order for it to make any sense at all. Just so with the spirit: you must be primed for it, set to receive its intelligence.

It soaks in little by little. You keep forgetting, and have to go back to the beginning to remember just how it goes. Sometimes you think the whole thing is your imagination—that's when it pains you that it's *not* information, like scientific or mechanical things are, not something you can just explain and comprehend immediately. You wish there were surefire techniques for spiritual growth, and there are many practices that assist it. But none of them are information. None of them are measurable. None of them.

Months go by. Years. You turn and realize that you are very different from the person you used to be, that you have learned a lot. That you have grown a great deal, in such small increments that you never saw it happening. Until it already had.

WEDNESDAY IN PROPER 3

Pss 38 * 119:25–48
Deuteronomy 4:25–31
2 Corinthians 1:23–2:17
Luke 15:1–2, 11–32

"But while he was still far off, his father saw him and was filled with compassion; he ran and put his arms around him and kissed him."
LUKE 15:20

His father must have been watching for him. Perhaps he went to his front door every morning and looked into the distance, hoping to see his lost son approaching. He may have looked down the road every morning for years: we don't know how long the young man was gone.

Clearly, the prodigal son was in the wrong. No doubt about that. His more righteous brother was absolutely right: he didn't deserve to be treated so well when he slunk back home with his tail between his legs.

But his dad's love was greater than the son's failure. No matter what, he loved his boy and wanted him back. *No matter what.* That's the way most of us feel: our hearts ache at their mistakes, because they usually don't hurt anybody more than they hurt themselves, and it hurts us mightily to have to watch them do it. *Come home and let's try again. What did you learn from what you did to yourself?*

Love requires nothing so much as it requires patience. Patience in quantities you can't begin to imagine before it's needed and you must summon it, and then you call on God to make you some, quick. Because you're fresh out of patience. The cupboard is bare.

God's got more than you have. Lots more. And the wisdom to go with it: there are times when the best thing to do may not be the most immediately kind, and the task of discerning that is formidable. It takes courage to say that kind of "No!" to someone who wants very much what he should not have.

The father in the story is usually taken to be God, and it is a story about our free will and how badly we can mess things up for ourselves with it. But the father might also be us, real mothers and fathers and friends. Either way, we learn good things from this old story. Maybe the father shouldn't have given in to his foolish son's initial request. He should have said "No." He didn't, and the boy learned the hard way. But both of them got a second chance.

THURSDAY IN PROPER 3

Pss 37:1–18 * 37:19–42
Deuteronomy 4:32–40
2 Corinthians 3:1–18
Luke 16:1–9

*"And I tell you, make friends for yourselves by means
of dishonest wealth, so that when it is gone,
they may welcome you into the eternal homes."*
LUKE 16:9

Well, *this* is different: Jesus seems to be recommending something like insider trading.

I wonder though: is it possible that the last line of today's reading might have been an attempt by a later copyist to make some sense of what must have been a very puzzling assignment? Is this really a recommendation from Jesus himself that we behave like the sly, unrighteous steward? Or is it something else?

What if Jesus' actual last words on the subject are the ones *before* these words? *The master commended the dishonest steward for his shrewdness; for the sons of this generation are more shrewd in dealing with their own generation than the sons of light.* Ah. The swindler spends a lot of energy and intelligence planning his crime. The innocent victim is just walking down the street. She is not aware of what might happen. She is not careful. She trusts her world.

Be smart, Jesus tells us. Be as smart as people have to be to commit a crime, only be that smart in the service of righteousness and love. Put the same energy into improving race relations in America that the KKK puts into ruining them. Spend the same amount of wit raising your children to be creative and interested in life that you would spend at a gambling casino.

You have a certain amount of intelligence. You decide how you'll use it. Maybe that's what Jesus is saying.

FRIDAY IN PROPER 3

Pss 31 * 35
Deuteronomy 5:1–22
2 Corinthians 4:1–12
Luke 16:10–17 (18)

Therefore, since it is by God's mercy that we are
engaged in this ministry, we do not lose heart.
2 CORINTHIANS 4:1

I can't imagine being anything but the priest I am. I have lived this life so long that it has simply become part of my body. Whatever it means to be called, it must at least mean this: the same God who formed me in the womb formed me for this.

But being certain of my call does not mean that it isn't hard. Even work you love, even work you know is really your calling, above all others—it can make you lose heart sometimes. You make mistakes and wonder if you're really any good at it at all. You look at someone else who does what you do and feel inferior: he is more successful, she is better at it. Or you work yourself to death and your heart fills with bitterness: you can almost die of it, if you don't remember that your heart is your responsibility and that you'll have no heart for anybody if you don't take care of your own first.

I am positive that these moments of real anguish are part of any vocation—priest, teacher, mom or dad, athlete, horse trainer, nurse, waiter. They don't invalidate the call, but they do display the cost of following it. They are warnings: *Be sure you line up the resources you will need to do this job. Don't be ashamed to admit it when you're in trouble, out of some misplaced sense of self-reliance. That's not what self-reliance is.*

So when do you know that what you're experiencing isn't just the normal disappointments of a right vocation? That it's something more, a sign that you're in the wrong place? You don't know that because you have a string of bad days. No job is a grin and a giggle all the time.

But your spirit should be more joyful, more of the time, than it is in misery. You may have misery, to be sure, but it should not be steadily in the majority. More joy than sorrow, over time. Bring someone else into your analysis if you still aren't sure on your own. And then don't be afraid to seek your true destiny, for you will not be at home until you find it.

SATURDAY IN PROPER 3

Pss 30, 32 * 42, 43
Deuteronomy 5:22–33
2 Corinthians 4:13–5:10
Luke 16:19–31

*"No, father Abraham; but if someone goes
to them from the dead, they will repent."*

LUKE 16:30

Will they? Do we really do what we think the beloved dead ask of us?

We do for a while. The relatives of someone who is gravely ill often show up in church again, very faithfully, for a while—and some of them do remain after the person has died, permanently comforted by the comfort that the one they loved enjoyed all her life. But many fall away after a time—sometimes in some anger, as if their church attendance were a failed bargaining chip intended to change the outcome of the illness.

Actually, we mostly don't change our behavior permanently for anyone else, living or dead, no matter how much we love them. We do it for ourselves, because we want the joy we think the change will bring, or can no longer endure the misery our current life brings us every day. *Sick and tired of being sick and tired* is how the alcoholics put it, and the pain of that state is the first step to the goodness of getting better and leaving the hell of addiction behind.

Maybe we don't change for their sake, but they do rejoice in it when we finally leave hell behind. They have prayed for this for years. They have longed to change us and, sooner or later, realized they could never do that. We can only change ourselves, and we can only do that with God's help. But afterwards, we'll remember what they told us so many times with their warnings. Even those in complete denial hear the truth, and they remember it.

SUNDAY, PROPER 4

Pss 63:1–8 (9–11), 98 * 103
Deuteronomy 11:1–12
Revelation 10:1–11
Matthew 13:44–58

"Prophets are not without honor except in
their own country and in their own house."
MATTHEW 13:57

That's the truth—other people respect you, but the home folks know where you came from. And what you used to look like. And what you did that time when you were nine years old and set the lawn mower on fire by mistake, burning down the garage.

Nobody comes into this world knowing everything they need to know—not even Jesus. He was a kid once, too: we have one snapshot of him, conversing with the elders in the temple, but we don't have snapshots of the other things he did when he was little. I think we can imagine, though: he was a little boy. He probably did what little boys do.

We have to *grow* into our full stature. We have to learn how to be the selves we will become, and we don't learn that all at once. It's a great privilege to accompany a young person in that journey, but it's hard: ask anyone who's raised a teenager.

Most people of a certain age realized something long ago: they have never really stopped learning. The more you know, the more you know you don't know. You learn humility along with everything else you learn, and it comes in handy, the more you know.

MONDAY IN PROPER 4

Pss 41, 52 * 44
Deuteronomy 11:13–19
2 Corinthians 5:11–6:2
Luke 17:1–10

"Do you thank the slave for doing what was commanded?"
LUKE 17:9

When we compliment someone, we are apt to say that he has done something "above and beyond the call of duty." We acknowledge, when we say that, that duty has a call—that doing your duty is not an extra bit of good behavior, for which you should get a prize. It's not extra. It's expected. It's your duty.

You're going to be so proud of me, a young man tells his mother on the phone. Everyone else in the dorm got ripping drunk, and I didn't. It was hard to know what to say to that: people don't really deserve a prize for not doing something self-destructive. That's expected—part of one's duty to oneself. Part of having brains enough not to make yourself sick or even dead.

We're so anxious about our children's self-esteem that it is typical, in school competitions, for everyone to get a prize. That way no one's feelings are hurt. Maybe. But the result is that we feel entitled to a commendation for everything, don't know the delight of competing, of trying to be the best.

I think we see through the inflation of congratulations. I think we know that if everything wins a prize, nothing is really prize-winning. And I think we can learn about the call of duty, if we want the satisfaction such knowledge brings to life, even if well-meaning adults who were trying to spare our feelings didn't get around to teaching us.

TUESDAY IN PROPER 4

Pss 45 * 47, 48
Deuteronomy 12:1–12
2 Corinthians 6:3–13 (14–7:1)
Luke 17:11–19

"Were not ten made clean? But the other nine, where are they?"
LUKE 17:17

I guess they were just excited and forgot. But one of them didn't. Who knows why? He was struck by the knowledge of where his miraculous healing had come from, and it stopped him in his tracks. And so his joy was doubled: first when he was healed, and then again when he realized that it was not by accident. That the love of God that had healed him intentionally.

God's intention for all of us is healing and wholeness, and yet there is illness in the world, and injury. People suffer. Sometimes people get better and sometimes they don't. Sometimes they get better when no one expects they will, and sometimes they don't. There is no way to tell which it will be. Contemplate this, and you may become fatalistic. It doesn't matter what I do. I have no control over anything.

Unless you approach it from the other direction. No, you don't know. And you don't have all the power over events: you have some, like the power to live a healthy life, but you aren't in charge of who lives and who dies. And since it could go any one of a thousand different terrible ways, it's a miracle when things go well, when people are healed. That we're here at all is one, that our hearts beat and beat for so many years without any help. We're miraculous. The capacity of our bodies to heal is a miracle.

I suppose you'll praise God for healing if you're used to praising God already. If you've already given some thought to how miraculous life itself is.

WEDNESDAY IN PROPER 4

Pss 119:49–72 * 49, (53)
Deuteronomy 13:1–11
2 Corinthians 7:2–16
Luke 17:20–37

"Remember Lot's wife."
LUKE 17:32

I remember her. She just wanted to take one last look at her home, and she was turned into a pillar of salt. I always thought that was sad, and quite unfair. I'd want to look back once, too, if I had to leave my home forever. *Just one look.*

Don't look after you have opened the door, the crew of the *Enola Gay* was told. *Don't look at the city below. Just turn the plane sharply to the right and get out of there as fast as you can.* And so they didn't look. Didn't see 100,000 souls vaporized in less than a second. Didn't see what happened afterward, either. They were long gone.

If you hear an explosion, don't open your eyes, the teacher told us. *You'll go blind if you open your eyes.* I had the feeling, even then, that going blind might be the least of our worries.

You can't hang onto what you had. Sometimes you just have to leave it behind. Sometimes somebody takes it from you. Sometimes it just explodes, without any warning. But even if it doesn't explode, you may try to go back, but you can't. You no longer live there. No point in looking for it. It isn't there. Not for you. Not for anybody, sometimes.

It hurts us that history only moves forward. So much love ties us to the past, and we can never visit. We must keep moving. We can't even look back. There's nothing there for us to see.

THURSDAY IN PROPER 4

Pss 50 * (59, 60) or 8, 84
Deuteronomy 16:18–20; 17:14–20
2 Corinthians 8:1–16
Luke 18:1–8

We want you to know, brothers and sisters, about the grace of
God that has been granted to the churches of Macedonia . . .

2 CORINTHIANS 8:1

If this chapter of 2 Corinthians has a familiar ring, it may be
because it's an ancient fundraising letter. The Gentile churches—
which included some very prosperous communities along the trade
routes of the ancient near east—were being asked to contribute to
the welfare of the poorer church in Jerusalem. People they had never
met and never would meet.

Like it or not, we are linked to everyone else in the world. We
don't get to decide whether or not to participate in a global economy; we already do, and we already have for a long time, whether
we knew it or not. It's only recently that we understood that the
person answering our technical question about the computer isn't
in an office nearby, that he's in Bangalore. That the must-have
American brands aren't made in America, and haven't been since
just about forever.

This incenses some of us: our money, our jobs, going elsewhere!
And concerns some of us: the faraway people with whom our economy is so deeply involved may be commodities in the eyes of decision makers here, of no more intrinsic importance than the sneakers
or designer jackets they make. What will happen to them when they
are of no more use to their wealthy overseas employers?

But here is an ancient Christian, entreating the strangers he has
met and come to love to care about faraway people simply because
they are Christians and they are in need. Paul's sense of our related-
ness is powerful, and it was much more spiritual and much less economic in his day than it is in ours. Might we regain his love for the

faraway, whose work serves us now, whether we have chosen it or not? And might not doing so, one day, change the imbalance between us into something more closely resembling fairness?

FRIDAY IN PROPER 4

Pss 40, 54 * 51
Deuteronomy 26:1–11
2 Corinthians 8:16–24
Luke 18:9–14

With him we are sending the brother who is famous among all the churches for his proclaiming of the good news . . .
2 CORINTHIANS 8:18

Now Paul is advertising a special guest preacher: he's sparing no expense in this fundraising campaign. The people of Corinth won't know what hit them.

People often complain about this when they talk about their clergy. *All he ever does is talk about money,* they say. It's hard to know how to respond to that. Maybe it's true that he never talks about anything else, but somehow I doubt it. I think his mentioning it at all is what troubles them. Money should be magic, we think, in religious settings. You shouldn't need to talk about it. We should just trust in God that the proper amount will come in.

Well, yes. But God ensures that by moving people's hearts, and one of the tools God uses to do that is the preacher.

Maybe some people don't know that church costs money; if they don't, somebody needs to tell them. And maybe some people don't know how blessed they are; somebody has to tell them that, too. And maybe some people don't know that our money isn't really ours, that we hold it in trust and are accountable for what we do with it. We're not supposed to keep it all for ourselves. We're supposed to share. Somebody's got to tell them.

And maybe some people don't know that if you can't give money, you can't. People can't do what they can't do. If you can't, somebody else will, and you need to accept that as the gift it is. Sometimes we carry others and sometimes others carry us. When you get back on your feet, you'll give again.

SATURDAY IN PROPER 4

Pss 55 * 138, 139:1–17 (18–23)
Deuteronomy 29:2–15
2 Corinthians 9:1–15
Luke 18:15–30

"Truly I tell you, there is no one who has left house or wife or brothers or parents or children, for the sake of the kingdom of God, who will not get back very much more in this age, and in the age to come eternal life."

LUKE 18:29–30

The people in the congregation were very proud of the warmth and love that was so visibly present in their congregation. Most of all, they liked it that the priest said each of their names and looked them in the eye as he gave them communion. "Mary, the Body of Christ." "Susan, the Body of Christ." "Frank, the Body of Christ." He would go down the line of people, each one known and named. *We are so close,* people used to say. *We're like a family.*

One Sunday morning, the priest drew a blank on a woman's name. "The Body of Christ," he said, after an awkward pause. It was obvious he'd forgotten her name. She was devastated, and went to see him afterward to tell him how hurt she was. Oh, dear. That is why I don't do the name thing when I distribute the bread.

People make mistakes. As nice as it is to be known and loved, the liturgy is really not a private event. It is not a ceremony solely about our intimacy with one another. It points beyond us and all the things we do, to the God who includes all those things.

Perhaps it is not always one another's eyes into which we need to gaze. Perhaps we need, at the moment in which we receive it, to gaze at the bit of bread we have received, so ordinary and unimpressive. So not about us alone, or even about our families and friends alone. So fragile and temporary. So mysterious.

So Christ.

SUNDAY, PROPER 5

Pss 24, 29 * 8, 84
Deuteronomy 29:16–29
Revelation 12:1–12
Matthew 15:29–39

... a woman clothed with the sun, with the moon under her feet, and on her head a crown of twelve stars. She was pregnant ...
REVELATION 12:1–2

This is the description of the Virgin of Guadeloupe: she is always pictured in a starry robe that shines so brightly her entire body is surrounded by a nimbus. She stands on a crescent moon, and she wears a crown of twelve stars. She wears black bands on her sleeves: in Mexico, a sign that she is pregnant. She is a virgin of color: Guadeloupe's skin is always brown.

In Hell's Kitchen, the children and I used to have a procession on Guadeloupe's feast day in December. We carried her icon and big bouquets of roses and handed them out to passers-by, to shopkeepers, to the people waiting at the traffic lights in their cars. We would have to tell those who were not Mexican what day it was, but the neighborhood people all knew. Then we would return to the church for a Mexican dinner. By that time their parents had finished work, and filtered into the shabby parish hall to join us for the burritos and the Spanish songs on the radio.

Juan Diego was a poor Indian man, a man who counted for little. One winter day, though, while he was out in the desert, he had a vision of the Virgin Mary. *Go and tell the bishop you saw me,* she instructed him. But Juan Diego knew the bishop would never believe that the Mother of Christ had come to him, a peasant, and not to the bishop himself. *I need a sign that he will believe,* he told her. *Hold out the hem of your blouse,* she said, and he did, stretching his arms out in front of him to accommodate the loose-fitting tunic he wore. Immediately, his tunic was full of flowers. In the dead of winter. The bishop saw the flowers and believed. Guadeloupe is the patron saint of Mexico, the virgin beloved of the poor, the one to whom they turn. Because she is one of them.

I would wonder, often, what the future might hold for the children we served. They came from Guatemala, from Ecuador, from Mexico. Their parents worked in the restaurant kitchens. Some of them have had only a couple of years schooling themselves. Some of them are here illegally. Their lives have been hard, and will remain so.

But their children will finish high school. Some will go to college. Flowers in the winter.

MONDAY IN PROPER 5

Pss 56, 57, (58) * Pss 64, 65
Deuteronomy 30:1–10
2 Corinthians 10:1–18
Luke 18:31–43

I who am humble when face to face with you,
but bold toward you when I am away!
2 CORINTHIANS 10:1

You get into trouble so easily with e-mail. You pound off a smart-aleck response to something with which you strongly disagree, the keys tapping like a machine gun, and then you press "send" while you're still mad. As it darts off into the ether and lands immediately in the inbox of your target, you realize with horror that you shouldn't have sent it. That you should have counted to ten. That your e-mail was a huge overreaction to something that really wasn't worth a hill of beans. That you misspelled "idiot." And that you can never get it back. Your e-mail will live forever in cyberspace. The Department of Homeland Security can read it. With one click, the person to whom you sent it can circulate it to an infinite number of people who you might very much rather didn't see it.

Emotions ride high on the Internet. The natural consequences of rudeness in conversation don't happen to you online: you don't see hurt collect in a person's eyes, you don't see someone's lips tighten. Nobody turns on her heels and walks silently away from you. Maybe she writes back a rebuke of her own. Maybe she doesn't write back at all. If she does not, you sit in the bluish light of your computer monitor, aware that you have hurt someone you cannot reach. You cannot pursue her, reach out and take her hand.

You can tell her you're sorry in an e-mail.

But she may just press "delete" when she sees who it's from.

TUESDAY IN PROPER 5

Pss 61, 62 * 68:1–20 (21–23) 24–36
Deuteronomy 30:11–20
2 Corinthians 11:1–21a
Luke 19:1–10

"Zaccheus, hurry and come down;
for I must stay at your house today."
LUKE 19:5

Zaccheus was thrilled to have a celebrity guest. But before they even got to his house, he found himself saying something he may not have planned to say when he set out that morning: I'll give to the poor, I'll stop cheating people, I'll repay the ones I have cheated. I'll repay them fourfold.

Just as I am. It is powerful to think that Christ comes to us just as we are, that our sins and errors are not enough to keep him away. That there is nothing that cannot be forgiven. Nothing that cannot be changed by his power.

Not that we always want to be changed. *Just as I am* sounds good, but nothing in the radical acceptance we are offered suggests that we should expect to stay there. God has intentions for us: that we grow in kindness and compassion, that we learn how to transcend our lonely self-absorption, that we come closer to the divine love. We're accepted just as we are, but we won't stay the same. God will work in us, and we may become quite different before God is finished with us.

We don't know what became of Zaccheus. His sudden repentance— did it last? Did he have a hard time sustaining it? Could he remain in his profession, or did he have to leave it in order to follow Jesus? Was there a way to be a Christian tax collector? We never find out.

We are cynical about the conversions of crooked business people. We don't believe in them, as the people who knew Zaccheus didn't believe in his capacity to change. But conversion is never a matter of our own capacity for goodness, all by itself: if it were, there would be no reason for conversion. We'd already be holy.

WEDNESDAY IN PROPER 5

Pss 72 * 119:73–96
Deuteronomy 31:30–32:14
2 Corinthians 11:21b–33
Luke 19:11–27

Remember the days of old, consider the years long past; ask your father, and he will inform you; your elders, and they will tell you.
DEUTERONOMY 32:7

Tomorrow, the dedication of the World War II Memorial in Washington, D.C. Already the Mall is full of veterans and their families. Dozens of volunteers have been trained to take oral histories from the grey-haired men and women. We must hear from them now: eleven hundred of these veterans die every day. Soon they will all be gone.

My father was one of them. I have a photograph of him with my mother, taken in 1942 by a street photographer in Duluth. He strides along in his uniform, she walks beside him, one slim foot just about to touch the sidewalk for her next step. She has just spoken; the forgotten word still shapes her mouth, and he is smiling at what she has said. *My first furlough*, he wrote on the back.

They have been married less than a year. Even my older brother is two years away. She will soon move to the East Coast and begin to work as a secretary on a military base while he is in Officer Candidate School. Later he will go to Japan and she will stay there in Maryland, waiting for his return.

There are things I don't know and now cannot ask them. Sometimes I accepted their guidance and sometimes I resisted it; almost always, I would have been better off if I had listened sooner. There are things I am glad they are missing. There are things about which I would like their advice. In prayer, I often have the sense that they are with me.

Call them today, if yours are still alive. Allow yourself to let go of the fact that they weren't perfect and made mistakes, giving them the forgiveness you want for yourself: doing anything else will cause you pain. Remember what was good in your life together. And be gentle with the world they left you; you'll be passing it on yourself some day.

THURSDAY IN PROPER 5

Pss (70), 71 * 74
Ecclesiasticus 44:19–45:5
2 Corinthians 12:1–10
Luke 19:28–40

I know a person in Christ who fourteen years ago
was caught up to the third heaven . . .
2 CORINTHIANS 12:2

Paul is talking about himself here: a mystical experience of the presence of God that he had and remembered for the rest of his life. These are not experiences people have every day, and they are not experiences we can summon up at will. We do not *do* them; they happen to us.

But we can learn practices that will make such experiences more likely. We can claim time and space for the quiet listening of the spirit for the voice of God: we can sit and think, we can read scripture and puzzle over it, we can listen to music or pray with an icon, sit in a church or lie on our backs and look at the blue sky through a screen of green leaves. With humility and hope, we can go to the places in which God has spoken to us before, or to the places in which God has spoken to others. God loves us and longs to connect with us, so our chances are pretty good.

And we can listen to the experience of others who have lived lives of connection with God. The Christian mystical tradition is old: many people have done this before, and have written about it. And many live this life today, and are willing to talk about it. We are not without help.

There is a place in our spirits that lies underneath all our busyness and noise. It is a quiet, expectant place, a silent place of openheartedness. It is a place with no agenda. We can learn to recognize this place within ourselves and we can learn to go there.

Fourteen years after Paul had this experience of heaven, he was the same cranky person he'd always been. We don't become perfect because we encounter God: we remain very human. But we never forget what we have seen and heard. And we will see and hear it all again.

FRIDAY IN PROPER 5

Pss 69:1–23 (24–30) 31–38 * 73
Ecclesiasticus 45:6–16
2 Corinthians 12:11–21
Luke 19:41–48

For I fear that when I come, I may find you not as I wish,
and that you may find me not as you wish . . .
2 CORINTHIANS 12:20

I have married more than one couple who met on the Internet. This seems risky, at first: anybody can claim to be anything online. But often they seem to work things out through the ether, and when at last they meet, neither is disappointed. After all, people have long relied on the introductions of friends and relatives: maybe the Internet is like that, a sprawling extended family with lots of cousins you don't know about yet.

It may have been so long ago that you've forgotten, but there was probably a time when you had an ideal in your mind of the perfect partner. Physical specifications: hair color, build. Maybe you had certain professions in mind, and certain likes and dislikes that were essential in your ideal mate. Maybe you even fantasized about the perfect name.

And now? Perhaps you're alone. But if you are not, it is likely that the person to whom your life is joined isn't your ideal. Doesn't resemble him or her very much. Because your ideal was never a real person. It was just an idea.

We never really know each other. We are unexpected. Even after years of marriage or friendship, we surprise each other. People are too complicated ever to be reducible to an ideal; getting to know a real person takes a lifetime. It's good that we can't act on our youthful desire to design the perfect mate. Faced with the real thing, the ideal looks silly, one-dimensional. Boring.

SATURDAY IN PROPER 5

Pss 75, 76 * 23, 27
Ecclesiasticus 46:1–10
2 Corinthians 13:1–14
Luke 20:1–8

*The grace of the Lord Jesus Christ, the love of God,
and the communion of the Holy Spirit be with all of you.*
2 CORINTHIANS 13:14

Church people have heard this phrase so many times in church that it's a shock to see it somewhere else—like at the end of a letter. But that's what it is.

All the things we know as liturgies were fresh and new once. Secular liturgies and sacred ones—"The Star-Spangled Banner" wasn't always the national anthem. It was just a new song. The Lord's Prayer was just the answer to a question.

In a way, the institutionalization of these things is a pity. We use them so much that they have lost their power to intrigue us. *Oh, that's the Creed*, we say, and we stand up and repeat it from memory. We can do that without wondering what "True God from True God" might mean and why it's there, or why they had to say both "God from God" and "Light from Light." What's that about? your child asks. *Oh, it's the Creed.* You just say it.

On the other hand, the capacity of the spirit to make words part of its fiber is itself a spiritual tool. Many, many times, your feelings and your intellect do not lead you anywhere near the heart of God. Sometimes they lead you in the opposite direction. At such times, it is heartening to know that there are holy words lodged in your very brain stem.

My mother-in-law had Alzheimer's disease. She couldn't answer a question or recognize her son. But she could repeat long prayers from the 1928 Prayer Book, and she could take comfort in them. From beneath a capacity for memory she no longer possessed, there they were. Waiting for her. Their very presence in the midst of her confusion was all the meaning they needed to have.

SUNDAY, PROPER 6

Pss 93, 96 * 34
Ecclesiasticus 46:11–20
Revelation 15:1–8
Matthew 18:1–14

*"If any of you put a stumbling block before one of
these little ones who believe in me, it would be better for you
if a great millstone were fastened around your neck and
you were drowned in the great depth of the sea."*
MATTHEW 18:6

We owe a peculiar debt to the innocent. It is not a debt of their negotiating: they are inexperienced in life. They have laid no claim on us. But we sense it, this debt. We are angry when one of them comes to grief. What did that little guy ever do to anybody? we inquire indignantly when a child suffers. But we inquire of no one: we know it's not like that.

We have a duty to protect them. They are smaller than we are, and weaker, and they claim us by their need. The visceral intensity of our response to their claim on us is obvious in parents, but it is not absent in any of us: we will stretch forth our hands to help the small and the weak, and feel bound to explain ourselves if we do not. Without a moment's deciding, most parents would give their lives, if doing so would spare the lives of their children. And they would count it a fair trade. They would consider themselves lucky.

A crime against one of them is graver in our eyes than a crime against one of us. I've lived my life, we will say, but she never even got a chance. A crime against one of them robs us of a little more of the future he would have carried in innocence. One fewer among the spotless. We cannot bear to see their ruin.

But here is the truth: no one is ruined. The injured innocent do not carry the sin of their injury, even if they think they do, even if they wear their scars like shame. Sin there was in the injury, all right, but the sin was not theirs, and there is comfort for them: preference, in the healing love of God. They will never be spotless again:

none of us remains spotless. But they will not be soiled. They will be clean.

And even if they die, their lives are complete and precious in the eyes of God. Just because they were brief doesn't mean they weren't everything they should have been. Even if they were sad, they were always beloved.

MONDAY IN PROPER 6

Pss 80 * 77, (79)
1 Samuel 1:1–20
Acts 1:1–14
Luke 20:9–19

*. . . but to Hannah he gave a double portion, because
he loved her, though the Lord had closed her womb.*

1 SAMUEL 1:5

Multiple wives, and a definite hierarchy of worth among them: the one who produced the most children was the honored one. But the human heart is not bound by hierarchy, and Elkanah loved Hannah no matter what.

Am I not more to you than ten sons? he asked. Wasn't it enough that they had each other? Apparently it was not enough, not if Hannah had to endure the jibes of her co-wife. And so Elkanah tried to compensate for what Hannah did not have. But the longing remained.

Twice as much of what you don't need doesn't make up for not having what you do need. Hannah had a double portion of food, but it was not food for which she hungered. It was a child.

We try to make up for things. We feel empty and think that shopping will help. We already have two of everything; perhaps we'll feel better with three. Maybe having more things will help. How about another drink? Another piece of cake?

But I can shop and eat and drink all I want, and the hunger inside me will not be satisfied. It will only be quiet when I have been given what I need. Is it a child? For Hannah it was; perhaps it is not for everyone. But everyone hungers for something.

Hungry? Not sure what it is you seek, but very sure that you do not have it now? Ask God to tell you, and then listen patiently for the answer. Don't get ahead of yourself; don't do what religious people often think they should do and ask "What am I supposed to be doing?" First ask yourself what it is you *want*, and listen carefully to your thoughts. It is in there, no matter how absurd it may seem to you. No matter how unexpected. Ordinarily, your desire is a means by which God draws you. Don't ignore it.

And then ask God to clear the way in accordance with his will. A sign will appear: your sign may be nothing more than a thought that comes to you, but it is your sign. Follow it. Follow the trail, keeping your desire in mind. Affirm often your willingness to be led by God, and pay close attention. Something is about to happen.

TUESDAY IN PROPER 6

Pss 78:1–39 * 78:40–72
1 Samuel 1:21–2:11
Acts 1:15–26
Luke 20:19–26

". . . Therefore I have lent him to the Lord;
as long as he lives, he is given to the Lord."
She left him there for the Lord.
1 SAMUEL 1:28

And after all that—Hannah gives up her child. After longing for him all those years, she leaves him in the temple to live. Her heart's desire. No one asked her to do this. It was her idea.

I suppose it was enough to give him life. Somehow, for Hannah, the act of becoming a mother was enough, and it was separate from the work of nurturing a child to adulthood. Most of us would not feel that way, but she did.

Could you give up the thing you wanted most in the world? Give it up to God? The whole point of sacrifice is that what we sacrifice is precious to us: sacrifice is meaningless if we only give things we neither want nor need. It must be our best, our most precious. Our only one.

And what is that for you? Perhaps it is your life. Perhaps it is your life you leave in the temple—not by dying, but by living in a state of surrender to God and trust in God's care for you, right up to and including the day of your death. Perhaps you give God your life, and then God gives you back all the things you need to live it with integrity and joy. Then you don't worry about what will happen, because you will know that whatever happens, your life already belongs to God. Nothing can change that. Good and ill fortune come your way, and you still belong to God.

WEDNESDAY IN PROPER 6

Pss 119:97–120 * 81, 82
1 Samuel 2:12–26
Acts 2:1–21
Luke 20:27–40

Now he is God not of the dead, but of the living . . .
LUKE 20:38

It's hard to say if Shirley knows that I am here or not. I say hello and tell her who I am, as always, but she makes no response. They can hear you, I've been told often enough by nurses to believe it, and so I always talk a little: about the weather outside, about how sorry I am that they are ill. I always say a psalm—usually the twenty-third—and a prayer about the presence of God and the love of God. And I almost always touch a hand, a shoulder, if it looks to me that doing so will not cause them pain.

Time disappears in the ICU. Its hushed bustle is constant, quiet, vigilant. The clink of metal instruments from one cubicle. The whirrs and beeps of the monitors, the whoosh of the ventilators, the half darkness.

Here, people cross from life into death. Some of them. Many of them. And some people linger a while at the threshold, as if unsure whether or not to enter. You just don't know.

Sleeping, Shirley looks young and unanxious. Her life is not visible here: her son, her dead husband, her girlhood, what she thinks about God and the war, what music she likes. Is that all still in there, or is it gone now?

I do not know which way Shirley will go: back into our world, for a time, or on into the next. I also do not know where all the memories and secrets that have composed her life will go. We desperately want to think that our personalities continue in heaven, that we are recognizably ourselves there. This I also do not know. The risen life is different from this one, and we don't know how. We haven't lived it.

We can only trust that it is good. This life was: hard, sometimes, and disappointing, sometimes, but almost all of us want to stay here for as long as we can. Either way we are headed, back home or on into the future, the Lord of this life is the Lord of that one, too.

THURSDAY IN PROPER 6

Pss (83) or 34 * 85, 86
1 Samuel 2:27–36
Acts 2:22–36
Luke 20:41–21:4

"Truly I tell you, this poor widow has put in more than all of them; for all of them have contributed out of their abundance, but she out of her poverty has put in all she had to live on."
LUKE 21:3–4

People watch when you put your money in, you think as the collection plate comes closer. The people taking up the offering will notice what you put in. That's why they have envelopes, so nobody will see. You fold your money up tight, in a little roll, so nobody can see its denomination.

Americans are very shy about money. We watch television programs that talk about sex in very graphic terms, or even depict it, but die a thousand deaths if someone asks us how much money we make. It isn't that way everywhere in the world. It's the other way around in some places.

It was the other way around in Jesus' time. People made their donations publicly, rich and poor. If we are to believe scripture, rich people sometimes sounded trumpets before them as they made their way to the treasury; Jesus says so, although maybe he's being ironic. And here came a widow with nothing. Two pennies, she puts in the plate. That's it.

People can't give equally. That's why a flat tax, which sounds so equitable, isn't fair at all: 10% of a poor person's income means more to him than 10% of a billionaire's. He already doesn't have enough, and the billionaire already has more than he needs. Some attention must be paid to how giving affects the life of the giver, and its effect on the rich is different from its effect on the poor.

But everyone should do something. Do what you can. Do the most you can. More than our best, nobody can do. But you lose an important sense of worth if you elect to do nothing except what benefits you directly.

FRIDAY IN PROPER 6

Pss 88 * 91, 92
1 Samuel 3:1–21
Acts 2:37–47
Luke 21:5–19

The word of the Lord was rare in those days;
visions were not widespread.

1 SAMUEL 3:1

What do you suppose that means? Maybe it just means what it appears to mean: *we have lots of visions now, but it wasn't always so. Here's a story about when God didn't speak to us in visions.*

Or maybe it's something else. Maybe there are *lots* of visions today—too many. Maybe everybody thinks God is on his side. Maybe everybody thinks that his own self-interest is God's will. And maybe there was a time when we had a higher standard for what the word of God might be.

Does God speak to people? Sure. How does God do that? In lots of ways. Sometimes it's directly in words, although this is rare, and we must always be aware, in claiming such a thing, of the undeniable fact that there are a fair number of people in state hospitals who also think God speaks to them. So your conviction that it's God speaking to you may not convince everyone.

But God speaks to us in other ways, too, more frequently. In dreams, sometimes, and in the peace of prayer and meditation. In the insistent moral voice that counters your self-absorption, your negativity, or your hopelessness. In the new idea. In the minority opinion. In the odd coincidence that suddenly seems to have more meaning than mere coincidence would warrant.

Can you prove that any of these are the voice of God? No, we're far beyond the realm of proofs. We're in the realm of faith. That we even ask about the voice of God is a sign of our faith. That we doubt it means little: every biblical prophet doubted his call, had trouble identifying the voice of God. But they kept asking until they were sure, kept puzzling it out until they got it right. As we must do with whatever vision we receive.

SATURDAY IN PROPER 6

Pss 87, 90 * 136
1 Samuel 4:1b–11
Acts 4:32–5:11
Luke 21:20–28

There was not a needy person among them,
for as many as owned lands or houses sold them
and brought the proceeds of what was sold.
ACTS 4:34

Or, at least, that was the plan. Two of the new Christians held back some of their earnings, though, for a rainy day. Oops— one was caught and died on the spot, and his wife came in a little later and was also caught. She dropped dead as well. Serious business—I doubt if anybody else tried to fudge his donation after that.

It would be hard for most of us to sign away our entire estates to the Church, so we can sympathize with Ananias and Sapphira: they were taking care of family business in a responsible manner.

But the first Christians were creating a community that was little short of heaven on earth. You didn't need to own property or put things away for the future: they didn't think there would be a future. They were going to heaven right away, they were sure.

So you would think they also wouldn't need disciplinary measures: surely people who think they're going to heaven are already on their best behavior. Or maybe they were like us: maybe their faith ebbed and flowed a little. Maybe they were more genuine about it at times than at others. Maybe they were so sure of themselves that they thought they could get away with anything, or maybe some of them wondered if the whole thing might not be a fantasy.

That was a long time ago. We weren't all swept up to heaven at once, as they thought we would be. We're still waiting. Money still causes us all manner of difficulty. We still try to rely on it beyond the strength of its reliability. And we still can't take it with us.

SUNDAY, PROPER 7

Pss 66, 67 * 19, 46
1 Samuel 4:12–22
James 1:1–18
Matthew 19:23–30

*But Jesus looked at them and said, "For mortals it is
impossible, but for God all things are possible."*
MATTHEW 19:26

Hearing Jesus say this reminds me of what the angel told Mary when she wondered how on earth her unusual pregnancy would come about: with God, the angel said, nothing will be impossible.

Perhaps—more than anything else—our God is the God of possibility. Of unseen potential for good in the midst of puzzling and intractable evil. In story after story, scripture pulls salvation from the jaws of death: just in the nick of time, Joseph saves his family, Pharaoh's daughter finds the baby, David slays the giant, Esther saves the Hebrews, and Daniel curls up safely with a hungry lion for a good night's sleep.

We keep forgetting that we are not alone. That everything we know isn't all that is known. That all we can do isn't all that can be done. Our hopes and plans do not come to pass, and we think that nothing good can happen because the good for which we prepared did not.

But new things happen all the time. Every day, something happens that has never happened in quite that way before. Sometimes we discover them. Sometimes they discover us. Whichever it may be, we do not predict them. They are surprises.

It can be a bumpy ride, here on the earth. Some of life's surprises aren't happy ones. But some are. *Oh, thank God!* we say without even thinking about it, when something completely unexpected saves us. *Thank God!*

MONDAY IN PROPER 7

Pss 89:1–18 * 89:19–52
1 Samuel 5:1–12
Acts 5:12–26
Luke 21:29–36

"Look at the fig tree and all the trees; as soon as they sprout leaves you can see for yourselves and know that the summer is already near. So also, when you see these things taking place, you know that the kingdom of God is near. Truly I tell you, this generation will not pass away until all things have taken place."

LUKE 21:29–32

People try to explain this away: Oh, he didn't mean his own generation, they say. He meant the human race throughout time. They don't want Jesus to have been mistaken about something. They think it would mean that he wasn't the Son of God.

But would it? Does the historical Jesus have to have known everything in order to be the messiah? I am not so sure. We believe him to be truly God and truly human, and we can't understand how those two things can blend together in a person. So we make him into a superman.

But if he was a true human being, in a specific time and a specific place, he allowed himself to be delineated by the limitations of the life into which he entered. Our life. Including our limited vision. Jesus of Nazareth may not have known what the Trinity knows. He came into our world from heaven, and when he came, he shed his power. Became weak and partial, like us, not to return to his power until the Resurrection.

Thinking about things like this makes some of us feel guilty, as if we were being rude. We are not, though: God gave us curious minds, and I am convinced he doesn't mind our stretching them. All will be revealed, one day, and we can ask Jesus what he knew and when he knew it. If we still want to know . . .

TUESDAY IN PROPER 7

Pss 97, 99, (100) * 94, (95)
1 Samuel 6:1–16
Acts 5:27–42
Luke 21:37–22:13

"What shall we do with the ark of the Lord?"

1 SAMUEL 6:2

Some prizes are like that: once you win it, you wish you hadn't. Capturing the Ark turned out to be way more trouble for the Philistines than it was worth: it made everyone develop tumors, no matter which town they tried to keep it in. They couldn't get rid of it fast enough.

Sometimes you need to leave well enough alone, I guess. I read somewhere that almost all the people who win the lottery end up in worse financial shape, within a few years, than they ever were before they won. It turned out that coming into a big pot of money was the worst thing that could have happened to them. Go figure.

You wander into something that just isn't you. You think it'll be one way, and it's a disastrous *other* way. Getting out of the trouble you got yourself into can be laborious and embarrassing. But that doesn't mean you don't have to get out. Whatever the cost, the pain of being in the wrong place at the wrong time is worse.

A friend of mine was in love with a man who was all wrong for her. He was all she wanted, and she was willing to do anything in order to be with him. It felt to her, at first, as if he were one of the necessities of life, like air or water. What he really was, though, was a disaster, and remaining with him was making her terribly depressed and even physically ill.

It was humiliating to face this truth, but it was worse not to. Eventually, she got free: from the distance her freedom gave her, she could see just how hard it had been. We long for things because we think they will bring us joy. Sometimes they do. But when they don't, no amount of longing makes them right. We have to put them back where we got them.

WEDNESDAY IN PROPER 7

Pss 101, 109:1–4 (5–19) 20–30 * Pss 119:121–144
1 Samuel 7:2–17
Acts 6:1–15
Luke 22:14–23

For the Son of Man is going . . . but woe
to that one by whom he is betrayed!
LUKE 22:22

There are abundant hints of blessing in medieval hymns about the sorrows of the cross—*Sweetest wood and sweetest iron! Sweetest weight is hung on thee!* goes the Latin hymn *Pange lingua*. The sacrifice of Christ was the gift of God, source of all blessing and all redemption.

Well, if Jesus had to be betrayed in order for salvation to happen, why do we hate Judas Iscariot? someone asked me once. *Why isn't he a saint, if it was by his betrayal that something so good happened?*

Because, although God always brings good out of evil if we know how to look for it, evil still exists. That it has a joyful ending doesn't make it good: it's still bad. And the good God brings from great evil isn't usually its reversal—Jesus was really dead, the millions killed in genocides the world over were really dead, and no quickening of the heart of humanity that has or might occur in response to those things can make them good things. They're still bad.

God's goodness is larger than our largest evil. But our evil is large, nonetheless, and we have choices about whether or not to throw in our lot with it. Can God not accomplish his purpose unless I cooperate with it? Of course he can. But I will not be part of it, of its brave struggle on earth, even if I can still hear its happy song at the end of time.

THURSDAY IN PROPER 7

Pss 105:1–22 * 105:23–45
1 Samuel 8:1–22
Acts 6:15–7:16
Luke 22:24–30

When Samuel became old, he made his sons judges over Israel.
1 SAMUEL 8:1

Well, it made sense, didn't it? They had grown up in the business, as it were, and knew what it entailed.

But they didn't do a good job, it turned out. You don't inherit skill and wisdom; you must develop it.

It's hard to be the son or daughter of a prominent person. People assume you're good at what you mom or dad was good at. That you think and do the same things.

Domestic diva Martha Stewart planted twin avenues of trees on her property when her daughter was born: they were to become an outdoor aisle for Alexis to walk on her father's arm on her wedding day. That sounds like Martha: she probably got up from the delivery table and started to dig that very afternoon.

But Martha's daughter wasn't Martha. She didn't go for the same things her famous mother was famous for: she grew up to be a much cooler, hipper character. She bought a 1950s motel and renovated it in pink and turquoise. And when she got married, she didn't walk down the avenue of trees. They went to City Hall, and she wore a grey trouser suit.

That must have been hard on Martha, but she took it well. She reported on the wedding in her magazine, and she had a big party for the newlyweds. And later, when her legal troubles were in all the papers every day, her daughter accompanied her to court faithfully. She wept when her mother's guilty verdict was announced.

Samuel should have asked himself if his boys were really up to it before he installed them in his old job. We can't be fresh versions of our parents, for good or for ill. We each start out on a path that is ours alone, and we must make it on our own.

FRIDAY IN PROPER 7

Pss 102 * 107:1–32
1 Samuel 9:1–14
Acts 7:17–29
Luke 22:31–38

*There was not a man among the people of Israel more handsome
than he; he stood head and shoulders above everyone else.*

1 SAMUEL 9:2

So the first king of Israel was really good-looking. And really tall.
Figures: looks still matter more than they should in the selection
of political candidates, and so does height. Presidents of the United
States are usually tall men. There was an old rumor that IBM had a
minimum height requirement for managers, something that came
to light when women began to viewed as promotable: *What are we
going to do about the height requirement?* Oft-repeated, although it
may not really have been the case. Maybe it's just office apocrypha.

The expectation that physical attractiveness mirrors moral excel-
lence and intelligence is old. Shakespeare's Richard III—not a sym-
pathetic character—is given a withered arm in the play that bears
his name, the only evidence of that disability we have. We are to
understand that his deformed outside mirrors a deformation inside.
We're supposed to be able to tell, just by looking at him, that he's
one of the bad guys. *But he's so nice,* I used to say to my girls about
this or that suitor. But, at a certain age, they were each reluctant to
entertain one who was not conventionally handsome, and a couple
of times they were sorry they had bought into a handsome face.

It's false, of course. You really can't judge a book by its cover.
A person can be absolutely gorgeous and really incompetent,
healthy-looking and physically strong but morally weak. Happens
all the time.

There is no shortcut to knowing a person personally. You really
do have to inquire beneath the surface of things. Appearances can
be deceiving, and your mother was right: it's what's inside that really

counts. Besides, love makes people lovely anyway. In the end, we think the one we love is beautiful, no matter what the world thinks. Because we no longer see as the world sees. We see much more.

SATURDAY IN PROPER 7

Pss 107:33–43, 108:1–6 (7–13) * 33
1 Samuel 9:15–10:1
Acts 7:30–43
Luke 22:39–51

*"Take off the sandals from your feet, for the place
where you are standing is holy ground."*
ACTS 7:33

This is a quote, of course: we are reading the words of one who is reciting a story both he and his hearers have heard ever since they were children. It is already a thousand years old when Stephen tells it. It's a story about Moses, but it's not Moses telling it. The tradition is telling it.

How does the tradition hang onto the details of a story? Anyone who has ever told a bedtime tale to a child knows that they are fierce little custodians of tradition: you have to tell it exactly the same way, every time you tell it. They will brook no interference with its proper cadence and proper sequence. Everybody knows just what Papa Bear says when he sees that somebody has been eating his porridge, and just how he says it. No paraphrasing allowed.

This was a detail: that Moses should remove his shoes because the ground where he saw God was holy. It's not a line without which the story can't hang together. But it had survived for a thousand years already when Stephen spoke it, and it has survived another two thousand since then. Just that way: take off the shoes from your feet, for the place where you are standing is holy ground.

How does the tradition hold a story? Through those who listen to it. The story belongs to them. It is they who hold it and pass it forward. Their devotion to its very word order—an irrational devotion in itself—is a sign of its importance.

We think tradition is about the past, and it does deal with things that were done and said in the past. But it belongs to the future, and it lives or dies in the hands of those who will inhabit tomorrow.

SUNDAY, PROPER 8

Pss 118 * 145
1 Samuel 10:1–16
Romans 4:13–25
Matthew 21:23–32

"He answered, 'I will not,' but later he changed his mind and went."
MATTHEW 21:29

Not every adolescent goes through it, of course, but many do: that era somewhere in the teens when they just have to defy us. When your desire for a certain course of action is reason enough, all by itself, not to do it. Your advocacy is the kiss of death, your approval certifies unacceptability. From the outside, it looks like real pain and suffering is a fair price to pay for the sweet taste of defiance; it looks as though they willingly deny themselves genuine pleasure rather than seem to agree to something you want.

Or maybe they're not like that. Maybe I've just gotten old. Because I remember believing that my parents' principal desire in life was for me not to have any fun, and that they forbade me things for that reason and that reason alone.

The defiant son in the story changes his mind. He does go, after all, and works in the vineyard for reasons only he knows. He doesn't, it seems, come to his father and tell him, "You know, I've been thinking, and I realize I was being disobedient. Please accept my apology." They don't apologize. Not mine, anyway. Not until they're all grown up, years later. Sometimes it's when they have teenagers of their own. And sometimes it's never, not out loud.

And maybe we don't need their apologies. Whatever they think, our rules and demands aren't about us. They're about them, about helping them grow into the responsible adults the world will insist they become. I don't need my child to be sorry out loud for being immature and obnoxious. I can wait forever to hear those words. I only need for her to be all right, to grow up into an adult who can manage without me.

MONDAY IN PROPER 8

Pss 106:1–18 * 106:19–48
1 Samuel 10:17–27
Acts 7:44–8:1a
Luke 22:52–62

"Which of the prophets did your ancestors not persecute?"
ACTS 7:52

Tie-dyed tee shirts and bellbottoms. Cool long hair and great music. The sixties were really cool. At least, that's what people who weren't there think. And they were creative, it's true. They were cool. But people forget that they were also terrible times. America was polarized about race and then about the war in Vietnam. Soldiers were dying by the hundreds each week. And three public figures, men whom young people admired, were gunned down in cold blood.

What would John F. Kennedy and his brother have become had they lived into old age? Robert was more a prophet than was his elder brother, whose more Machiavellian side is now public knowledge. What about Dr. King? Where would his prophecy have led him had he been permitted to continue it into the seventies, into the eighties, into the present time? What would they say about this war? What would they say now about African Americans' struggle for an equal share of our society, each from his own perspective as an activist?

It was the last straw. It seemed, after Robert Kennedy was killed, that death must certainly claim anybody who was any good if he came anywhere near public life. We became fatalistic about it, macabre in our humor—there was a band in the eighties called "Dead Kennedys."

At dinner with some young people a year or two ago, I heard one of them refer to something as having happened at around the time Kennedy was killed. *Wait a minute,* I said, *you weren't even born when Kennedy was killed.* But of course, she meant JFK the younger, the handsome son of the slain president. Not the Kennedy I meant. Oh. We were talking about different Kennedys.

It annoys us that they don't remember, that they didn't make the same sacrifices we did, that they didn't have to. It shouldn't: weren't we hoping for a world in which those things their elders fought for could be confidently expected by the young? We are closer to that world than we were years ago. Isn't that good? Sure. But once you've been shocked by violence, ambushed by it, you're jumpy forever after. Some events in history are too large ever to consider again with anything like neutrality. Some events cry out for comfort, years after they happen. Q and I watch a documentary about Dr. King and are both in tears by the end of it, tears we do not shed when we watch something about, say, the death of Napoleon. We want the young to know. We want them to care. Maybe we want them to comfort us, even. And tell us that the sacrifice was worth it. Because they, the hope of it all, are the only ones who can.

TUESDAY IN PROPER 8

Pss (120), 121, 122, 123 * 124, 125, 126, (127)
1 Samuel 11:1–15
Acts 8:1–13
Luke 22:63–71

*Now a certain man named Simon had previously
practiced magic in the city and amazed the people
of Samaria, saying that he was someone great.*
ACTS 8:9

This must be why Jesus himself was more than a little circum-spect about his own miracles: he wasn't the only one perform-ing them. There were wandering wonder workers in the Holy Land in those days. There were other people proclaiming themselves the messiah, and pointing to their magic tricks as proof of their claim. To be the Son of God meant more than walking on water, even more than healing the sick. So Jesus sometimes tells people to keep his wonders to themselves. Sometimes he chides his friends for believ-ing because of them.

To be the Son of God is to be more than the Lord of history and the events of history, although God is, indeed, the Lord of history and does, indeed, participate in its events. But although God is Lord of history, history does not contain God. It does not certify God. It's the other way around. History does not prove God's existence, or even God's goodness, although we say it does all the time. *God is good!* we say, when a parking place appears just when we need one, or when we get a job we've hoped for. But God is good, no matter what happens to us.

The truth is that life is hard, but God is good. Nobody ever said believing Jesus to be the Son of God guaranteed us a smooth sail through this difficult life. It does assure us, though, that this life—as lovely and painful as it is, by turns—is not all there is. There is much more here than meets the eye.

WEDNESDAY IN PROPER 8

Pss 119:145–176 * 128, 129, 130
1 Samuel 12:1–6, 16–25
Acts 8:14–25
Luke 23:1–12

That same day Herod and Pilate became friends with
each other; before this they had been enemies.
LUKE 23:12

There's an unholy alliance for you. Evil, lazy, or negligent—we don't know which they were, but they recognized each other as having something significant in common: it was with their permission and cooperation that the Son of God was taken prisoner and killed.

But, of course, this death is, for us, part of the great project of redemption. *So why do we condemn them*, someone asks me, *if it all ends up in the resurrection anyhow?* They were linchpins to the larger drama.

God brings good from evil. The resurrection is a sign of this, although it is much more than such a sign. Together with the coming of Christ to live among us as a human being, his victory over death joins earth to heaven in a way that fuses them together forever. The holiness of the world is restored in Christ.

But not everything that has happened in the world since the birth of Christ, or since his resurrection, has been a good thing. Evil continues here. God's triumph is ultimate, but the story continues as long as there is a physical world for us to fight over. The divine mercy resolves everything, but human sin will require the meting out of human justice as long as there are human beings. It is an earthly reality, this justice, and it is our uneasy task.

THURSDAY IN PROPER 8

Pss 131, 132, (133) * 134, 135
1 Samuel 13:5–18
Acts 8:26–40
Luke 23:13–25

See, here is water! What is to prevent me from being baptized?
ACTS 8:36

When this was written, the nascent Church was already getting picky about who could get baptized, and how: you didn't just drive by a river and do it on a whim. You needed preparation, and there was a long period of preparation. It got longer still, soon, until it took about two years to become a Christian. In this story, Philip prepares the eunuch, but the eunuch was already pretty well prepared to hear what Philip has to say: he was reading Isaiah as he rode along in his chariot. Expecting a messiah, though not at all clear about who that messiah might be. Teachable. Wanting to know.

The centuries of normative infant baptism made it difficult for baptismal preparation to happen: most newborns are poor listeners at best. For the last thirty years, though, more attention has been paid to it. Mostly, it's still babies, but more and more adults are preparing and choosing it. More and more, it's a big deal.

Usually, this is not because they knew about baptism all their lives and decided to wait until they were ready. Usually, it's because they didn't know about it at all—their parents, still smarting from the religious wars of their youth, decided to skip the whole church thing and raised them without any religious training at all. We'll let them decide, they told each other, when they're older.

And they do decide. Decide they want a community usually, at first, a haven from the anonymity of modern life. Then notice that the community they have found is gathered around something greater than themselves, than the community itself, around the God who brings everything into being and yet somehow loves us each, with all our faults. Something calls them to participate in the eternal, and they respond.

FRIDAY IN PROPER 8

Pss 140, 142 * 141, 143:1–11 (12)
1 Samuel 13:19–14:15
Acts 9:1–9
Luke 23:26–31

For if they do this when the wood is green,
what will happen when it is dry?
LUKE 23:31

In their efforts to control the population of Israel, the Romans were actively making things worse. Public executions designed to inspire obedience seemed not to be working. They seemed, in fact, to be having the opposite effect, inspiring rebellion instead. Things would get worse: forty years after the events Luke describes, they leveled the temple and expelled the Jews, scattering them throughout the world.

In general, violence doesn't heal violence. It makes it worse. It generates a never-ending spiral of itself, an endless tit-for-tat of offense and reprisal that can't end. It raises up a generation—or two or three or more—that imbibes hatred of the enemy with its mothers' milk. Pick up any newspaper and get the latest news on the Israelis and the Palestinians if you want to see the result of answering violence with violence.

Relationships can be molded into life-giving forms when they are young and pliable. But they don't remain malleable for very long: they harden into a more permanent shape as time passes, and it's much harder to change the terms of them after a pattern has been established. It's worth getting it right the first time.

SATURDAY IN PROPER 8

Pss 137:1–6 (7–9), 144 * 104
1 Samuel 14:16–30
Acts 9:10–19a
Luke 23:32–43

*"Lord, I have heard from many about this man,
how much evil he has done..."*
ACTS 9:13

If Ananaias had had his way, I guess we wouldn't know about St. Paul. And probably we wouldn't be Christians. Our faith would have remained an obscure sect of first-century Judaism.

His objections were nothing if not reasonable. He checked Paul's references: this guy was nothing but trouble. Paul was the most inappropriate choice in the ancient Near East for the job of Apostle to the Gentiles. Or to anyone else. The very last person anyone with any sense would propose.

So, of course, he is the one who got the job.

What are we to take from this? That poor credentials ensure good performance? Should we go directly to the place where we are least welcome and entreat entrance, assuming God to have called us there by virtue of our inappropriateness?

Well, the usual way of discerning one's direction is usual for a reason: usually, you consider your natural gifts and proclivities and look for a place hospitable to them. Usually you don't go to the hardware store for oranges. Usually, that's the way the world works. You should check the usual entrances first.

But once in a while, something unusual happens. If we can never lift our eyes from the templates we ordinarily use, we will miss those unusual times.

SUNDAY, PROPER 9

Pss 146, 147 * 111, 112, 113
1 Samuel 14:36–45
Romans 5:1–11
Matthew 22:1–14

"Friend, how did you get in here without a wedding robe?"
MATTHEW 22:12

My dress is blue. It has stripes of beading on the top and the skirt is just blue. I liked it when I picked it out, but I've been afraid to look at it again, in case I don't like it any more.

I suppose I could always buy another one. Then I would have two expensive long dresses hanging in my closet. Maybe I could be buried in this one. People would say, "She looks nice in blue, doesn't she?"

Corinna's dress is beautiful, of course: she's the bride. She and Anna look beautiful in anything. They could walk down the aisle in black plastic garbage bags and look good. I'm a little more of a challenge.

I do lots of other people's weddings, of course, and I never have to stop and wonder what to wear: I wear a black suit and a clerical collar. I could do a quick funeral on the way to the wedding and not have to change clothes. Staring uneasily at the long plastic dress bag hanging in my office closet, I am nostalgic for that simplicity. You blend into the background as the officiant at a wedding. Nobody's looking at you. It's the couple they want to see.

But wait a minute—nobody's looking at the mother of the bride, either. They're not coming to see me. It's not about me. It's about a new family beginning in joy and hope. And it's not even about clothes, as I've been telling stressed-out brides for decades. It's a promise before God and the community to try and be faithful and kind. No easy thing, no matter how good you look.

Maybe I'm the one who should wear a garbage bag.

MONDAY IN PROPER 9

Pss 1, 2, 3 * 4, 7
1 Samuel 15:1–3, 7–23
Acts 9:19b–31
Luke 23:44–56a

"Certainly this man was innocent."
LUKE 23:47

A mong the many reasons for outlawing the death penalty, surely the most compelling is the fact that at least twenty-three people were executed in America in the last century who were subsequently proven not to have committed the crimes for which they paid with their lives. No system of investigation and trial will ever guarantee that no innocent person will ever slip through the cracks, and we have all read stories of bored, incompetent public defenders allowing their unfortunate clients to be killed by the state. Everyone is sorry when that happens. But sorry never brought anybody back from the dead.

Does opposing this barbaric practice mean we are soft on crime? That we don't believe people should answer for their misdeeds? Of course not. It's just that the overwhelming body of evidence is that capital punishment accomplishes none of the things its fans hope it will. It doesn't deter crime. It doesn't save money. It doesn't help victims heal. It certainly doesn't bring back the dead. It just adds another corpse to the pile.

Everyone has feelings of vengeance. Everyone who cares to can look inside himself and find fierce longing for revenge for a terrible crime. That's human. But so is the capacity for restraint. So is the thought that tempers impulse. So is the capacity of our more animal passions to yield to the gentler counsels of our minds. I don't have to act on every feeling I have, and I should not act on the baser ones.

If I do, I become just another killer. And the innocent would still have died for nothing.

TUESDAY IN PROPER 9

Pss 5, 6 * 10, 11
1 Samuel 15:24–35
Acts 9:32–43
Luke 23:56b–24:11

All the widows stood beside him, weeping and showing tunics and other clothing that Dorcas had made while she was with them.
ACTS 9:39

The fabric store is full of women. Most of them, I have noticed when I have gone there in recent years, are not American: they are from somewhere else. Somewhere where women learn how to sew as a matter of course, because they have to. Years from now, someone will hang onto the garments they will make from the bright fabric they choose today, just because it was they who made them.

I have table linens embroidered by my grandmother: napkins, a tablecloth. And another set, a luncheon cloth and luncheon napkins, embroidered by the oldest living member of my church. I have a beautiful cream-colored lace tablecloth made by the mother of our Bosnian foster daughter. And I have a set of linen napkins embroidered with different flowers that I made myself, years ago when my mother was still alive, as a gift to her. And a Christmas tablecloth she made, painstakingly, for she did not like to sew: the fact that she struggled through it moves me every year when I bring it out.

Most handmade things are more beautiful than they need to be. It takes so much time that you settle into it, as if it were a prayer. You don't want to rush. You want it to be as fine a thing as you can make. Exactly as if it were a prayer. Maybe it is.

The fabric with which you work cooperates with you as best it can. It tells you what it can and cannot do. It is flat, but you make it dimensional, shaping it to fit its eventual wearer. You make it look like what it will be, little by little, and what it will be is shaped like a human being: a waist, arms, legs.

Dorcas's friends remembered her kindness in sewing for them. Honored her giftedness: apparently not everybody, even back then, could sew as well as she did. Wept, when they saw those things she made, missed her when they looked at them. Those garments were very special. And that was a long time ago. When every woman sewed.

WEDNESDAY IN PROPER 9

Pss 119:1–24 * 12, 13, 14
1 Samuel 16:1–13
Acts 10:1–16
Luke 24:12–35

"What God has made clean, you must not call profane."
ACTS 10:15

W*hen I find out that Jesus has changed the rules,* a woman writes to me icily, *I'll change.* She is angry because I wrote something about the inclusion of gay people in the Church's life and she disagreed with what I wrote. *Until then, what right have you to pick and choose what you'll abide by in what the Bible says?*

The same right people have always had, I guess. People have always weighed the obligations scripture imposes, relative to one another. Keep the Sabbath holy, it says, and don't do any work. But you must feed your animals anyway. Keep the dietary laws, it says at great length in the Hebrew Scriptures. And the Christian ones find a way to move beyond those laws, a major story in the New Testament, a way to see them as part of a time and a people that need not be universal. Do not kill, God says to Moses, and yet the Bible is full of killing. It says in Leviticus that women aren't supposed to braid their hair.

Sometimes we get our choices right when we do this and sometimes we don't. We read and ponder, argue with other readers and ponderers, and still our way is often unclear. We choose in the midst of unclarity all the time. If the Bible were a recipe book, I guess that would not be the case. But there's not a recipe in it.

THURSDAY IN PROPER 9

Pss 18:1–20 * 18:21–50
1 Samuel 16:14–17:11
Acts 10:17–33
Luke 24:36–53

And they worshiped him, and returned to Jerusalem with great joy;
and they were continually in the temple blessing God.
LUKE 24:52–53

In the *temple*? The place in which animal sacrifices were offered every day? Where the scribes and the Pharisees and Sadducees came and went? I wonder if the people in the temple were glad to hear them rejoicing about Jesus' ongoing life. The Romans were still suspicious of Jesus' followers. Things hadn't calmed down so much that talking about him a lot was a safe thing to do. I imagine that some people in the temple just wished they'd be quiet.

So this thing that made them so happy must have been something truly amazing. Something that just wiped their fear right out of their hearts. This sense of theirs that Jesus was with them still must have been so powerful that no human force arrayed against it counted for much of anything. It just didn't bother them if people didn't like hearing it. They barely noticed.

Our excitement can be tedious to those who must live with us, as anyone who has been in love knows. All you want to talk about is your beloved, and the people who love you are tired of hearing about her. *Give it a break*, someone says, and you try. But you just can't.

Many Christians in America have experienced Christ in just this way—as something brand new. Others don't know what it's like not to be a Christian: they've been in the Church since they were baptized into it as babies.

It must have been just like that. Like being in love. They must have been full to overflowing with what had happened to them.

FRIDAY IN PROPER 9

Pss 16, 17 * 22
1 Samuel 17:17–30
Acts 10:34–48
Mark 1:1–13

The beginning of the good news of Jesus Christ, the Son of God.
MARK 1:1

This is an abrupt beginning to an abrupt gospel: events unfold quickly in Mark, one scene following another without much in the way of transition beyond the word "immediately," which occurs dozens of times in this shortest of the four gospels. It is urgent, blunt, as if the writer can't get the words down quickly enough.

No genealogy. No annunciation. No Joseph. No birth narrative. No visit of a twelve-year-old Jesus to the temple to instruct his elders. And, in the oldest extant manuscript of Mark, no appearance of the resurrected Jesus. Just some very frightened women running, as fast as their legs could carry them, from an empty tomb.

Mark is so brief, in comparison with the other three gospels in scripture, that several prominent actors have undertaken to perform it as a monologue. The ones I have seen have captured the urgency well, telling the story as if it had just happened to them, as if they had just seen and heard the events it describes.

But of course, none of the gospel writers witnessed the events they describe. Mark, the earliest, dates from the seventies, forty years after the crucifixion and resurrection. It may be that some very elderly people remained to tell about what they had seen, but by far the greater part of these books were certainly compiled from the tradition to which the writers were heir.

They had to do what we have to do: examine the experience of those who came before them, and combine it with their own experience of the Lord in their lives to form a faith they could own and share. In every generation, the same task awaits those who seek life in Christ.

SATURDAY IN PROPER 9

Pss 20, 21:1–7 (8–14) * 110:1–5 (6–7), 116, 117
1 Samuel 17:31–49
Acts 11:1–18
Mark 1:14–28

*And the unclean spirit, throwing him into convulsions
and crying with a loud voice, came out of him.*
MARK 1:26

Things often get a lot worse before they get better. Whatever it is that causes evil in the world ordinarily doesn't give up without a fight. My addictions, my anger, my self-indulgence—whatever has me in its grip wants to keep me right there. Something in us doesn't want to be free and healthy. It wants to remain in jail and stay sick.

And we are certainly in its grip. Anyone who has dieted, has given up cigarettes, alcohol, gambling, gossiping, sexual compulsivity knows that the demons are bigger than we are. We struggle in vain against them, quitting not once, but many times. We make hollow, unfunny jokes about our doomed efforts, sneaking cigarettes and drinks, hiding our shopping receipts, laughing about it all. But inside, we are sick at heart.

We know one more thing, though, besides the formidable strength of the demon. We know that while the demons are stronger than we are, Jesus is stronger than they are. They know it, too: they are no match for him. Regardless of how glib a rationalization we can give for our behavior, our guts know the truth about it. *I am out of control. The things I have tried have not worked. I can't do this alone.*

And we aren't alone. Our help is here with us, ready to act and fight the demon on our behalf. The fight may be lifelong, but its outcome is not in question if we hold onto the truth and never let go.

SUNDAY, PROPER 10

Pss 148, 149, 150 * 114, 115
1 Samuel 17:50–18:4
Romans 10:4–17
Matthew 23:29–39

"If we had lived in the days of our ancestors, we would not have taken part with them in shedding the blood of the prophets."
MATTHEW 23:30

We think we'll be brave. We think we can do things that frighten us. *Of course I have the courage of my convictions,* we say indignantly. *What do you take me for?* But then comes the test, and we fail it. We do not step up to the plate. We hang back, hoping nobody will see us and ask us to stand for what we believe. And nobody sees us. The moment comes and goes, and we are safe.

But we know. And God knows. And we are ashamed. *I am not the person I thought I was.*

It's worth remembering that none of the twelve disciples, so close to Jesus during his earthly life and so important later on, passed the test, either. Even Peter did not, the rock upon whom Jesus built his church. Not that time. But later on, he did step up to the plate. Many times before he died, he was brave: able to endure imprisonment, able to speak out to a hostile crowd. Able, finally, to embrace a death very like that of his Lord.

Did you fail a test of courage in a matter of ethics? Do you know that particular anguish? You are not alone. While you are still alive, it is never too late. Another chance to find courage will come to you, as it came to Peter, and this time you will be more informed about the actual cost of a principled stand. This time you will not be over-confident. This time you will ask God for the courage you need, and not count on yourself to supply what you may not have when the time comes.

MONDAY IN PROPER 10

Pss 25 * 9, 15
1 Samuel 18:5–16, 27b–30
Acts 11:19–30
Mark 1:29–45

*Now Simon's mother-in-law was in bed with a fever,
and they told him about her at once. He came and
took her by the hand and lifted her up.*

MARK 1:30–31

A nd they were still friends? a wag in seminary will always say. We don't hear any mother-in-law jokes in scripture. Simon Peter seems to love his wife's mom—and why not? She's so nice to him and his friends. As soon as Jesus heals her, she gets up and fixes everybody a snack. And remember Ruth? Ruth adores her mother-in-law, and wants to live with her, even after her son's death.

We, on the other hand, think that conflict and suspicion are built into the in-law relationship. It is utterly different from the unconditional love and continuous affirmation we expect from our mothers, a steady stream of blessing no single human being could possibly deliver.

But the in-law bond is not necessarily uncomfortable. It's just complex. We all want happiness for our kids, and idealize their futures. Their careers, homes, children, and certainly their spouses should be perfect. And we idealize our past, too: I was a perfect housekeeper when you were little, a perfect mother, never crabby, always consistent in discipline, never made a mistake. It's amazing what we can fool ourselves into either remembering or expecting.

And nobody is perfect. Not us and not our kids and not our kids' spouses, when they come along. The same breaks you need—when you're tired, when you're ill, or even when you're just obtuse and simply don't get it—are the breaks you need to give others.

TUESDAY IN PROPER 10

Pss 26, 28 * 36, 39
1 Samuel 19:1–18
Acts 12:1–17
Mark 2:1–12

*When [Jesus] returned to Capernaum after some days,
it was reported that he was at home.*
MARK 2:1

No sooner has he arrived than word is out, in that age before radio and cell phones. He is almost a prisoner in his own home. Things won't calm down until Elvis leaves the building.

You see celebrities on the street when you live in New York. We used to live down the street from Gwyneth Paltrow. Sometimes we used to see Madonna.

When you see them, they are not alone. They have large men with them—their bodyguards. It's probably a matter of contract for some of them, this protection: they are valuable properties for whatever show they're in, and they cannot be replaced. People feel as if they know them, and some people just can't keep their hands off the merchandise.

It's hard on them. Maybe we don't think so, because they're rich and famous: maybe we think the loss of privacy is a fair price to pay for that. They also must court publicity, in a careful way: in order to continue working, you have to keep your name out there. So people think they don't really want privacy. That they're lying when they say they do.

But everyone needs to be alone sometimes. Just because we want to talk to them doesn't mean they have to talk to us. Even Jesus needed his privacy, and he sometimes had to sneak away from people to grab some solitude.

This time he wasn't safe even at home: his fans broke through the roof. But it wasn't just hero-worship that brought them there: they longed to help their friend walk again. They were willing to do what it took to get what they wanted, even to the point of breaking and entering. We are not told if Jesus sighed when he saw them through the new hole in the roof. There goes my quiet evening at home.

Maybe he did. But even if he sighed and wished for peace and quiet, it didn't stop him from giving the man what he needed. Truly human. Truly God.

WEDNESDAY IN PROPER 10

Pss 38 * 119:25–48
1 Samuel 20:1–23
Acts 12:18–25
Mark 2:13–22

"Those who are well have no need of a physician, but those who are sick; I have come to call not the righteous but sinners."
MARK 2:17

We keep forgetting: we don't have to earn Jesus' love by being good. Jesus loves us, whether we're good or not. Because we keep forgetting, we stop praying whenever we're conscious of something in our lives that is not as we know it should be—as if we were afraid he might find out. We hide. But that's dumb: you can't hide from God, and besides, he already knows.

Knows what and knows why. We have no secret from the one who created us out of love alone, who was content to leave our animal nature, with all its urges and instincts, intact within us. And who was also content to assume it himself

Mixed beings that we are, we need some help from time to time in sorting things out. We get out of balance rather easily, find ourselves miles from where we thought we were going without a clear sense of the way home. This is not surprising to God and it should not surprise us. It goes with our nature.

We needed saving, once for all, and Christ has done that. And we need comfort and guidance every day, and the Holy Spirit does that. Rome was not built in a day, and the life of a Christian is even more complex than the city of Rome! It takes Christ a lifetime to mold us into the full stature of who he would have us be. Perhaps it takes longer: maybe many of the things we carry unnecessarily—prejudices, grudges—are peeled off us at the end, so we enter a new life unencumbered by them.

THURSDAY IN PROPER 10

Pss 37:1–18 * 37:19–42
1 Samuel 20:24–42
Acts 13:1–12
Mark 2:23–3:6

*. . . so Jonathan knew that it was the decision
of his father to put David to death.*
1 SAMUEL 20:33

Jonathan's friendship with David was the most intimate friendship of his life. More intimate than his friendship with his own wife. And his father didn't understand it and didn't approve. His disapproval was so intense that he threw a spear at his son. Saul threw spears a lot, when he was mad, it seems. You didn't want to get on his bad side.

I knew a young man who was dying of AIDS in a New York hospital, and his own mother wouldn't come to see him. It was his own fault, she said, for living a sinful life. And he did die. And she never did come.

She thought she was being very religious and upright, but she fell far short of the love of God. I think of her now and then, of what she must have thought when she saw herself in the mirror each morning. I wonder if she looked in her own eyes and saw a woman who turned away from her own son when he needed her. A bitter thing to see in the mirror: an aging woman with sagging eyes. I am alone, and he is gone forever, and I let him die without my love.

Maybe she looked in the mirror and saw something else—a courageous woman of faith, brave enough even to sacrifice her son for her beliefs. Okay. But when Abraham thought he was being called to sacrifice his son, God showed him otherwise.

She thought she was right. But rightness untempered by love is a lonely place. The place of love and life is far from pure rightness, sometimes, and it leaves the judgment to God, who alone is competent to judge.

FRIDAY IN PROPER 10

Pss 31 * 35
1 Samuel 21:1–15
Acts 13:13–25
Mark 3:7–19a

And he appointed twelve, whom he also named apostles,
to be with him, and to be sent out to proclaim the message,
and to have authority to cast out demons.

MARK 3:14–15

So those were the twelve apostles: we call them "disciples" during Jesus' earthly ministry and "apostles" afterwards. Those who follow and those who are sent.

The Archbishop of Atlanta decided this year that women couldn't get their feet washed in the annual Maundy Thursday liturgies, because it says in scripture that Jesus washed the feet of his disciples and those disciples were all men. My goodness. There was a time when the pope used to wash the feet of a beggar in Rome.

What does it mean that the disciples of Jesus of Nazareth were all men? To begin with, it's not the case. Just these twelve were. There were others, including some women, of whom Mary Magdalene was the most prominent. But several other disciples, men and women, are named in the gospels. Jesus had followers and admirers beyond that small circle of twelve men.

But even if they were all men, what would it mean? Would it mean that priests could only be men? Jesus is not recorded to have used the word priest to apply to anybody but the priests of the temple in Jerusalem; he didn't consider his twelve disciples to be priests. Neither did the earliest Church: that word is not applied in the New Testament to anyone but the temple priests. That office was not part of the earliest Christian communities.

We are protective of our religious structures. We insist that they remain exactly the same, and we imagine that this happens. But nothing remains the same in this world. We think Jesus created the Church we see around us, but he did not. He left a small band of friends, ready to receive the Holy Spirit in all of its power. This small band of people began the work, and their descendents have done the rest. Who knows what our descendents will do.

SATURDAY IN PROPER 10

Pss 30, 32 * 42, 43
1 Samuel 22:1–23
Acts 13:26–43
Mark 3:19b–35

When his family heard it, they went out to restrain him,
for people were saying "He has gone out of his mind."
MARK 3:21

This a sad aside: Jesus' family thought he had lost his mind. They didn't get what he was about at all. They wanted to drag him home until he came to his senses. Even Mary, whose understanding and fidelity to her son's mission we have always assumed, didn't get it. She didn't always understand. She acted like many another parent has acted: "You get yourself home right this minute, young man, and I don't want to hear another word!"

To the neighbors, he must have looked like a promising young man who had, tragically, lost his way. They whispered about him, probably, about his troubles with the law. They looked at Mary with pity. The poor thing! Her son's gone off the deep end, they would say behind her back. But she always knew they were talking about her.

Eventually, she did get it. She remained, when almost everyone else had fled, at the foot of the cross. Love made her brave the soldiers, the crowd. She was close enough to Jesus' beloved friend that she lived with him for the rest of her life. *Woman, behold your son,* her own dying son told her, the last words he ever addressed to her. Love made her understand him, because love made her hang in there with him. My son wasn't crazy. Not at all. No matter what people thought.

SUNDAY, PROPER 11

Pss 63:1–8 (9–11), 98 * 103
1 Samuel 23:7–18
Romans 11:33–12:2
Matthew 25:14–30

*". . . so I was afraid, and I went and hid your talent
in the ground. Here you have what is yours."*
MATTHEW 25:25

Rule #1: If you don't grow, you shrink. Nothing stays the same. Life is a series of risks. All of us must learn to tolerate them, to ride the wave of them. We must learn to do this even if we are scared. We may seek to minimize risk in our lives, but the really big gains always involve a fair amount of it.

And even modest gains require some.

And there is no such thing as standing still: if you don't move forward, you will move backward.

So the frightened steward's cautious plan backfired. He didn't break even. He lost. His timidity cost him the whole of what he had. In every part of life, the same. Can you keep your kids from getting into trouble by locking them in a closet until they grow up? Yes, but then they won't grow up; they'll be stunted. Can you keep your spouse from straying by checking up on him all the time? Perhaps, but then you will lose his love. Can you avoid a mistake at work by researching your project carefully? Yes, but you can't research your project forever; there will come a time when you must get on with the actual work, accepting the risk that you overlooked something. Can you avoid the wrong choice by not choosing?

Not forever.

MONDAY IN PROPER 11

Pss 41, 52 * 44
1 Samuel 24:1–22
Acts 13:44–52
Mark 4:1–20

"Listen! A sower went out to sow."
MARK 4:3

Most seeds germinate, but some don't. And some of the ones that do are stronger than others, so you have to thin them, pulling up the weak ones, to give the strongest the best chance of making it. Thinning them is a bit painful; it's hard to pull up a living plant, however tiny. But if you don't thin them, all of them will remain small and weak.

You can't do everything. Not in church and not in life. Try to do everything and you won't do anything very well: the breadth of your effort will dilute the quality of it. And it's even harder to thin your life than it is to thin your row of carrots. You have to say no to good things, things you might very much like to do, important things that really should be done. *Somebody really should do this,* you think. But sometimes that somebody just can't be you.

Jesus' sower parable isn't about thinning. It's about differing qualities of soil. He used harvesting of wheat as an example of a spiritual principle once, too, and he used flowers, and he used weeds. His hearers were familiar with farming, gardening, growing things, and he met them where they were.

He used the world to teach us about God. We can see the things of God in ordinary things, and so nothing is ordinary.

TUESDAY IN PROPER 11

Pss 45 * 47, 48
1 Samuel 25:1–22
Acts 14:1–18
Mark 4:21–34

The woman was clever and beautiful,
but the man was surly and mean . . .
1 SAMUEL 25:3

Well, women didn't choose their own husbands back then. On the other hand, we do choose our own mates today, and some unions still leave onlookers shaking their heads.

My husband and I take turns being surly and mean. He is hard to get along with when he has too much to do in too little time; I am ugly when I think I have failed at something. Patience is required, in both instances: it will pass if you let it. Then you can get back to normal, which is when you're both clever and beautiful.

One of my most consistent struggles is in developing this patience. Nobody is as bad as his or her worst moment all the time; we all have good days and bad days. Both are true of us. If our goodness doesn't cancel out our badness, neither is the reverse true: we are simply a mixture of good and evil. Catch us on a bad day and we'll bite your head off. But we grow more mature, if we are blessed with people early on who insist on it, and learn to control our behavior when we're in one of our bad moods; if we don't, they cause us way more trouble than they're worth. It can save a relationship if we can over-look the occasional lapse of good humor, and it is certain that a time will come when we need the same favor in return.

All of which is different from being a doormat. You have to let people know when they're behaving badly, or they may never find out. You may have to refuse the request they have made of you in so demanding a fashion until such time as they can, um, *rephrase*. But you can do it in a way that asserts your strength, rather than a way that reacts to their weakness.

WEDNESDAY IN PROPER 11

Pss 119:49–72 * 49, (53)
1 Samuel 25:23–44
Acts 14:19–28
Mark 4:35–41

"Why are you afraid? Have you still no faith?"
MARK 4:40

I wonder if anybody in the boat was annoyed at the question. The scripture says they were all filled with awe, and I'm sure they were, but they had also been scared out of their wits, and Jesus knew it.

Nobody answers him back, so we'll never know. But I would have been angry. Grateful for being saved, of course, but a little angry just the same.

Why didn't you tell me? your friend asks, angry. Her engagement is broken, her ex is revealed to be a cad, and you volunteer that you had reservations about the two of them from the start. *Well, why didn't you tell me?*

Well, lots of reasons, but the main reason is that she would have discounted your warning. People in love don't take in warnings like that. They know better. Even when they're wrong. There's only one way to learn these things, and that's the way she's learning it right now.

How could the disciples have learned faith if they were not allowed to be in a place in which they needed it? *Poof! You've got faith now?* How do you get strong if you never test your muscles against a load too heavy for them? That's how they grow and strengthen. It's the mechanism of growth God has given us. We don't have another one for muscles.

Faith is the same. You can only learn it from experience. God saves you—a few thousand times—and you suddenly realize that God is good, as if it were news.

THURSDAY IN PROPER 11

Pss 50 * (59, 60) or 66, 67
1 Samuel 28:3–20
Acts 15:1–11
Mark 5:1–20

"Why have you disturbed me by bringing me up?"
1 SAMUEL 28:15

All the mediums and wizards are out of work and out of sight, but Saul needs one, and so he pays a call on the Witch of Endor. He wishes he hadn't before the end of the story; the *séance* brings him nothing but grief. Samuel can't help him any more. The dead must stay dead. They have no job here any more. We are better off not knowing what they know.

But we want them back. We think we could pick up where we left off with them. One of our most painful truths is that we could not, not even if they were here, no matter how close we were in life. We were close only in history when they were here, and they are out of history now.

By focusing all our longing on what we can no longer have with them, we delay receiving the gift of what we can have. For we are on our way out of history, too. We, too, will not stay forever. We will know what they know, too, someday, and they relate to us in a new way *now*. We can have an experience of this new way.

For starters, we no longer worry about them. If they were terribly ill, we know that dread as well as we know our own names. It was weeks, maybe months, before the sound of a telephone ringing late at night didn't make us jump. It was never out of our minds. We woke every day with dread: *Is it today?* And we never knew. But now we know. It is not today: it will never be again. It has already been.

We know the completeness of their lives. We know their ending here on the earth. After we spend the first months of shock and sorrow remembering the sad last days, we know their whole life. All their good remains with us.

And a mystery beckons. We'll be as they are someday. Now they *know* things we can only guess about. We sit tight, right here on the earth where they left us, and begin to listen acutely. And we begin to hear in a new way.

FRIDAY IN PROPER 11

Pss 40, 54 * 51
1 Samuel 31:1–13
Acts 15:12–21
Mark 5:21–43

*She had endured much under many physicians,
and had spent all that she had ...*
MARK 5:26

She treated her leukemia with vitamins. She was in chemotherapy for a year and a little more, but her insurance ran out. It was interferon—tough stuff. And $20,000 per year if you pay yourself. Which you could do if you were the Shah of Iran, but not if you were an undocumented worker who cleaned people's houses for a living, which is what she was.

So she read up on vitamins and began to treat herself. Her joints ached terribly, at times, and sometimes she was so tired she could barely move. Some days she just stayed in bed. Sometimes she had fevers, and awakened drenched with sweat. Her cleaning was slow but steady: she wasn't winning any races at it. But it wasn't a race. *I just pray*, she would say. *And take my vitamins.*

She became ill eight years ago. Last I heard, she was holding her own, walking the tightrope between catastrophic illness and poverty and her own rigorous self-care. So far, so good.

The elements of healing that she used in combating her illness were not much beyond what the woman in this ancient story had at her disposal. Rest, the best food obtainable. And the healing power of God, which both of them knew enough to ask for.

The woman in the story had a dramatic and immediate healing. The woman in this modern story hasn't had that. *Yet*, she says. But as she points out, she's still here.

SATURDAY IN PROPER 11

Pss 55 * 138, 139:1–17 (18–23)
2 Samuel 1:1–16
Acts 15:22–35
Mark 6:1–13

He said to me, "Come, stand over me and kill me; for convulsions have seized me and yet my life still lingers." So I stood over him, and killed him, for I knew that he could not live after he had fallen.
2 SAMUEL 1:9–10

A mercy killing. David understood this, I guess, but it didn't change his response: he had the young man put to death.

He waited, though—didn't do it right away. Waited until his day-long period of intense mourning for Saul and Jonathan was over. Perhaps he was also waiting to puzzle over the strange ethics of mercy killing: Saul wanted to die. His life was unsupportable. In fact, he *was* dying: this translation says "convulsions have seized me," but others have it differently: "I am in the throes of death." Ending his agony was an act of kindness.

But not an unmixed one. There are laws permitting mercy killing in some places: the state of Oregon has one at this writing, although it is hotly contested. The Netherlands permits it. Sometimes the courts find in favor of someone who wishes to allow nature to take its course in the case of a dying love one, and the papers call it a mercy killing. And sometimes an unbalanced nurse takes it upon himself or herself to end lives that seem not worth living. Such people go to jail: in some places, they are killed themselves.

And yet we understand it. There are things worse than death, we sense, especially when death is inevitable and imminent. When a husband or wife is convicted of such a killing, everyone in court is shaken by something that does not feel exactly like a crime but most assuredly *is* one. The inevitable guilty verdict satisfies no one, although everyone understands it: *Of course. We can't take the law into our own hands. It does not belong to us. It isn't ours to take.*

And yet. And yet.

SUNDAY, PROPER 12

Pss 24, 29 * 8, 84
2 Samuel 1:17–27
Romans 12:9–21
Matthew 25:31–46

*Do not repay anyone evil for evil, but take
thought for what is noble in the sight of all.*
ROMANS 12:17

The week after hundreds of photographs and hours of videotape records of dreadful abuse and even killing of Iraqi prisoners by their American captors were made public in the west, an American civilian was beheaded—on videotape—by his Iraqi captors. People didn't know how to relate the two horrors: some were angry that they were mentioned in the same breath, others thought they were an eye for an eye. Clearly, the men who performed the beheading were of the latter opinion: they said so on the videotape.

One thing is clear: doing the math won't bring resolution, peace, or closure to these incidents. How do you weigh out atrocities and add up the totals? How many sexual crimes equal one murder? When do you know if you're entitled to kill in retaliation for another killing? And then what? Just more of the same.

I struggle to bring to mind a situation in history in which tit-for-tat retaliation settled a dispute between nations, or within a nation among its warring people, and I find that I cannot. All such retaliation has ever done anywhere has been to spawn more violence. Whether it is justified or not, it simply doesn't work in the long run.

Terror is the weapon of people who don't think ordinary engagement works. It happens after civilized negotiation has failed, and sometimes even before it begins: despair engenders it. Terror, and retaliation for terror, represent the complete failure of human interaction on a large scale.

What works? Nonviolence. It freed millions of Indians from a colonial overlord, and a nation of South Africans from their apartheid oppressors. It is true that violence was a part of each of those struggles, but it was not a part that worked. What worked was the huge, insistent mass of people who simply wouldn't go away.

MONDAY IN PROPER 12

Pss 56, 57, (58) * 64, 65
2 Samuel 2:1–11
Acts 15:36–16:5
Mark 6:14–29

*But when Herod heard of it, he said, "John,
whom I beheaded, has been raised."*

MARK 6:16

Herod was like Lady Macbeth: he knew of his own sin, and so it seemed to follow him everywhere. Guilt is like that—not only do you know what you did, but you come to imagine that everyone else knows, too. The innocent observations of other people seem somehow pointed. Coincidences seem planned.

Mostly, we suspect in others what we know to be present in ourselves. We think other people are like us. It is part of our mistaken conviction that we are at the center of our own moral universe, that everything is somehow about us. It is not. But it can take us a long, long time to figure that out.

There are no curses. That's only in fairytales. Our immediate actions are usually what have immediate consequences, not our horoscopes or our ancient misdeeds. I am not doomed because of something I did wrong long ago, but I am informed by it. I have had ample time to examine it and my role in it, and I have had time to resolve to repair the damage I have done and follow another course next time.

If I do that, my ancient error is more than redeemed: although it is still an evil in itself, in the context of my whole life, it has become an occasion for good. I now know better, and I will take special care in this error of old weakness and sin. I know myself, and sadly, I know what I am capable of. And so I guard myself, and so guard the world—not against a curse, but against what I know. Immediately I am cut down to size, both my power and my sin, in order that the modest goodness of which I am capable may flower as God intends.

TUESDAY IN PROPER 12

Pss 61, 62 * 68:1–20 (21–23) 24–36
2 Samuel 3:6–21
Acts 16:6–15
Mark 6:30–46

When they had come opposite Mysia, they attempted to go into
Bithynia, but the Spirit of Jesus did not allow them.
ACTS 16:7

Early in a person's life in Christ, it can seem as if Jesus is dictating
every move. Where does Jesus want me to go to college, and who
does Jesus want me to marry? Does Jesus want me to take this job,
or does he want me to wait for another? WWJD, those bracelets say:
What Would Jesus Do?

I'm not getting a sign, someone complains. I don't know what
God wants.

Well then, what do *you* want? Maybe God wants you to embark
upon the delicate task of discernment. I think it is often not clear
what Jesus would do. Discerning the will of God is subtle business,
a matter of prayer and study, of the clear-eyed weighing of options.
It is always done with humility: I may be wrong in my assessment of
what I should be doing. I could have read the signs wrong. Maybe I
allowed self-interest to inform me more than it should.

There are signs in life—oddities that crop up when we are
attempting to make a choice, oddities that inform that choice. These
things happen. But they happen to us in the context of doing our
own part: not waiting for God to dictate to us and then blaming
him for our immobility, but using what God gave us to find our
path, and trusting God to help us correct it if we make a mistake.

WEDNESDAY IN PROPER 12

Pss 72 * 119:73–96
2 Samuel 3:22–39
Acts 16:16–24
Mark 6:47–56

*One day, as we were going to the place of prayer, we met
a slave-girl who had a spirit of divination and brought
her owners a great deal of money by fortune-telling.*

ACTS 16:16

It is striking that this girl, who possessed a gift her owners did not possess, was nonetheless still trapped in a system of slavery. Her gifts didn't make anybody think maybe she should be free. They really weren't her gifts, in the eyes of her owners: she and her gifts belonged to them.

Oh, they value our art, a friend told me once. We were talking about what it's like to be gay in the Church. They let us design their cathedrals and arrange their flowers. We can play their organs and direct their choirs. They love our music and they'll take our money. It's just us they don't want. But we come with our gifts. We're not separate from them.

Women, too. It was fine for women to work in the Church, to teach the Church's children, to make the Church beautiful, its linens white and crisp, its silver gleaming. Fine.

Our work belongs to us. Our gifts are ours, given to us by God. Only to us: your gifts are yours alone. Nobody else's gifts are quite like yours. Nobody can do what you can do, the way you do it. It is unique to you. Unique and valuable. Irreplaceable, in the Church and in the world.

When the disciples took away the little girl's soothsaying abilities, her owners didn't care about her any more. Of course, they never had.

THURSDAY IN PROPER 12

Pss (70), 71 * 74
2 Samuel 4:1–12
Acts 16:25–40
Mark 7:1–23

". . . in vain do they worship me,
teaching human precepts as doctrines."
MARK 7:7

There were theologians in Nazi Germany who made it their life's work to find support in scripture for the totalitarian regime and its genocidal mania. They found it, too: in Romans, Paul counsels obedience to the government as instituted by God. In the gospel of John, the Jews cry out for Jesus' execution and ask that his blood be upon them and their children. Jesus says that the wheat and the tares grow together, and only after they are grown are they separated—and the tares are thrown into the fire.

These things seemed to them clear enough: it's okay to kill the Jews—they killed Christ. They are the tares that are thrown into the fire. It's okay to follow a violent government headed by a madman. He's not mad: it's all in the Bible.

Their writings are chilling. So even-handed, so intellectual. Not hysterical. Well-reasoned. Hate was well-mannered there. Murder was efficient. All the records were in order. There were photographs.

If it seems to us that God counsels killing, that God endorses bigotry, that God divides person from person—we'd better check our reading of scripture. The letter kills, sometimes, and the spirit gives life. We have taken ourselves at our very worst as the model for God, crediting God with our vindictiveness and prejudice.

The church that went along with Hitler was called the German Christian Church. Its underground alternative was known as the Confessing Church. To confess is to take seriously the cost of one's beliefs, and to be willing to pay them. Some of the leaders of the

Confessing Church were killed: Dietrich Bonhoeffer was one. We remember his name.

And those who rode the wave of Nazi power? Not a single one of them survives in the popular memory. None is read in seminaries today, except as an example of what happens when the Church is co-opted. They perished as if they had never lived.

FRIDAY IN PROPER 12

Pss 69:1–23 (24–30) 31–38 * 73
2 Samuel 5:1–12
Acts 17:1–15
Mark 7:24–37

"Sir, even the dogs under the table eat the children's crumbs."
MARK 7:28

Here we have Jesus behaving in a most un-Jesuslike way. He is rude to the poor woman who approaches him for a healing for her daughter, and his rudeness is based on her ethnicity. Is this our egalitarian Jesus, who impresses us by being so nice to Samaritans, to prostitutes, and tax collectors? Our Jesus, the Civil Libertarian?

The woman was surprised, too, but she didn't give up. She challenged Jesus, and she won.

Does it trouble you to consider the possibility that Jesus made a mistake here? That he was corrected by a woman, and that he accepted her correction and changed his mind and then his behavior?

We are used to a Jesus who knew everything and never made a mistake. I doubt if that is the Jesus we really have: not if the Incarnation is true, and Jesus was truly God and truly human. Truly human means learning the way humans learn, which is primarily by making mistakes and learning from them. It is true of us that we learn best when we learn the hard way. That must also have been true of him.

And does such a possibility interfere with Jesus' Godhood? Isn't that as mysterious as ever, regardless of whether or not he was smarter than everybody else? Limiting himself with our limits, all of them? And then empowering himself with God's power—all of it?

SATURDAY IN PROPER 12

Pss 75, 76 * 23, 27
2 Samuel 5:22–6:11
Acts 17:16–34
Mark 8:1–10

Now all the Athenians and the foreigners living there would spend their time in nothing but telling or hearing something new.
ACTS 17:21

Modern-day Athens is a remarkable combination of great beauty and real tawdriness: the Parthenon presides over it from the Acropolis, lit at night to reveal it as what it is: the most beautiful building in the world. But crude political placards plaster ancient walls and chain link fences alike, all over the city, and graffiti is everywhere. It contains many monuments, but Athens is not itself a monument. The Parthenon, which we think of as pearly white, pristine, austere, was painted many bright colors. The *Parthenon* was *painted*. Athens is the same today: it is a living city—dirty, loud, argumentative. Alive.

Even children watch political debates on television. The politics of their parents is not boring to them, as ours is to our kids. Real passion about public life fills the air, and everyone is excited by it. The place that invented democracy 2500 years ago continues to live with the rowdiness that accompanies democracy to this very day.

One of America's great scandals is our boredom with public life. Many, many people in this great country have never bothered to vote. They usually say something self-serving, like, "All politicians are crooked," to explain their lassitude, but it's just that. Laziness. Reaping the benefits of freedom without paying any price at all.

When God related to Abraham, it was on behalf of a people yet unborn. Moses gave his entire life to his people, at God's command. The nation of Israel was of concern to God, the people and all their dealings with one another. Politics was religion then, and very serious. Politics is not religion now, but it is still serious. It still matters how we arrange ourselves in order that justice may be served among us. There is still no such thing as an individual all by himself. We are not alone. We live together, and bear a debt to one another and to the future to protect one another's rights. Or no one will be left to protect ours.

SUNDAY, PROPER 13

Pss 93, 96 * 34
2 Samuel 6:12–23
Romans 4:7–12
John 1:43–51

. . . Michal daughter of Saul looked out of the window,
and saw King David leaping and dancing before the Lord;
and she despised him in her heart.

2 SAMUEL 6:16

Marrying David had not been Michal's idea: her dad had just given her to him like one might give a friend a prized horse, to cement their friendship. And, of course, to join the two houses in the person of the heir who would be born of the match.

And now he was embarrassing her, dancing half-naked in the street. In a better marriage, the reproach might not have been so bitter: who has not been embarrassed in public by a spouse's behavior at least once? Such things can be survived.

But a weak union can't endure what a strong one can. Eventually Michal was given to someone else. She never did get to choose. Her marriage to David faded into history.

I don't know that love had much to do with it. People didn't expect that romantic love would precede marriage then: that seems strange to us, since marriage does involve immediate sexual intimacy, and we think it would be nice to be in love when that happens. But that's the way it was. A very different time and place.

The writer makes sure we remember whose daughter Michal is: this is really a story about the fall of the house of Saul and the rise of David's house. Michal is barren: the house of Saul has nothing more to give Israel. The daughter of Saul is angry at David's happy intimacy with God, for God's favor has left her house.

I guess it was never meant to be, someone says sadly of his broken marriage. *It was no good from the start.* Sometimes. And sometimes it dies later on, a victim of neglect or violence or faithlessness. Lots of reasons. Maybe it was meant to be, but many things God means do not come to pass. Ours is an imperfect world.

MONDAY IN PROPER 13

Pss 80 * 77, (79)
2 Samuel 7:1–17
Acts 18:1–11
Mark 8:11–21

"See now, I am living in a house of cedar,
but the ark of God stays in a tent."
2 SAMUEL 7:2

David wants to build a temple: God should live at least as well as I do, he thinks. But a consistent memory of the wandering in the wilderness has established a different principle: God doesn't have a house. He has a tent. God is portable. God can go anywhere.

Transcends everything. It didn't last, though. David didn't build the house of God, but his son Solomon would.

Early on the children of Israel hold to this important distinction between themselves and other nations, but in the end, they succumb: the God of Israel has a temple, like every other god. The God of Israel has arrived.

But the God of Israel never arrives. He leads. Even in the temple, there is no figure of YHWH, as there is in every other god's temple. Not here—God cannot be imagined or portrayed. God is beyond this.

And in the end, all the temples are destroyed. A few pagan temples are left, here and there—in France, in Italy, a few in Rome. But the statues of the gods that stood in them are gone. And the temple of the God of Israel is gone. Those gods are gone.

And, alone of all of them, the mobile God of Israel remains. Nathan the prophet was right: God didn't need a house after all.

TUESDAY IN PROPER 13

Pss 78:1–39 * 78:40–72
2 Samuel 7:18–29
Acts 18:12–28
Mark 8:22–33

"If it were a matter of crime or serious villainy, I would be justified in accepting the complaint of you Jews; but since it is a matter of questions about words and names and your own law, see to it yourselves; I do not wish to be a judge of these matters."
ACTS 18:14–15

The Roman version of our separation of church and state: settle your doctrinal disputes yourselves, and let the civil authority confine itself to civil matters.

We imagine that earlier ages were more religious than our modern one, but they were not. In colonial America, for instance, the largest demographic group in the population was not Puritans or Anglicans: it was the unchurched. Then, as now, most people were not animated mainly by considerations arising from their religious faith. They thought more about other things.

Not everyone lifts his eyes from the day-to-day tasks of living. Some don't know there's anything to see apart from them. Others don't feel qualified to explore. Some feel unworthy. Some are too angry.

And nobody has to.

But for those who want to begin, there is another world. Unfettered by the categories of secular life, yet loving the secular world. Praying for it.

It is probably not the case that the civil authority can further religious goals. The government cannot convert us, or even protect our conversions. It is more the other way around: a prayer for the world offered daily and in great earnestness, we bring the spirit in to cover the secular. Maybe they don't pray, and maybe they never will. But—in part, precisely because they do not—we pray for them.

WEDNESDAY IN PROPER 13

Pss 119:97–120 * 81, 82
2 Samuel 9:1–13
Acts 19:1–10
Mark 8:34–9:1

Now he was lame in both his feet.
2 SAMUEL 9:13

The writer tacks this bit of information about Mephibosheth, Jonathan's only surviving son, onto the end of the story. We are to know who he was, and we are to be moved by David's own emotion: he weeps upon seeing him. But why do we need to know that he was lame?

Because the people who wrote scripture believed that physical deformity was a punishment from God, and so we are told this to remind us—yet again—that David has triumphed over Saul and his whole family. Just in case we didn't understand the significance of Michal's barrenness a couple of chapters back. They thought these things were curses.

How silly. But half the time, we think so, too, sophisticated as we are. "What did I do to deserve this?" we mutter about our arthritis, our shingles, our ulcers. Sometimes we can point to something: *I smoked. I overate. I drank too much.*

But sometimes, there's no such reason. Sometimes we just get sick, and it's not our fault. And usually we don't know which is true.

Not much good comes of blaming people—or their parents—for their illnesses. Life is hard enough for them without an added burden of reproach from us, and we really don't have any privileged information about the reasons for other people's afflictions. Or our own.

THURSDAY IN PROPER 13

Pss (83) or 145 * 85, 86
2 Samuel 11:1–27
Acts 19:11–20
Mark 9:2–13

The thing that David had done displeased the Lord.
2 SAMUEL 12:1

How cruel, this deed of the great king of Israel, Jesus' most famous forebear. How could one who enjoyed such favor from God stoop to such deceit?

It is a sign of real honesty on the part of the biblical writer to have included this story: it doesn't make David look good at all. If he were writing a boss's biography today, you can bet he would have left it out. But he doesn't. He has a responsibility to report this ancient crime, and he fulfills it.

Unlike the gods of Greek myth, for example, the characters of 2 Samuel are real people. This is history: not all scripture is history, but this is. And very honest history it is, too. Which should give us some confidence in its veracity. This isn't an essay on why the boss is brilliant. It's a candid story of a great man guiltily involved in a terrible scandal.

And Jesus, the messiah, is the son of David—called that dozens of times, in the gospels. Son of the great king, heir to all the power in Israel. But also heir to all its messes. Jesus received the fruit of all our good work and all our sins. He absorbs it all. The good is recognized as God's work in us.

And the rest is redeemed.

No matter what you've done or who you've been, God can work in your biography, too, to renew your little portion of the whole redeemable earth. The good that God finds in you and the good that God makes in you outweigh your sins, and you can still have the enjoyment of it, if you can bring yourself to admit what they are.

FRIDAY IN PROPER 13

Pss 88 * 91, 92
2 Samuel 12:1–14
Acts 19:21–41
Mark 9:14–29

"Why could we not cast it out?"
MARK 9:28

My neighbor's cancer is in remission, but mine has returned. My friend's wife has stopped drinking, but mine refuses even to talk about it. And both of us pray. We pray together, in fact: we've been in the same prayer group for years, and we've been praying for healing all this time.

My niece is an honor student, but my daughter won't even get out of bed in the morning. She's missed thirty days of school this year. I am so jealous of her mother I can barely stand to see them.

Miracles happen in this world. There are healings with no reasonable explanation. But you can't order them up, like pizzas. Healing is mysterious. It is not a magic trick.

So when Jesus answers his frustrated and puzzled disciples—*This kind can only be cast out with prayer*, he says—are we enlightened? Not much.

It sounds like the disciples were in trouble: a crowd had gathered to watch the healing they couldn't seem to perform, and some scribes were scolding them about their failure as Jesus approached. Who is to say what they were doing wrong? Whatever it was, Jesus fixed it. And then he made that remark about "this kind" of demon—as if it were a special breed of the beast.

However the disciples performed their healings, we only have the one Jesus mentioned. We only have prayer. It is our only weapon. We pray for those who need healing without knowing what will happen. We never know.

We know that God wills health. We know that God hears us. We know that, sooner or later, everyone dies.

But we never know what will happen this time.

SATURDAY IN PROPER 13

Pss 87, 90 * 136
2 Samuel 12:15–31
Acts 20:1–16
Mark 9:30–41

*A young man named Eutychus, who was sitting in the
window, began to sink off into a deep sleep while
Paul talked still longer. Overcome by sleep, he fell to the
ground three floors below and was picked up dead.*

ACTS 20:9

Poor Eutychus, the patron saint of those who must listen to sermons. He actually died of one. It was only fair that Paul, the person who put Eutychus through all this, was the one appointed to heal him miraculously.

The sermon is one of the few places left in public life in which someone comments on God's ways in the world. For a dozen minutes, you have the chance to change people's lives with your words. But the truth is sad: most people don't remember what the preacher said.

You ought to be able to tell someone who wasn't there what the preacher said and you ought to be able to do it in one sentence. If you can't, the sermon probably wasn't tight enough—it may have had lots of good ideas in it, but they may not have held together well enough for someone to grasp the direction of them. You ought to be able to remember a word that touched you, or a string of them. You ought to have encountered some emotion or strong sense of commitment within yourself in response to the preacher's words. The scripture from which it was taken should remind you of it when next you read it—they should go together.

If these things happen, you've heard a good sermon from a good preacher. And you'll stay awake for it.

SUNDAY, PROPER 14

Pss 66, 67 * 19, 46
2 Samuel 13:1–22
Romans 15:1–13
John 3:22–36

"Now therefore, I beg you, speak to the king;
for he will not withhold me from you."
2 SAMUEL 13:13

Interesting—incest is not the crime Amnon has committed in this story, although modern readers always assume it is. Tamar is his half-sister: David fathered both of them, but they have different mothers. His crime was rape, violating the daughter of the king. If he had only asked, Tamar points out, David would have permitted their marriage and all would have been well.

But we still suspect that the relationship between the two is the reason that the story is included. It was titillating and faintly perverse. Tamar wasn't just any virgin or any king's daughter. She was Amnon's *sister*.

How incidental she is in the scheme of things. It is Absalom and Amnon who are the main characters in this sorry play. Her weeping is sorrowful: she disfigures herself, pouring ashes on her head, and rips the robe that proclaims her virginity. Her wound is denied by her powerful brother; *Do not take this to heart*, he tells her. After all, Amnon is her brother. Surely she owes him something.

Don't tell anybody. We'll handle this ourselves. She lives in Absalom's house, "a desolate woman," it says. That's the last we see of her.

Until later on. Much later on, when we meet Tamar again. She is on the list of forebears of Jesus of Nazareth.

Do you have a secret shame? Your own doing, or someone else's? Is there something that makes you doubt your own worth? Is there something you know you must hide from the world?

Maybe so. But don't ever think your life is meaningless because of it. God brings good from evil every day.

MONDAY IN PROPER 14

Pss 89:1–18 * 89:19–52
2 Samuel 13:23–39
Acts 20:17–38
Mark 9:42–50

*Salt is good, but if salt has lost its saltiness,
how can you season it?*
MARK 9:50

He's too old to change, a woman says about her husband, shaking her head. But it isn't true that old people can't change. They fall in love, move to a different house, begin new careers in a volunteer capacity. They change their politics, sometimes, and develop new friendships. They remarry. They make the adjustment to physical limitation, and most of them make it with good humor and grace. They discover their own venerable status: they are the sages now, the ones who remember, the wise ones. All of their youthful mistakes have become treasures, ways in which they learned important things.

This is not a bad deal.

Another important thing often happens in an older person's life: a rediscovery of faith. Sometime it happens when tragedy strikes: the death of a husband or wife. The very ground of life has been yanked from under their feet, and they must find a new ground or go mad. God waits for these terrible moments with comfort and the promise of return: you can come back to the community of faith you may have been too busy for when you were young and your life was too full to think much about it. The church at which you dropped your children off for Sunday school may have something that *you* need now—and your children may be the ones, with their jobs and houses and children and hectic schedules—who do not have time. You may have time and space to listen, now, and you may have need of listening. You may be about to be born again.

TUESDAY IN PROPER 14

Pss 97, 99, (100) * 94, (95)
2 Samuel 14:1–20Acts 21:1–14
Mark 10:1–16

When our days there were ended, we left and proceeded on our journey; and all of them, with wives and children, escorted us outside the city. There we knelt down on the beach and prayed and said farewell to one another. Then we went on board the ship, and they returned home.

ACTS 21:5–6

At first, they call you rather more than you would like: *Where is that report? How did you estimate mailing costs for the year—should we use the same figure for next year? Do you remember which of the three plans we looked at came in second? And where did we put the other proposals we decided not to put in the final three?*

They're in one of those cardboard file boxes in my office, over near the window, you answer with good humor, and then you say, *I told you you'd be lost without me,* and you put down the phone. You're glad you're not on the train this morning—you're sitting in your kitchen, reading the paper, and then you're going out to the garden for a little while, before it gets too warm. In the afternoon, maybe you'll read a book. You haven't decided.

In a few weeks you go in for lunch with the old gang and everyone crowds around you. They ask a few questions and a few whisper a familiar gripe. You have a good lunch and then you go home. You're home by three in the afternoon.

You go in for lunch every now and then. Less often, soon: somebody else is sitting at your desk, and there are a couple of other people you don't know. Nobody has anything to ask you, any more: the place where you were has closed up, and sometimes it is as if you were never there. They're not lost without you. They're doing fine.

The tiniest twinge of jealousy nips at your heart. You wanted to retire, you planned for it all these years, but it hurts to see your importance diminish in a place where you used to be so central to everything. So much a part of everything.

If John the Baptist felt that twinge, we don't read about it in the Gospel of Mark. He is graceful and generous in his yielding to what must replace him. We don't know if it was easy for him to be that way, or hard. It just doesn't say.

WEDNESDAY IN PROPER 14

Pss 101, 109:1–4 (5–19) 20–30 * 119:121–144
2 Samuel 14:21–33
Acts 21:15–26
Mark 10:17–31

*And he took them up in his arms, laid his
hands on them, and blessed them.*
MARK 10:16

We had a picture of this moment in Sunday School: Jesus sitting on a rock in a meadow, surrounded by children, with two of them in his lap and more sitting or standing beside him, talking to him. Our picture didn't show the annoyed disciples—we never really heard about the people who didn't want Jesus to bother with children.

It was a pretty picture—all the children strong and healthy, well-fed, all smiling. Mark, though, is thinking of their weakness when he tells us about Jesus and the children: they are little, vulnerable. Children are in need. Jesus' preference for the children is just like his preference for the hungry, the sick, those in prison, those sick of their own sin—Jesus wants to be with people who need his presence, no matter who they are. People in need don't quibble about details when help and comfort is offered. They accept immediately. *Thanks. I needed that.*

So maybe entering the kingdom like a little child means entering it with immediacy, eager for its healing, longing for its peace. Maybe we enter it clumsily, falling all over ourselves in our longing. Maybe we are not elegant in our redemption. Maybe we are childlike.

Kids always take it on the chin, a man told me sadly, having heard about a little girl who was terribly injured. Here on the earth, they're in danger. Children die if someone doesn't see to it that they don't. Maybe it is really our need, more than our innocence, that is the childlike quality that endears us to Christ.

THURSDAY IN PROPER 14

Pss 105:1–22 * 105:23–45
2 Samuel 15:1–18
Acts 21:27–36
Mark 10:32–45

Fellow Israelites, help! This is the man who is teaching everyone everywhere against our people, our law, and this place . . .
ACTS 21:28

Paul was a strange kind of evangelist: argumentative, anxious about his reputation, easily angered. His dramatic story antagonized both Christians and Jews.

But he did his part, and it was immense. He set whole communities upon their road to Christ. He started them out—that's all any of us can do for anyone else: give them a beginning. Nobody can give another person faith. We can't really convert one another. God does the converting. Faith is such an important thing that no one can give it to another. We must find it for ourselves.

What we can do is put it in front of people. Let them see it, as best we can. Some of them will pick it up and examine it. And some who do pick it up will make it their own.

Others won't pick it up. After all, most people who lived in Jesus' day did not—seeing him did not produce instant belief. But those who were ready, who wanted to know, who wanted to spend the time puzzling and listening and weighing for themselves: they embraced who he was.

In large measure, faith is a matter of desiring. It is never a matter of proof: Paul had poor credentials as a Christian witness, and we constantly see his struggle for credibility in what he writes. But he witnesses anyway. You long for God to be manifest to you in any way possible, and you live your life in anticipation of the signs that this is so. And you see them.

Wishful thinking, say the skeptics scornfully. Of course. I wish it with all my heart. And my wish becomes prayer, and—in the stillness of the night, or the morning intake of breath before the sun comes up—God answers.

FRIDAY IN PROPER 14

Pss 102 * 107:1–32
2 Samuel 15:19–37
Acts 21:37–22:16
Mark 10:46–52

"My teacher, let me see again."
MARK 10:51

We used to play a game when I was little. *Which would you rather lose, your hearing or your sight?* we would ask one another, and then we would have to tell why we'd made the choice we did.

Never to see the flowers again. Never again to see my husband or my children or my grandchildren. Never to look at a painting; when I am in Minneapolis, I try to get to the Walker Art Center to spend a little time with Rembrandt's *Lucrezia,* because I can never get enough of the sadness in her eyes. Never to see that.

But then, never to hear. Not hear Q's rich rumbly voice? Not hear my daughters on the telephone? Never hear music? I have a friend with tinnitus, a disorder of the ear in which sounds are scrambled, or repeat unceasingly. Music sounds terrible to her—a great loss, since she loved music. Now music is agony.

One thing is certain, something that was not nearly so obvious to me when I played this game as a child: one day we will lose both sight *and* hearing. And everything else. I never thought of that then.

So when blind Bartimaeus received his sight, he was too overjoyed to reflect on the fact that he would lose it again someday. But he did: one day the world narrowed to a tunnel of black, and then the light went out. Until that day came, though, he wanted to experience as much of the world as he could. He wanted to see it and hear it and feel it and do it all.

We all want that. Until our very last moment here, we want to do it all.

SATURDAY IN PROPER 14

Pss 107:33–43, 108:1–6 (7–13) * 33
2 Samuel 16:1–23
Acts 22:17–29
Mark 11:1–11

And while the blood of your witness Stephen was shed,
I myself was standing by, approving and keeping the
coats of those who killed him. Then he said to me,
"Go, for I will send you far away to the Gentiles."
ACTS 22:20–21

Ah—*now* we understand. The reason Paul was the Apostle to the Gentiles was that his own people wouldn't have anything to do with him. They knew his history too well, and they couldn't get past it.

Sometimes that happens: what you want to do is closed to you, and so you go and do something else. And it turns out that this is what you were born to do.

I have a friend who wanted, from the time he was a little boy, to be a priest. He went to minor seminary at a young age—fourteen?—and was scrupulous in the performance of all his duties. Faithful in prayer and fasting: too faithful, his superiors kept telling him, trying to pull him back from too rigorous an adherence to holiness. He could not restrain his zeal. But he would not be pulled back. He put his health in danger, his fasting was so rigorous. Finally, his superiors asked him to leave the seminary.

He was crushed. The only dream he'd ever had was broken. His life went on, of course, and he continued to practice his faith with great rigor. The changes brought to the church by Vatican II didn't sit well with him: he felt his church had left him behind. But God continued to call him, and after many trials he found a way of living his faith that was full of love and joy as a lay person.

What would he have been if his youthful dream had come true? A rigid priest who could only see things one way. God spared him this fate. He was called, all right—just not in the way he thought he was.

SUNDAY, PROPER 15

Pss 118 * 145
2 Samuel 17:1–23
Galatians 3:6–14
John 5:30–47

*"You search the scriptures because you think that in them
you have eternal life; and it is they that testify on
my behalf. Yet you refuse to come to me to have life."*

JOHN 5:39–40

*B*ut don't you believe in the Bible? someone asks me. He is in evident distress: it is the week after the General Convention of the Episcopal Church has voted to recognize the election of the first openly gay person as a bishop. My friend has serious questions: it says in Leviticus that it is an abomination for a man to lie with a man as with a woman. It says in Romans that sodomites will go to hell. He has been told all his life that homosexuality is sinful, and he has been told that it says so in the Bible. And it does: anyone can go and read it. And yet he knows that I am pleased with the decision, that I am proud of my church for having had the courage to make it. *Don't you believe in the Bible?*

My belief is in God. I believe that the writers of the many books that comprise our Holy Scriptures were inspired by God to write them. I have been reading it long enough to know. I see more evidence every day that this is so: the way in which reading scripture together brings people into close and loving relationship, the way you always find something new in a passage, no matter how many hundreds of times you have read it before. The Bible is filled to overflowing with the Spirit to which it bears witness.

That is a very different thing, though, from *believing in the Bible.* Like Jesus—who says in today's gospel reading that just as he does not bear witness to himself, the Bible does not bear witness to itself. It bears witness to God. It will not save us: God saves us. Remember what Jesus' name means? *Jesus. Yehu-shuah. God saves.*

Saves us from what? From a life of meaninglessness and despair. From a too-small view of the world and of time, as if the way things are now were the way they have always been and always must be. As if what we see is all there is. What we see is utterly *not* all there is. It is a tiny fraction of what there is.

MONDAY IN PROPER 15

Pss 106:1–18 * 106:19–48
2 Samuel 17:24–18:8
Acts 22:30–23:11
Mark 11:12–26

*"We find nothing wrong with this man.
What if a spirit or an angel has spoken to him?"*
ACTS 23:9

You can pet a bumblebee when it is busy drinking nectar from a flower. It buries its head deep in the flower's throat, covering itself with yellow pollen in the process. While it is feeding, you can touch its furry yellow-and-black-striped back with your fingertip. It will be so busy drinking that it won't care what you're doing.

Its back is as furry as that of a kitten. Just that soft and silky. It is not dangerous. It doesn't even have a stinger: it is in the class of bee society that goes out foraging in flowers, not the group that guards things. But the bumblebee shares the public relations burden of all bees where we are concerned. We're scared of all of them. But not all of them are dangerous.

Life is hard enough without generalizing every danger we meet. Some new things are hard and unpleasant, but not all new things are. Some people are, indeed, falsehearted, but we do ourselves and others a great disservice if we assume bad faith on the part of everyone we meet. If self-protection becomes my only goal in life, I doom myself to chronic isolation. Sometimes you have to venture into an arena in which you feel neither comfortable nor safe, and sometimes you have to go someplace where you've been hurt before.

Not all men are two-timing jerks. Not all women have dollar signs in their eyes. Not all children are rude and noisy. Not all Christians are judgmental. Not all anybody is anything. We have to take each case as it comes.

TUESDAY IN PROPER 15

Pss (120), 121,122, 123 * 124, 125, 126, (127)
2 Samuel 18:9–18
Acts 23:12–24
Mark 11:27–12:12

A man planted a vineyard . . .

MARK 12:1

There are only twelve of them: a dozen Bibles, published in Oxford in 1717, in which this parable was printed incorrectly. The printer mistook "vineyard" for "vinegar," and it appeared that way throughout the story about the man and his problematic vineyard. A scrupulous proofreader soon discovered the mistake and they corrected the run. That's why there are only twelve.

So, of course, the Vinegar Bibles are priceless. Nobody who owns one—churches own most of them—would ever let it go, and they are all kept under lock and key.

Interesting: what makes it priceless is a mistake. Like stamps with a mistake in the run, or coins with an irregularity on the rim—priceless. We don't feel that way about most of our mistakes: we think they cancel out all our other excellences. They loom large in our assessment of ourselves. One of them outweighs a dozen things we do well.

This is heresy. It invades what we know to be true: God made us in his image, and we are good. Not perfect, apt to stray, have our faults, to be sure, but we are not junk. The mistakes that plague us and keep us up at night can all be fixed: God is bigger than my biggest fault. Our actions have consequences, and they range from the excellent through the silly to the terrible, but God can handle them all. And what is true of the Vinegar Bibles is true of us, too: the thing that we most rue about ourselves can be the very thing that makes us most useful and lovely if we lift it to God and allow God to work within it.

WEDNESDAY IN PROPER 15

Pss 119:145–176 * 128, 129, 130
2 Samuel 18:19–23
Acts 23:23–35
Mark 12:13–27

*"Teacher, we know that you are sincere, and show deference
to no one; for you do not regard people with partiality,
but teach the way of God in accordance with truth.*

MARK 12:14

Be wary of people who begin a conversation with a series of compliments: they may be about to ask you to do something you might think more than twice about, if the only thing you had to rely on was your own judgment. Maybe Jesus is sincere, but these guys certainly aren't.

What they hope is that they will trap him with words. And, as always, he cannot be trapped that way. Nobody ever gets the best of him. Even his silence is more eloquent than most of us ever get.

It's interesting, in this encounter, that the things they compliment Jesus about are things they lack themselves. I wonder if that isn't often the case with those who wish to deceive: they fool us best when they appear to share our values, and so they take pains to seem like us. It is on our home turf that we feel most safe: *This person is like me, cares about the things I care about. I can trust him.*

Most of us don't go into a conversation thinking that the other party might be insincere. Mostly, we think that what you see is pretty much what you get. We're always shocked when that turns out not to be so, shocked and a little ashamed of our own gullibility. *What an idiot I was not to have suspected something*, we think, and set about repairing the damage somebody else's craftiness has caused. *Next time I'll be smarter.*

But maybe you won't. And maybe you shouldn't be too smart and suspicious. There is something to be said for a trusting attitude toward the world, even if you sometimes get burned.

THURSDAY IN PROPER 15

Pss 131, 132, (133) * 134, 135
2 Samuel 19:1–23
Acts 24:1–23
Mark 12:28–34

"But this I admit to you, that according to the Way,
which they call a sect, I worship the God of our ancestors . . ."
ACTS 24:14

The first Christians didn't call themselves Christians, of course. They called their new faith "the Way," and to them it was a way of serving God within the boundaries of the faith they already knew. They weren't starting something new, not at first. They were completing what they already believed. God had come near them, and they had a Way to follow because of it.

It didn't look that way to those who opposed them. It looked different, different and offensive. What was wrong with the old way, that there had to be something new?

America has seen its fair share of sects. Unitarians and Mormons were both viewed as dangerous enemies by the Episcopal Church in America in the nineteenth century: you can trace the fear of them as you read old resolutions of the Church's General Conventions. We don't handle diversity in matters of faith very well. Everyone thinks his or her own faith is uniquely true, and that must mean that others are false.

Well, maybe. But maybe they have a truth to tell, and maybe there's something to learn in just about anything.

FRIDAY IN PROPER 15

Pss 140, 142 * 141, 143:1–11 (12)
2 Samuel 19:24–43
Acts 24:24–25:12
Mark 12:35–44

"David himself calls him Lord; so how can he be his son?"
MARK 12:37

Without even questioning it, Jesus shows us the way things are in the ancient Middle East: respect for the elder, a hierarchy of honor that cannot be disturbed. How can the messiah be the son of David? He would have to outrank him, and you can't outrank your father. It seems a weak point to us, but it would have been self-evident to the people at the time. And to modern people in that part of the world, even now. Men over women, older over younger, always; these things went without saying.

Yet in his own life, he disturbed it now and then: he quietly instructs his older cousin John, who yields to him gladly. He talks with the scribes in the temple as an equal, when he is just a boy. He speaks directly with a foreign woman, and interacts sympathetically with a prostitute. The hierarchy of honor doesn't appear to concern him much.

In heaven, there is no such hierarchy. All the things that separate us for each other here do not, there. *All will be in Christ,* Paul said once, *and Christ will be all in all.*

When Jesus poses this question—almost like a riddle—Mark tells us that "the large crowd was listening to him with delight." I bet they were. He was providing a feast of the imagination, a feast of fools, in which the power principles with which they had lived all their lives are inverted. He was giving them a glimpse of something they had never seen. Maybe love can make us all equals, he was suggesting.

And they liked it.

SATURDAY IN PROPER 15

Pss 137:1–6 (7–9), 144 * 104
2 Samuel 23:1–7, 13–17
Acts 25:13–27
Mark 13:1–13

"Look, Teacher, what large stones and what large buildings!"
MARK 13:1

Even now, I could walk you through the entire ground floor of the World Trade Center. Say you enter from Liberty Street and go down a flight of stairs. There's a bank on the right, and an ATM. Then there's a bookstore, and some other stores. On the other side of the hall is a store that sells nothing but hosiery. You turn right and head for the escalators to the Path train. Or you go straight to the E Train. Or maybe you head for the E train at first, but change your mind, grab a slice of pizza instead of stopping for lunch and walk through the tunnel and up the steps onto Church Street. Or maybe you entered from West Street, through the hotel lobby, and you take the elevator—whoosh!—all the way up to Windows on the World.

No, you don't. Not any more. Not ever again. Even now, I can't believe it's gone.

It seemed impossible to the people walking with Jesus in the bright sunshine that the time might come when the temple was no longer there. And it did, and it's not there: one part of one wall remains. That's it.

They last longer than we do, most buildings—although the World Trade Center was only thirty years old. But they don't last forever. You don't realize that you loved them until they're gone, but you did love them. They seem to keep a hint of the souls of everyone involved with them: the footsteps, the whispers, the hoots of laughter, the blueprints, and the cleaning solutions, the mops, the click of the keys, the fluorescent lights, inanimate things that they are, it seems now that they loved you, too. Now that they are gone.

SUNDAY, PROPER 16

Pss 146, 147 * 111, 112, 113
2 Samuel 24:1–2, 10–25
Galatians 3:23–4:7
John 8:12–20

But when the fullness of time had come . . .
GALATIANS 4:4

Figs are not native to the Geranium Farm: we are in Zone 6, and figs favor a more Mediterranean climate. But they are grown here, mostly by Italian men who remember their little towns and the gardens in them, and long for the sweetness of a fresh fig. And by Q, of course, who, though not Italian, also remembers.

It takes some work. You must cover the roots heavily with about a foot of mulch, so they won't freeze, and you must put evergreen branches over that, so that the alternate freezing and thawing of the ground doesn't heave the thing right out of its hole, roots and all. Last year we left the top branches bare during what turned out to be our coldest winter in five or six years, and the top branches were so thoroughly dead that we thought the whole tree was a goner, until one June day when the little fiddle-shaped leaves appeared at its base. Rarely have we been so glad to see a pair of leaves.

What we call summer is already here, for North Americans. But this fig is from somewhere else, somewhere where summer really means business, where you have to have bright sun and intense heat before anybody knows it's summer. It just wasn't warm enough until now.

The spiritual life—the life of the world, the life of an individual— is largely a matter of ripeness: the fullness of time. The time must be right. Things can't happen before their time, no matter how much you long for them to hurry up and get here. *How could I have been such a fool?* you think when you look back upon a chaotic time in your life. Well, you just *were* back then, that's all. You weren't ready then to become the person you have become. You couldn't. Not until you were ripe for it.

MONDAY IN PROPER 16

Pss 1, 2, 3 * 4, 7
1 Kings 1:5–31
Acts 26:1–23
Mark 13:14–27

I saw a light from heaven, brighter than the sun,
shining around me and my companions.
ACTS 26:13

Most conversions are not so spectacular. Many of us don't have *conversions* at all, having been raised from infancy in the faith we profess as adults. What we have is something else: *deepening,* one might call it—the gradual awareness that words we've heard all our lives are more than words. Born-again people are often insistent on knowing the exact date and time of the conversion, which leaves those of us who have experienced our faith differently a bit uncomfortable.

Are you born again? someone asks you eagerly. You know they want to hear a story about a life of spiritual lassitude or downright hostility to anything religious ending abruptly in a beautiful melt-down of the Savior's love, given so explicitly and so suddenly nobody could possibly mistake it for anything else. But you don't have a story like that. You have a rather nondescript road to faith, bumpier at some spots than at others, paved mostly with your own mistakes, with a fair amount of what remains still a mystery to you. Is that good enough?

Some folks feel that those without a dramatic conversion story aren't real Christians. That you have to be knocked off your horse and go blind, like Paul. No, you don't. God can come however he wants to, and it doesn't have to be dramatic. It just has to be genuine.

How do you know? Well, your life deepens, for one thing. The things of faith interest you more than they ever did before, and they interest you more than some things in which you used to be very interested indeed. You want to pray, and you want to learn how to want to pray when you don't want to. You begin to think of forgiving people you haven't thought of in years. You're not as afraid of death as you used to be. You read different things. Lots of things in your life grow to be very different.

Jesus knocks some of us off our horses. Others he beckons gently and we look up and follow. Neither is better than the other. Both roads lead to the same place.

TUESDAY IN PROPER 16

Pss 5, 6 * 10, 11
1 Kings 1:38–2:4
Acts 26:24–27:8
Mark 13:28–37

"You are out of your mind, Paul!
Too much learning is driving you insane."
ACTS 26:24

Can that really happen? Is there such a thing as too much learning? "He has book sense, but no common sense," a woman I knew used to say of her brilliant son. In his presence. I knew them both well, and always suspected a certain resentment at her own lack of education lay beneath the surface of this unkind remark, for her son possessed abundant common sense.

But it *is* a common stereotype: the absent-minded professor, the egghead who forgets his own address. The astrophysicist who can't work a can opener.

In this case, though, Paul is on trial for bringing his considerable store of traditional knowledge to an untraditional task. A task antithetical, most Jews would say, to that with which a Jew ought to be occupying his time. They thought he was crazy. Dangerous. And he was dangerous: he was thinking outside the box. Doing something new.

Is education supposed to make us better practitioners of what already is, or is it to make us able to imagine what could be? Both—but not always united in the same person. Not everyone tills new ground. There must be people left to till the old ground.

And us, millennia later: we educate our children to be independent thinkers, and then we are uncomfortable when they think independently. Depend on it: they won't be just like you. They won't think exactly as you think. How could they? The world they enter is not the world you entered.

Can I listen intently to the one who has come to a conclusion different from my conclusion? Can I believe that two people can look at the same thing and see it very differently?

Hardly anyone who was alive when Jesus walked the earth knew who he was. Paul didn't. At first, he did what most people do when confronted with something new: he lashed out at it in suspicion and hostility. But then Paul changed radically.

But he always remembered what it was like not to know. Always kept in mind what would have held him back from the faith, what objections would have come to mind for him—and *had* come to mind, and been acted upon many times, before his conversion.

Few of us learn Christ as suddenly as Paul learned Christ. Most of us come to faith gradually, with time to integrate what we are learning into our old selves, so the disjunction is not so drastic.

WEDNESDAY IN PROPER 16

Pss 119:1–24 * 12, 13, 14
1 Kings 3:1–15
Acts 27:9–26
Mark 14:1–11

*Then Judas Iscariot, who was one of the twelve, went
to the chief priests in order to betray him to them.*
MARK 14:10

It sounds like the affirmation Jesus gave to the nameless woman who anointed him with costly ointment was the last straw for Judas; the writer makes it sounds like he got right up and left, to find the priests to whom he would betray Jesus.

From time to time, people have wondered about this. Some have thought that Judas was a radical believer in the messiah, and that he expected Jesus to win an earthly victory over the Roman oppressors and establish the kingdom of the poor. Thus, Jesus' willingness to be anointed with such expensive oil, instead of opting to give the money it cost to the poor, was evidence to Judas that he had been wrong about Jesus: this couldn't possibly be the messiah foretold in prophecy.

Others think that Judas was just a bad'un from the beginning, a thief and a liar from the start. That he had long been plotting to have Jesus killed, and this was just his first opportunity. John thought this: he refers to Judas as having had the habit of stealing from the ragtag group's tiny treasury, and puts the protest about the expensive ointment in Judas's mouth (John 12:4–6).

We'll never know. We do know, though, that people swept along in a great cause bring themselves with them: their frailties, their sinfulness, their inability to understand. Tempt them with money, power, something else they want, and some of them will yield.

A playwright friend of mine wrote a play once about Judas. It was set in a time about a dozen years after the crucifixion. In the play, Judas didn't succeed in killing himself, but lived, broken and crippled. Pontius Pilate is in it, too, and Mrs. Pilate. It is a play about what it was to go on living after having been involved in the killing of the Son of God. About the character of the divine forgiveness, and the coming of peace into lives that have known no peace for years.

It's a good play, the work of a superb imagination. Imagination it must remain: the inner workings of people's souls are not ours to know; we don't even know our contemporaries' minds, let alone those of people long dead. We imagine, instead, and cast ourselves into their roles to see what it would be like. In meditating on a story from scripture, it is as if we're in a play, bringing to life the things we wonder about as we read.

THURSDAY IN PROPER 16

Pss 18:1–20 * 18:21–50
1 Kings 3:16–28
Acts 27:27–44
Mark 14:12–26

He ordered those who could swim to jump overboard
first and make for the land, and the rest to follow,
some on planks and others on pieces of the ship.
And so it was that all were brought safely to land.
ACTS 27:43–44

A harrowing story of shipwreck. An ancient story, but not a story that has disappeared: even today, a ship goes down somewhere in the world every three days. So many sleep at the bottom, men who left home for any one of a number of reasons—the most common of which was to make some money because there was no way to do that at home—and never returned. They left home young and never got old.

Second most common reason: to fight in a war. The most ancient law of the sea provides for any ship nearby to come to the aid of a ship in distress, regardless of who it is. To pick up anybody in the water, no matter who they are. These ancient duties apply during wartime, but they are often turned on their heads. Seafarers who made the North Atlantic run to Murmansk-Arcangel tell of being ordered to pass right by men in the freezing water, men who had, at most, five minutes or so to live in the unendurable cold. Those orders were given sixty years ago, but the pain of remembering them is fresh today.

Seafarers are philosophical, many of them. They have a lot of time to think at sea: the work is hard, but there are long periods at sea when nothing is available to do, and you have time to think. The watch in the wheel house is a stretch of four long hours, during which little happens, if God is good. They gaze at the limitless ocean, its never-ending waves, and they think of things: of where it came from, of who has sailed here before, right at this very place. Of what happens after death. Of what love is—whether there is really any such thing. They cross the days off on their pin-up calendars until it is time to go home to the families they miss so much, but that doesn't mean they don't misbehave in port sometimes. *No, it doesn't mean I don't love her*, they might say to themselves. *I'm not sure what it means. Maybe all it means is that I'm scared and lonely.*

They are forgiven their misdeeds, for the most part, if they happen to mention them. Those who love them understand their fear and loneliness, and mostly forgive.

FRIDAY IN PROPER 16

Pss 16, 17 * 22
1 Kings 5:1–6:1, 7
Acts 28:1–16
Mark 14:27–42

"... *the spirit indeed is willing, but the flesh is weak.*"
MARK 14:38

Most of the things we ought not to do are also things we suffer for doing. They carry their own unpleasant consequences, and the only way to rid yourself of them is to stop doing whatever it is that brings them on. We are curiously unwilling to do this, though: stubborn in our insistence on a course of action that everyone around us can see clearly is disastrous for us: we soldier on with it, denying every sign that it is not the path that is best for us. We invent all manner of things to make it better, new ways to carry this burden we shouldn't be carrying, new ways to make its ill effects not quite so painful—everything, in short, but setting it down. We won't do that.

A problem: most of the things we shouldn't do don't hurt us soon enough. There's a lag between ill action and ill effect. Smoking gives you cancer, but it doesn't give you cancer *today*. You could wait for twenty years. That's forever. It's easy to live in denial when the sword takes that long to fall. An affair will probably end your marriage, but it won't end it *this afternoon*: you're just going to have an interlude of forbidden intimacy this afternoon. Why not?

There must be a hurt besides the hurt of the inevitable consequences of our bad actions, and there is: the hurt of not being in control of ourselves. We are not centered and serene when we're chasing after other things: managing our own vendettas, stoking the fires of our religious hatreds, lusting after people or power or material possessions. There is no peace in these activities.

So we pray for the grace to seek peace where true peace is to be found, no matter what happens to us. For the love that can never be taken from us. For what we can never lose. A thousand fold, it is worth whatever we must forgo to keep it.

SATURDAY IN PROPER 16

Pss 20, 21:1–7 (8–14) * 110:1–5 (6–7), 116, 117
1 Kings 7:51–8:21
Acts 28:17–31
Mark 14:43–52

When they had examined me, the Romans wanted to release me, because there was no reason for the death penalty in my case.
ACTS 28:18

I can't believe we just caved like that, I said on the way home from the bird store. In the back seat rode a bag of compressed corn cylinders, each with a hole bored through it so it could fit on the spike of the squirrel feeder for which we had just paid fourteen dollars. We almost bought one for twenty-five dollars, until I realized that we were about to plunk down good money on something that included a *chair* on which a squirrel could sit to eat his food, for heaven's sake. We came *that* close. Good Lord.

This is the slippery slope of ethical compromise. One minute you're protecting your birds' expensive seed mixtures against marauding squirrels and the next minute you're putting in a squirrel nursing home. I believe this psychological phenomenon is known as the Stockholm effect, wherein a hostage begins to identify with her captors and to adopt their values. This has now happened to us. After many seasons of efforts to prevent the squirrels from stealing birdseed—cayenne pepper on the seed, a rigged feeder that swings wildly around and throws the squirrels into space, feeders with doors that shut under the weight of a squirrel, huge baffles intended to make it impossible for them to climb into the tray feeder—we have given up and decided to feed them ourselves.

Woodpeckers like this compressed corn a lot, too, the lady in the bird store says consolingly. I am too stunned by my sudden capitulation even to react to the temptation of more woodpeckers. *Whatever,* I say, fishing in my purse for some money.

What is troubling is that we didn't make this decision before entering the store. We made it there. A lady was buying an enormous amount of food for her squirrels, talking about how much she loved to feed them. *What?* But we were drawn in. We had no adequate answer for why it was good to feed birds and bad to feed squirrels. There is no good reason. It is just a preference. All are God's creatures.

We do have a certain codependent need to be tyrannized over by small animals. The cats have run us for years, and the birds can get me up out of a warm bed, if I think their hanging tray is covered with snow so they can't get to it. Soon the squirrels will be ordering Chinese food and billing it to my Visa. I know them. This is how it starts.

It is colonizing, some say, to feed them at all. Not a good idea. They need to forage. I say they *are* foraging. They're foraging in our garden. It's paradise back there.

Perhaps we should not have begun feeding anybody. That would have been a terrible loss to us, because we find the birds so delightful, but perhaps it would have been right. Since we have begun, though, it was right of the squirrels to continue their guerilla actions until we admitted them into the family. If we are a colonial power, they have forced us into becoming a more benevolent one.

What do you do when you're half way down a road you shouldn't have started out on in the first place? Sometimes you can't retrace your steps and go back where you came from. Sometimes you can't even make restitution if restitution would have been appropriate: it's too late, or your restitution would cause more hurt than healing. Sometimes you have to find a way to the good from where you are, no matter how you got there.

SUNDAY, PROPER 17

Pss 148, 149, 150 * 114, 115
1 Kings 8:22–30 (31–40)
1 Timothy 4:7b–16
John 8:47–59

So they picked up stones to throw at him,
but Jesus hid himself and went out of the temple.
JOHN 8:59

A man came by and dumped about a ton of stones in our drive-way the other day. Now we're sorting them—by size and by flat-ness or roundness—in order that we might build a garden wall. Every time I go out there, I pick up one or two stones and put them in their proper place as to shape and size. Little by little, the pile is going down.

Here is what I have learned in this project so far: stones are heavy. Some of them are really too heavy for me to lift, and I have to wait for Q to lift them. This continues to shock me, as long as we've been married: that there are things he can lift that I can't even though we're both about the same size. Why is that? But it is so: I must pass over several, and move little ones and medium sized ones into their places in the line.

So stoning somebody is not for sissies, I guess: just for maniacs. Strong ones. It would be a terrible way to die, being stoned, and it would be a terrible way to kill: calculating the impact of hard, heavy stone against soft flesh, over and over again, in company with oth-ers: nobody ever seemed to stone anybody all by themselves. They did it together.

And another thing: stones are old. These stones are billions of years old. Who knows—maybe somebody used one or two of them to stone somebody with, centuries or millennia ago. I hope not, but it's possible. Or maybe they were in another wall, a fort somewhere, maybe. They're old enough.

I think they will be permanent in our garden wall. Perhaps they'll be here for a hundred years. Maybe longer. Or perhaps the next person who lives here won't like the rustic look of them, and will have the whole front garden paved over, to make a place to park all his cars.

It'll be all in a millennium's work for the stones. They don't care where they go or who does what with them. They are inanimate, not troubled by ponderings about their own destinies, as we are. For good or ill, they are stones, pure and simple. Like all the building blocks of the universe, they are morally neutral. It is human beings who decide whether they will injure or protect.

MONDAY IN PROPER 17

Pss 25 * 9, 15
2 Chronicles 6:32–7:7
James 2:1–13
Mark 14:53–65

For many gave false testimony against him,
and their testimony did not agree.
MARK 14:56

When my husband was carjacked, I escaped out the back door of the car and began to scream for help. The carjacker forced him to drive off, and for two hours I didn't know if my husband was alive or dead. He made it home in time for supper, though.

When the police came the next day with a sheaf of mug shots, we were each asked to look at the faces separately. Rows of young men with blond hair stared morosely back at me as I struggled to find the carjacker, but I couldn't be sure which one was he. Finally I handed the pictures back to the detective. *I can't tell for sure*, I said, anxiously.

Q could tell, though. He'd spent two hours with the young man, at close range, and he identified him without hesitation. *That's him,* he said quietly, pointing to one of the faces. It wasn't long before the young man in the picture went to jail.

Eyewitness testimony is notoriously unreliable. People's memories play tricks on them. They want to identify the bad guy, so they choose a face they don't like. It turns out to be one of the detectives, not the bad guy at all. People think they see what they want to be true. They remember what they wish happened. It becomes fact in their minds. But it is fantasy. So a witness identification is an important piece of evidence, but it's never enough all by itself.

Human justice is sometimes unjust. That's what the trial of Jesus was like, so long ago. It was a forgone conclusion, what they would do: it was just a matter of getting there.

TUESDAY IN PROPER 17

Pss 26, 28 * 36, 39
1 Kings 8:65–9:9
James 2:14–26
Mark 14:66–72

"I do not know or understand what you are talking about."
MARK 14:68

This was hardly Peter's finest hour. But then, we're not totally surprised by his weakness here, because we know him: Peter gets it wrong about Jesus much more often than he gets it right. He consistently misunderstands. But it is Peter who identifies Jesus as the messiah, and it is that insight that carries him through his other mistakes, including this big one.

One of scripture's greatest gifts to us is its honesty. None of these writers tries to make Peter look much better than he is: his glory days happen after the events surrounding Jesus' life, death, and resurrection. He doesn't do any of these very well. It isn't until he is empowered by the Holy Spirit that he becomes the Peter who could found a church. Before that, he could barely catch a fish.

Why is this a gift? Because it means that I, too, am not defined by my mistakes alone. I have had unworthy moments in my life, too, and I regret them. I would hate to think that they sum me up in the eyes of God: I know God knows about them, but I would hate to think that they were all there was to me.

And they are not. Our sins and virtues aren't added up separately and then subtracted from one another. God is not an accountant. We have many chances to become the people God intends us to be, a new chance each day, no matter what we did the day before.

Peter must have been awash in shame when the cock crowed. Many people would never have shown their faces again. But Peter must have understood that he was forgiven for his cowardice, and that the gift he was given in exchange for it was its opposite: he was given great courage.

Give God your biggest fault. You just might get it back, in the form of its opposite virtue.

WEDNESDAY IN PROPER 17

Pss 38 * 119:25–48
1 Kings 9:24–10:13
James 3:1–12
Mark 15:1–11

Not many of you should become teachers,
my brothers and sisters, for you know that we who
teach will be judged with greater strictness.

JAMES 3:1

My husband has taught for—let's see—fifty years. His first teaching position was in Turkey, where they had to develop a new word for "teacher." The traditional one meant "revealer of the things of God" and Turkey in 1950 was a nation that wanted desperately to be modern and secular.

But the position of teacher was a sacred one, no matter what you called it. He was responsible for the moral training of his boys, as well as their growing English proficiency. In a society in which literacy is limited, the teacher is one who can read, can explain things, one who knows history and literature. A wise head, someone to consult. It is teachers, more than anyone else, who can lead us into the future. Without them, we are all but paralyzed.

He has said that he viewed his teaching calling as a priestly one, a *vocation*. It is a vocation calling for exemplary behavior: we don't just learn from what the teacher says; we learn from what the teacher does.

Priestly? That makes a certain sense: a priest is also a teacher. There is a *college* of educators, just as there is a college of priests, a community of people drawn together by virtue of what God has called them to do and be. They alone know exactly what it is to walk in their path. There is a peculiar body of knowledge, the knowledge of what it is to impart a portion of the truth to another human being.

But I imagine there is a priestliness to every vocation, a way in which it can be rendered sacred and exemplary. A way it teaches and leads. There is a college of mothers, of physicians, to be sure. There is a college of seafarers. There is a college of farmers, of waiters. A college of the only other people who know what it is to do what you do. A college that teaches the lore of the calling, whatever it may be, to the next generation.

THURSDAY IN PROPER 17

Pss 37:1–18 * 37:19–42
1 Kings 11:1–13
James 3:13–4:12
Mark 15:12–21

*Show by your good life that your works are
done with gentleness born of wisdom.*

JAMES 3:13

Why live a good life? The eighteenth-century philosopher David Hume sought to answer that question and, in answering it, to shed some light on that century's quest for reasonableness in religious matters. If there were no God, he asked, and you could arrange things so there were no bad consequences for you in behaving abominably, would you still have a reason to behave well?

Nope, Hume decided. There's no reason to behave well if there's no God. You should just do whatever you can get away with. But the "sensible knave," as Hume called him—a person with no conscience but a strong sense of self-interest—would think further than that. He would understand that life would be awful if everyone did as he pleased without regard for others. And so a sense of moral duty could be derived from enlightened self-interest alone. With no God involved at all. No heaven and no hell. No nothing, except what is here.

And he was right. Most of the things we do that are wrong carry with them consequences we don't like: maybe not immediately, not in the moment we do them, but later, if *everyone* were to do them. Nothing bad will happen today if you don't go to school, but you will fail tenth grade if you stay home every day. The landscape will not be destroyed if you throw a candy wrapper out the car window, but if everyone does it, the beauty of the landscape will be destroyed. No God. No heaven or hell. Just your desire to have a nice landscape.

But if God does dwell with us? If the world is moral at its core, created in beauty and full of potential for love and generosity? If even the Sensible Knave knows to behave himself, the rest of us really have no excuse.

FRIDAY IN PROPER 17

Pss 31 * 35
1 Kings 11:26–43
James 4:13–5:6
Mark 15:22–32

"Come now, you who say, 'Today or tomorrow we will go to such and such a town and spend a year there, doing business and making money.' Yet you do not even know what tomorrow will bring."
JAMES 4:13–14

What are you doing on Thursday, several people have asked. Thursday is the eleventh of September, the second anniversary of the bombing of the World Trade Center.

I'll be in New York at the convent, seeing people in spiritual direction. One woman has cancelled already: she doesn't want to be in the city that day. Others may cancel, too.

My appointments will fill the day—people catching up from having been away in the summer. My last appointment will be at 7:00 p.m. There is a service at the cathedral at 7:00 p.m. The convent is near the cathedral. Maybe I'll see if I can rearrange that hour. I'd like to be there.

Today is a beautiful September day, like that day two years ago. Last year the weather was beautiful, too—just the same. Last year I listened to the names being read in the morning, at the precise time when the planes had hit the towers the year before. Last year I could close my eyes and still see them burning. I still can.

Maybe there will be another attack on New York. Maybe there will not. I have arranged with my kids and grandkids to know where they are, and they have worked out a plan about where to go if "something happens." So we will all know. But, of course, we won't know. Nobody will know.

"The North Tower has collapsed," I heard someone yell as I came up from the subway. *That's ridiculous,* I thought, *and malicious, to spread falsehoods and scare people like that! If that's his idea of a joke, it's not very funny.* It was on the tip of my tongue to reprimand him, to tell him, *No, it hasn't. Don't spread rumors like that. I just saw it standing five minutes ago.* But something held me back. And the guy turned out to be right. The first tower had collapsed while I was underground.

We don't know what tomorrow will bring. But we'll find out—tomorrow. In the meantime, it could be that this day is our last day. Our last time to enjoy anything in this beautiful world. Or maybe it won't. But however many—or however few—tomorrows you have, you will only have today once. Stay in it.

SATURDAY IN PROPER 17

Pss 30, 32 * 42, 43
1 Kings 12:1–20
James 5:7–12, 19–20
Mark 15:33–39

Now when the centurion, who stood facing him, saw that in this way he breathed his last, he said, "Truly this man was God's Son!"

MARK 15:39

So what did he see, to make him say that? In Mark 15, Jesus calls out to God in Aramaic, the words of Psalm 22: *My God, my God, why have you forsaken me?* And he drinks some sour wine from a sponge on the end of a long stick. The temple veil spontaneously rips in half. Was that it? But how would the centurion have known about that? They were nowhere near the temple; Golgotha is outside the city wall. Mark tells us about the two thieves crucified on either side of Jesus, and about how they taunt him, along with everybody else. But Jesus' loving words to the thief who repented are in John, not Mark. So *that's* not what the centurion heard. All he heard was a loud cry, at the moment of death. He heard human agony. Little of the divine can have been evident in that.

But something made him understand that Jesus was the Son of God.

Many people were there watching, probably. They didn't all come to the same conclusion as the centurion. Many people heard Jesus preach, and they didn't all believe he was the Son of God. Even people who were healed by him didn't always believe it: they knew something wonderful had happened to them, but that didn't mean they grasped who Jesus was.

So I think it must have been in some other way, rather than in the usual sensory way, that the centurion came to his understanding. It wasn't something he saw, or something he heard. He saw a condemned man die a terrible death. He didn't deduce Jesus' divinity from what he saw. He didn't figure it out. It was *given* him.

Faith doesn't make sense? Not logical? Can't explain it to your skeptical friend in a way that satisfies him? Neither could the centurion. Realization came upon him. We are like him: faith is given us.

I don't know about you, but this helps me. Faith is a gift. It's not something we must come up with somehow: it is something we can ask for. And, because God desires our faith, we will receive it as is best for us. So we can relax, and not stress over whether we have enough faith. We have what we can receive from God. We can ask for more and more, and we will receive it as we are able.

SUNDAY, PROPER 18

Pss 63:1–8 (9–11), 98 * 103
1 Kings 12:21–33
Acts 4:18–31
John 10:31–42

The Jews took up stones again to stone him.

JOHN 10:31

My young friend wrote me an e-mail. He's been reading a passage from the psalms—one of those verses about God striking
our enemies dead in some horrible way. *How do you reconcile yourself to all this violence?* he wrote. *It seems to me that religion has been
the excuse for more violence than anything else.*

Well, it's certainly been an excuse for a lot. More than anything
else? I don't know: neither Stalin nor Pol Pot was religious, and each
of them killed millions of people. But still—of all the entities in the
world over which to kill, surely religion of any kind ought to be the
very last one. Instead, it's often the first.

Jesus is such a casualty—a person killed in the name of religion.
And here, in this reading for the gospel of John, the people prepare
to punish him for blasphemy, according to the ancient law of their
forebears. So he had more than one brush with a terrible death
before they finally got him.

What can we do with these parts of our scriptures? Sometimes the
Book of Common Prayer takes the easy way out: leaf through the lectionary pages at the back, and you'll see that some of the appointed
psalms are chopped up a bit. Why, just today, for instance—if we had
read the whole of Psalm 63 at Morning Prayer, we would have been
treated to these edifying lines: *May those who seek my life to destroy it
go down into the depths of the earth; Let them fall upon the edge of the
sword, and let them be food for jackals.* So the compilers of the lectionary made those pleasing verses optional: we can stop at verse 8,
and not have to pray for anyone to become jackal food.

Why do we keep this stuff around? Why don't we just edit the Bible, bring out a new edition? Purge it of objectionable things like these verses of Psalm 63? But we don't revise scripture. We leave it as it is, and struggle with it, with what it shows us about ourselves. Because it's good for us to remember that we have violence in our history, lest we fool ourselves into thinking that violence is always someone else's problem. It's ours, too, from ancient times. *Learn from history or you'll have to repeat it,* George Santayana said and it is so.

MONDAY IN PROPER 18

Pss 41, 52 * 44
1 Kings 13:1–10
Philippians 1:1–11
Mark 15:40–47

Then Joseph bought a linen cloth, and taking down the body, wrapped it in the linen cloth, and laid it in a tomb that had been hewn out of the rock.
MARK 15:46

That would be the Shroud of Turin, I suppose, that length of linen cloth. My father was fascinated with the Shroud, and read every book about it that came out. Once, toward the end of his life, a group of scientists examined it in some scientific way—a scan? A chemical analysis? An x-ray? I can't remember now.

My dad was thrilled: it seemed that the imprint of the face on the Shroud was caused, the scientists said, by some cataclysmic event, something electric, maybe, or something involving a lot of heat or light. Like a photograph, they said.

A photograph! Actual proof of the resurrection! Resurrection: a thing that can be weighed and measured, captured on film, as it were. An event like other events in our world: really spectacular, maybe, but an event in history nonetheless. Just what we want: historical proof. Proof positive.

Of course we want proof. It's how we think, how we compre-hend the things that happen in history. *Did it happen or didn't it? What happened? When? How did it happen, exactly?* we ask. On the strength of these information-gathering tools, we move through history as fish move through water.

But the domain of God is not located in history. It's the other way around: history is located in the domain of God. And the Res-urrection, like the Incarnation, is a moment when the two worlds touch each other. It's not *just* in history, like a war or a presidential term, and yet it *touches* history.

My father got a piece of the proof for which he longed. But what if he had not? What if the scientists had concluded, beyond doubt, that the Shroud was a fake?

It would not have destroyed his faith. He would have been dis-appointed, but his faith was in God, not in the Shroud. He found the idea of the Shroud thrilling, but it was not the Shroud that redeemed him, any more than the box of bones that, for a few famous months, falsely purported to be those of Jesus' brother James—another thrill. Such things are in history, and my dad was on his way out of it, into the larger world that contains it all. And there, as inconceivable as it is to us, nobody tries to prove anything to anybody. Ever.

TUESDAY IN PROPER 18

Pss 45 * 47, 48
1 Kings 16:23–34
Philippians 1:12–30
Mark 16:1–8 (9–20)

So they went out and fled....

MARK 16:8

It probably wasn't really an hour I spent online with the nice young man from my Internet service provider, but it was a long time. He was the soul of patience, talking me through an involved process of deleting things I didn't know I had. This, he assured me, would solve my problem.

It didn't, of course.

I had forgotten about the longstanding enmity between me and the Internet. Lately, I've gotten complacent. I haven't tried to do anything very fancy, and things have gone along with relative smoothness. But now that I have a website, I'm locked into doing things within its categories—including some things I really need to do, like send out my daily meditations to several thousand people.

This is like a column, you know? I type plaintively to my young webmaster. It has to get out. It's the most important thing of the day. It's more important than the website. I know he doesn't think many things are more important than the website.

He types back that I have a bad attitude. He doesn't know the half of it. *The hell with it*, I said after yet another failed sending attempt. I put on my running shoes and went out.

The street was wet. The late summer garden hung with suspended raindrops: enormous bright dahlias bending toward the ground, like the branching purple fronds of the butterfly bush. To run was to skip over puddles and sidestep mudslicks, to breathe cool, wet air deep into my lungs.

I don't run fast. I don't know what I look like when I run: I suspect that I look like someone in slow motion, seeming to run but not making much headway. I suspect many people walk faster than I run.

I don't care. Whether I'm fast or slow. If I look silly or not. I am a middle-aged lady with arthritis and a heart condition. Maybe I shouldn't run, but I'm running anyway. Just because I can. And when I am faced with things I cannot do—like mastering the computer task—it is glorious.

WEDNESDAY IN PROPER 18

Pss 119:49–72 * 49, (53)
1 Kings 17:1–24
Philippians 2:1–11
Matthew 2:1–12

And having been warned in a dream not to return to Herod,
they left for their own country by another road.
MATTHEW 2:12

I seem to be on the wrong train. No great harm done: they all stop at Newark, and I can change trains there.

The man next to me is confused, too: his ticket is inadequate for the trip he's taking. He is embarrassed when the conductor points this out to him. Whether his embarrassment is at his mistake or at being caught, I cannot tell.

Sometimes people hide in the restroom until the conductor has passed through to take everyone's ticket.

Sometimes someone stands in the vestibule and makes a little speech about being three dollars short of his fare to Princeton. This is suspect: hardly anybody in Princeton is three dollars short of anything.

Of course, you can ride between Newark and New York for the rest of your life, I suppose: there are no stops in between, and they're not going to toss you off the train into the river. I wonder if people do that. Surely not: the conductor would get wise after the first free ride or two.

Traveling brings out the worst in some people. Tempers fray. Honesty falls by the wayside.

And, in some people, light shines. Like the wise men from the east, making a long, long journey just to present three odd baby gifts. The main thing about them is not their number or their royal birth; none of these things are certain. What matters about them is that they are wise and that they come from far away. They are symbols of the light of Christ reaching far beyond its point of origin. Despite being scammed by Herod, they return home by another route and save the Christ Child's life.

Not everyone is honest. The world is a hard place. And the light of Christ shines on every inch of it.

THURSDAY IN PROPER 18

Pss 50 * (59, 60) or 93, 96
1 Kings 18:1–19
Philippians 2:12–30
Matthew 2:13–23

Do all things without murmuring and arguing,
so that you may be blameless and innocent . . .
PHILIPPIANS 2:14–15

I guess none of the Philippians were teenagers. *You'll do it and you'll like it!* parents used to say. I wonder if they still say that: it's so ill-informed. Because they won't like it, and you can't make them like it. No, I won't, they say. And they are right: you can make them do something, but you really can't make them like it. They have the right to their anger, even if their anger is silly and based on a complete misunderstanding of what you're trying to do. Which, between the ages of fifteen and eighteen, is about half the time.

You're not going to get hearts and minds, not every time. Probably not even half the time. Mostly, you'll get behavior you can live with, and you'll count yourself lucky to have gotten that. The hearts and minds will come later, assuming they survive the school of hard knocks in which most of them enroll so enthusiastically, so sure they can "handle" everything. Somewhere along the line—I'm not talking about later in their senior year; I mean when they're forty-seven—they will get that you were trying to help them stay alive and get through a terrible time. If you're still alive, they may seek you out and make some cryptic allusion to how hard it must have been for you and that they know it and that they're sorry.

But maybe not. Maybe they'll never get to that ready-for-prime-time moment of reconciliation. Some people just aren't built for it. Some people can't or won't do the work of self-examination such a moment requires. Maybe they'll always need to cast you as the bad guy in the drama of their lives. That's harder.

But even that is not without its reward. They lived through it, and you helped them live. You lived through it, grey hairs and all. And God—who knows a thing or two about ungrateful children—saw it all.

FRIDAY IN PROPER 18

Pss 40, 54 * 51
1 Kings 18:20–40
Philippians 3:1–16
Matthew 3:1–12

Then they seized them; and Elijah brought them down to the Wadi Kishon, and killed them there.
1 KINGS 18:40

A really cool miracle story, one of the best, recounted with much wit and merriment. The labors of the poor Baal prophets are so ornate, leaving them limping around their own altar in exhaustion. We cannot help but cheer when God sends down a mighty fire to consume the altar and everything on it—including the water Elijah has poured all over everything to make it even more spectacular. Score one for our side.

But what a bloody ending! Why did all the Baal prophets have to be killed after their vanquishing? Why couldn't Elijah have contented himself with his victory and their humiliation, which was utter? It seems so harsh. It was a harsh age, we tell ourselves, although our own age has its own harshness, and we have become much more efficient killers of many more people than those folks ever were.

Maybe the best use of ancient violence is as a lens to help us see our own modern violence in starker relief. Like it or not, we are continuous with them. We, too, want to vanquish the enemy, punish him beyond the boundaries of self-defense. We, too, invoke God to justify our violence, attributing to the Almighty prejudices only human beings have. God dislikes the people I dislike, we are pretty sure. Hanging is too good for them.

Father, forgive them, for they know not what they do. It's a different approach to violence, all right, and an example before which we must abase ourselves. We're a long way from that kind of love, most of us. But we know about it, and we know how to reach the one who loves us that way. Perhaps we are not there yet: perhaps we're not all that much farther along than Elijah was. But we have Someone ahead of us, drawing us beyond where we are now.

SATURDAY IN PROPER 18

Pss 55 * 138, 139:1–17 (18–23)
1 Kings 18:41–19:8
Philippians 3:17–4:7
Matthew 3:13–17

*I urge Euodia and I urge Syntyche to be
of the same mind in the Lord.*

PHILIPPIANS 4:2

Sounds like the two women had a feud of long standing. These things happen in churches today, and I guess they happened then, too. In fact, it seems to me that they happen a bit more often in churches than they do in the rest of life. That's very odd: why would it be true that one comes closer to God in an explicit way and yet also becomes more likely to engage in childish behavior?

I think it's because of who we know God to be. We say that God loves us unconditionally, and for most of us, that sounds like parental love, love like we knew when we were little, only limitless, unrestrained by parental flaws. God is the father who is better than the father we had, the mother whose love is purer than my mother's love. All of the *Nos* in growing up turn to glorious *Yeses*, and we are free at last of all the limits within which we have grown to adulthood. Free, spacious, unimprisoned. We can do anything.

Now, this is a fine thing. Or, rather, it would be if it were true. But the limitless freedom we have in Christ doesn't wear well on a large child: we still live on the earth, still must get along with other people, still function within the boundaries of earthly reality. Our freedom includes the freedom to grow up. We don't know everything. We know some things. We can't do everything. We can do some things. We can't have everything. We can have some things. The freedom we have been given is freedom that lives in this world: the freedom of heaven is something else again.

SUNDAY, PROPER 19

Pss 24, 29 * 8, 84
1 Kings 19:8–21
Acts 5:34–42
John 11:45–47

... because if this plan or this undertaking is of human origin, it will fail; but if it is of God, you will not be able to overthrow them.
ACTS 5:38–39

The ordination of women priests, same-sex marriage, the election of an openly gay bishop: these things were bitterly opposed at their beginning. They still are, in some places. Far from settled.

What does God want? We try to give a quick answer: just look it up in the Bible and do what it says. But that's not always as simple as it sounds: sometimes the letter of scripture wars with its spirit. Some things we experience today were unknown in ancient times. What seems obvious to one person is anything but obvious to another, and they cannot agree.

God works in history. That which can survive, does. A way opens where we saw no way. But the way opens in God's own time, and mostly we just have to wait until its time comes.

So we begin, in the knowledge that a correction may come to us. We strive to be as sure as we can and then we act, knowing that we may have gotten it all wrong. Trusting in God to let us know, and to help us repair the damage. If we do not proceed that way, in equal parts of bravery and humility, we will never do a new thing, for all new things beckon us into the future and the future is always a mystery until it arrives.

The main good effect of such humility is that it prevents religious wars. The time for them is past, we used to think, but it seems that we were wrong: considerable blood is shed over whether or not some religious proposition or practice is God's will. Enough people think God wants to kill unbelievers to have us all taking off our shoes in airports. The age of ecumenical politeness is not upon us, as we used to think it was. For many, it has not yet arrived.

MONDAY IN PROPER 19

Pss 56, 57, (58) * 64, 65
1 Kings 21:1–16
1 Corinthians 1:1–19
Matthew 4:1–11

Then the devil left him, and suddenly
angels came and waited on him.
MATTHEW 4:11

Now, nobody else was there. So Matthew did not actually see angels ministering to Jesus or, for that matter, the devil tempting him.

Well, then, what was the conversation like in which Matthew got this bit of information? *Say, Matt, did I ever tell you about the time angels ministered to me?* Somehow that seems a bit more self-congratulatory than we remember Jesus being. He is the one, remember, who tells his friends that he comes not to be served, but to serve.

I think it must be the case that Matthew invents this scenario. Invents the devil's conversation with Jesus and invents the angels, as a way of letting us—two thousand years later—visualize the struggle Jesus was beginning to undergo. Am I really going to live a life so devoid of the normal things everybody wants? Is what I suspect about myself true, that's God's destiny for me will take me into terror and pain? Am I really up to this?

We must believe his temptation was real if we accept the fact that his sacrifice was real. We must believe that he had his doubts about himself. That his journey was not a self-confident stride into an obvious moral victory. And if we believe in the reality of his temptation, we must gently let go of the notion that Jesus the man was perfectly well-behaved at all times. Perfect in faith. Had no doubts. No: he must have grown into his courage, as we do. Who he was must have dawned upon him over time. It must have been a struggle.

When you struggle with your own destiny, when you don't know what path to take, when you long for what you know you cannot have if you are to remain faithful, you are Jesus. We know we imitate him when we are good, but we are like him in our pain and uncertainty as well.

TUESDAY IN PROPER 19

Pss 61, 62 * 68:1–20 (21–23) 24–36
1 Kings 21:17–29
1 Corinthians 1:20–31
Matthew 4:12–17

"Let the one who boasts, boast in the Lord."
1 CORINTHIANS 1:31

And what are your strengths? the interviewer asks. A newcomer to the process is taken aback by the questions: Am I allowed to compliment myself? Won't I seem vain if I do?

But they really want to know. Who are we hiring, or accepting into our incoming class? What do you bring that we need? It isn't vain to know what you do well, and to say so. You're also expected to know that your weaknesses are: that's the next question in your interview.

To take delight in the things in which we excel is to praise God, for they are all gifts from God. It is we who hone and develop them, but God is the one who gives them.

There have been demonstrations of this. A pianist loses the use of one of his hands, or an athlete is paralyzed from the waist down in an accident. After the initial reeling, such devastation changes the character of the gift: the pianist specializes in work composed for one hand, or conducting replaces performance, for instance. The athlete becomes competitive in a sport requiring upper body strength. Something else arises: another gift.

The power to change from one state to another, to move into the world of a new gift when an old one disappears: this is like resurrection. Funny—we've never really thought about whether Jesus' resurrection was hard or not, but I'll bet it was. God raised him, but the willingness to be raised was his. God's creative work is the forming of good from evil, and it can be painfully slow. Life from loss. Strength from weakness. That's what God does.

WEDNESDAY IN PROPER 19

Pss 72 * 119:73–96
1 Kings 22:1–28
1 Corinthians 2:1–13
Matthew 4:18–25

Then Zedakiah son of Chenaanah came up to Micaiah, slapped him on the cheek, and said, "Which way did the spirit of the Lord pass from me to speak to you?"

1 KINGS 22:24

Every king had prophets who worked for him. Their job was to foretell the future. Court prophets learned quickly not to prophesy anything unpleasant, which made them all but useless in terms of actually advising the king in any helpful way. Such is human vanity that the king usually preferred good news to true news.

People who write for large corporations know something about this. Anybody who works for anybody knows, actually: sometimes it seems as if your only job is to make your boss look good and feel good about himself. As if reporting a negative finding were a disloyal act. Few things in an organization are more dangerous than this one.

It can be almost impossible for a person in authority to find people who will tell her the truth. The desire to tell her what she wants to hear is nearly irresistible. Fewer and fewer truth tellers surround her, and she grows farther and farther from an accurate picture of herself and other people. A leader must insist on receiving negative feedback along with the bouquets. Even if she hates it.

In authority? Don't trust "Why the Boss is Brilliant" memos from your people. Insist they do better. Solicit honest opinions, but then don't turn around and punish them when they're unflattering or scary.

Under authority? Tell the truth. You have to. Because a lie always manifests itself. And the truth is always demonstrated, eventually.

But what if you're right about what will happen? What if you're punished for telling the truth, like Micaiah is? It's true that you can be hurt for being honest. You can lose your job.

Ethics is hard in the real world. There can be serious consequences to being honest, and many of them are unfair. We each have to decide whether knowing you were honest is enough, because sometime that's all you get.

THURSDAY IN PROPER 19

Pss (70), 71 * 74
1 Kings 22:29–45
1 Corinthians 2:14–3:15
Matthew 5:1–10

Then he began to speak, and taught them, saying: "Blessed are the poor in spirit, for theirs is the kingdom of heaven."
MATHEW 5:2–3

Some translations used the word "happy" instead of "blessed." Good one—this is the Sermon on the Mount, in which Jesus upends all the ways in which we assume people are miserable and proclaims the hope of joy for them. In what way are the poor happy? Those who mourn? Those are sorrowful things. Where is the joy in these sad things?

You know someone whose outlook on life astonishes you. How on earth does she do it, you ask yourself, always so calm and open-hearted, when she has more things go wrong in her life than anyone

I've ever known. Seeming genuinely not to be bitter and self-pity-ing, when she has so much to pity herself about? How does she do it? And how can I do it?

I have read that contentment and optimism are, in part, a genetic matter. People are born disposed to a bright outlook, and others born disposed to see the glass half empty.

But, no matter how we came into the world, there are some things we can do to change the way we evaluate the bad things that happen in life.

1. Talk about them with people who have survived them. That's the secret behind the whole universe of twelve-step recovery: we can laugh together over the things we used to cry about alone. Don't isolate. Force yourself to affiliate.

2. Focus some attention on what you do have that you love. It is old-fashioned, but count your blessings.

3. Do something. Complete a task that you can finish and see that it's finished, like cleaning out one drawer. This keeps chaos at bay in your imagination, as well as in your house, and makes you feel less defenseless.

4. Consider psychotherapy. If you still think it's not something a person of faith should need, get over that belief, for heaven's sake. We're in the twenty-first century now. You don't have to view things the way you do if it's hurtful to you and inhibits your being the joy-ful person Christ intends you to be.

FRIDAY IN PROPER 19

Pss 69:1–23 (24–30) 31–38 * 73
2 Kings 1:2–17
1 Corinthians 3:16–23
Matthew 5:11–16

*". . . let your light shine before others, so that they may see
your good works and give glory to your Father in heaven."*
MATTHEW 5:16

Some people think it's not becoming in a person of faith to display talents, or to appear to be proud of them. Religious people should be modest.

Modest, maybe, but not full of self-hatred. If something is good, it's good—even if it's yours. Maybe it's not modesty we should be cultivating, but honesty. A realistic view of what we're good at and what we're not. There isn't anyone who lacks even one good quality.

Sometimes, though, you meet a person who seems compelled to blow his own horn. He is the authority on everything, has done everything at least once, and has always been the best at everything he has ever done. More than five minutes of him is excruciating.

He seems too self-confident, but actually the reverse is true: he doesn't trust his manifest gifts to be visible. He doesn't think people will love him unless he earns his keep by being more amazing than any human being could possibly be. All braggarts are really people who profoundly doubt their own worth.

This should make them easier to take. They are really quite sad. All that bragging is an attempt to conceal inadequacy. Perhaps compassion might take the place of some of the annoyance you feel in their presence.

But how do you make them stop?

One thing that might work is complimenting and supporting only the gifts, among the many they claim, that they actually possess. Maintain a composed noncommittal posture toward the grandiosity—resisting the temptation to puncture the balloon of their conceit—but endorse the good things that are real. If they get support for the real things, the temptation to claim the false ones will lessen.

SATURDAY IN PROPER 19

Pss 75, 76 * 23, 27
2 Kings 2:1–18
1 Corinthians 4:1–7
Matthew 5:17–20

The Lord is my shepherd; I shall not want.
PSALM 23:1

This is the psalm everyone knows. People who don't know any psalms know this one. Go to a funeral without a prayer book; the people will stand and sit and say nothing until the officiant begins the Twenty-third Psalm, and half of those present will join in.

When I was still a student, I visited an elderly priest who was gravely ill in the hospital. The doctor was there when I walked in the ICU; he was preparing a spinal tap. I stood on one side of the bed and the doctor stood on the other, he armed with the enormous spinal syringe, a child's nightmare of a needle, and I armed with nothing but my own inadequacy. The poor old man was so sick: feverish, shaking with chills, a little confused.

The doctor began to insert the needle. A painful procedure. Holding his hand and unable to think of anything else to say, I began to say the Twenty-third Psalm. After only a few words, the old priest joined me, whispering the ancient words he knew as well as he knew anything else. His body relaxed under the assault of the spinal tap. Soon it was over; the fluid in the glass tube looked clean and pure. Good. The old man and I finished the psalm together: "And I shall dwell in the house of the Lord forever." Within a few months he would begin that new life. He knew that, I think, that night as he lay there and found comfort in the ancient song during a moment of pain and fear.

Many passages from scripture are comforting; this one is uniquely so. Why that is, I cannot say. Its trust is utter, childlike—animal, even, since it likens us to sheep. Sheep. Walking under the care of someone we can trust. Never doubting. So unlike the way we really are. So like what we would like to be. "Surely goodness and mercy shall follow me all the days of my life."

SUNDAY, PROPER 20

Pss 93, 96 * 34
2 Kings 4:8–37
Acts 9:10–31
Luke 3:7–18

. . . the child sat on her lap until noon, and he died.
2 KINGS 4:20

A bald sentence—but what must the reality have been like? The hours holding her only child, searching his face in vain for some sign of improvement, but nothing good was coming. He grew weaker and weaker, his breath more and more ragged. And then, when the sun was high in the sky, there was no breath at all. Throughout his short life, every time she had held him on her lap, she had made everything better. But not this time.

I suppose it was a brain hemorrhage—sounds like it. This tentative diagnosis is as far as we can go and still be on familiar territory, though, because what follows isn't just rare: it's outside the range of our experience altogether. A child who has been dead for hours, if not days, is brought back to life by what sounds like mouth-to-mouth resuscitation.

But then, this nameless little boy was a miracle child to begin with. His parents had no expectation of being blessed with him: his father was very old, we hear, and there was no chance of having a baby in the normal course of things. But this is not a story about the normal course of things. The Shunamite woman knew that the gift of this child was too miraculous to dissolve like this, knew it so absolutely that she was able to answer Elisha's inquiry about her family with a simple "It is well," rather than bursting into tears and telling him everything right there on the road.

In the end, this is a story about trust. God has been good, and that goodness will not depart from us. We know that this story does not mean that our children won't die, our dreams won't ever shatter: it's a story. There are no guarantees in life except for the one that this story shows: life may be hard, but God can be trusted.

MONDAY IN PROPER 20

Pss 80 * 77, (79)
2 Kings 5:1–19
1 Corinthians 4:8–21
Matthew 5:21–26

So when you are offering your gift at the altar, if you remember that your brother or sister has something against you, leave your gift there before the altar and go; first be reconciled to your brother or sister, and then come and offer your gift.
MATTHEW 5:23–24

You have offended somebody, and you know it. There has been, as yet, no reconciliation: the grudge hangs between the two of you. Somehow, you can't bring yourself to set things right: you're embarrassed by your actions. The grudge becomes more and more permanent. You can't talk to him now. You literally cross the street in order to avoid him. I can't believe I'm doing this, you say to yourself. Why don't I just go up to him and apologize?

People do the same thing with God, when they think they've offended beyond repair. They stop praying when they know they've done something wrong. They no longer feel worthy to approach the goodness of God, feeling keenly the stain of their sin. And so they don't try: God knows what I've done, they think, and I won't be accepted.

But of course the reverse is true; God does know what we've done and we are accepted anyway. It is for this reason that Christ is among us: because we continually make a mess of things, whether through mistake or negligence or downright perversity, and we need help. God does not demand our perfection as a condition of engagement with us. God engages us first, and perfects us in time.

If shame is stopping you from calling on God, remember that he already knows it all. What we did, and also why. However foolish or even evil it was, it is not beyond the power of God to forgive and heal.

But you can't regain the relationship with God, or with anyone else, if you won't talk.

TUESDAY IN PROPER 20

Pss 78:1–39 * 78:40–72
2 Kings 5:19–27
1 Corinthians 5:1–8
Matthew 5:27–37

But I say to you that every one who divorces his wife, except on the ground of unchastity, causes her to commit adultery; and whomever marries a divorced woman commits adultery.
MATTHEW 5:32

Many of us remember a time when divorced people could not remarry in the Church. These are softer times, at least in this regard: now the priest performing the marriage must, in the course of the premarital counseling, ascertain what brought about the death of the first marriage, and make a judgment about whether or not it seems likely that the proposed one will fare better. His or her judgment is then presented to the bishop, who gives permission if it seems well to him or her. At least eighteen months must have elapsed between the two marriages. If there are children, care must be taken to ascertain that adequate provision has been made for their upbringing.

To some, this softening has seemed the toe in the door that opens to moral chaos. To others, it has seemed humane, a compassionate recognition that people make mistakes, grave ones, but that sexual mistakes are not grave beyond the love of God. Most divorced people know very well that they've screwed up, and that they have paid a high price for their errors. Many regret divorcing. Many feel set free. But nobody does it lightly.

As nobody marries lightly. There is a line at the beginning of the marriage service, a warning: *Therefore marriage is not to be entered into lightly, but deliberately, reverently and in accordance with the purposes for which it was instituted by God.* I've been marrying people for twenty-five years, and I've never met anyone who entered into it lightly. This, even though some of the marriages over which I've presided have ended in divorce. Nobody wanted that. Perhaps it could have been prevented; perhaps not. But the intention at the outset was always reverent.

Because you might fail is not reason not to make a promise. People fail in the things they intend all the time. They learn from the experience, pick themselves up painfully and continue living. Perhaps love comes again, a second chance. The experience of God's forgiveness is a good place to start living again.

WEDNESDAY IN PROPER 20

Pss 119:97–120 * 81, 82
2 Kings 6:1–23
1 Corinthians 5:9–6:8
Matthew 5:38–48

*"You have heard that it was said, 'An eye for an eye and a tooth
for a tooth.' But I say to you, Do not resist an evildoer."*
MATTHEW 5:38–39

Do not resist in equal violence, Jesus means. Don't participate in an arms race, in the tit-for-tat escalation of violence that such a thing always produces.

Meeting violence with violence rarely settles things. Oh, wars have been won and lost, of course. But when a nation has been vanquished, it has nursed the resentment of its defeat for centuries, sometimes, and they ignite in an instant at the first opportunity.

We think about all our wars: this was a "good" war, that was a "bad" one. The Second World War is usually the good war; Vietnam is bad. The American Civil War continues to cast its shadow over us, 150 years later. We can point to an actual evil that was eradicated in World War II, except that white supremacist groups in America and in Europe continue to remember the Third Reich nostalgically, so maybe we didn't wipe it out as thoroughly as we thought.

Never a clean victory, a sure thing. War is neither clean nor sure. Why we continue to think that war will bring peace is a puzzlement, all right, but we hold firm to that belief and act on it in every generation, sending our children off to kill and be killed, thinking that somehow this will bring about a more peaceful world. Forgetting that it never has.

THURSDAY IN PROPER 20

Pss (83) or 116, 117 * 85, 86
2 Kings 9:1–16
1 Corinthians 6:12–20
Matthew 6:1–6, 16–18

"All things are lawful for me,"
but not all things are beneficial.
1 CORINTHIANS 6:12

Corinth was a port city—the New Orleans of its day, with the same reputation for loose morals that the Big Easy enjoys. Life in Corinth was something like life in America in the 1970s, in case you were around for that. When Paul came there, fresh from a life as an observant Jew who had been faithful to more than six hundred careful laws, he preached the gospel that had liberated him: Hey, it's not about following the rules! It's about following Christ.

Context is everything, though: the Corinthians never *had* thought it was about following rules. They were not particularly oppressed by stern duty. Oh, good, they said to each other as they listened to Paul, now we can make a religion out of our hedonism.

So Paul had to go back and clean up after himself. Yes, indeed, it's not just about following the rules: God isn't waiting to pounce on you for all your sins. But that doesn't mean that sin doesn't draw you away from God in major ways. Maybe everything is lawful for us, but that doesn't mean you won't taste the consequences of what you do. And if you do nothing but stupid, self-indulgent things, what you taste may be bitter indeed.

An Irish proverb: God set Adam and Eve in the garden and said to them, "You can take anything you like here, and then you can pay for it." Nothing we do is without cost; deciding for something is to decide against something else.

And St. Augustine said, "Love God, and do as you like." Like Paul, he was certain that a love of the author of all good would naturally produce good in us.

FRIDAY IN PROPER 20

Pss 88 * 91, 92
2 Kings 9:17–37
1 Corinthians 7:1–9
Matthew 6:7–15

Now concerning the matters about which you wrote:
"It is well for a man not to touch a woman."
1 CORINTHIANS 7:1

A strong minority current of celibacy in the early Church, already. It made sense to Paul: the world is ending soon. Don't bother getting married: we won't *be* here. But later readers grabbed it and ran with it: sex is evil. Even the world is evil, because it is populated through sex. Everything here ends in death and decay. Our real home is in heaven, where we don't have bodies. The only true Christians are celibate Christians. And so, within a few centuries, all bishops were celibate, and then priests were, too, in the Western Church.

But the Eastern Church was different. Bishops were—and are—celibate, but priests could marry and have children. And the Anglican way is yet more hospitable to blending a life that contains sexual intimacy and family life with the life of service to God, without ranking one state above another. Celibacy is not held up as the highest good among us. It is merely a lifestyle to which some are called.

Human sexuality is complex. One size definitely does not fit all. And it is personal, a private matter: the Church does not own us. We own ourselves, and it is we who are responsible to God for an accounting of our lives. There is a way of life and health in living as the sexual being God made you, and there is a way of death, but these are not always the same way.

We have come a long way from Paul's grudging permission to marry if you were so out of control that you couldn't behave yourself, or from his horror of homosexual behavior. That was Paul. The early Church was the early Church. But we are part of history, too, and we have our contribution to make to it, just as they all did.

SATURDAY IN PROPER 20

Pss 87, 90 * 136
2 Kings 11:1–20a
1 Corinthians 7:10–24
Matthew 6:19–24

Wife, for all you know, you might save your husband.
1 CORINTHIANS 7:16

Well, she should know that she can't change him before they tie the knot. Save everybody some heartache and a whole lot of money. He's going to be who he is. People don't reform other people, and they shouldn't try.

But they do influence them. Everyone with whom we come into contact influences and shapes us, for good or ill, and we have a lot of contact with our spouses. They catch things from us, and we from them. We react against them, and they recoil from us. We shape each other profoundly over a period of decades. We grow up together.

Most devout people wish their families were more like them: in church, and happy being there. They reproach themselves often, for not having succeeded in hauling the old boy into a pew. He stays home with the paper while she gets the kids up and out, looking their very best. Or he prays daily and she is painfully embarrassed when he asks her to join him. It's just not her way.

Back off, but don't give up. God's love for the observant and the unobservant alike is equal: he loves us all. Longs for us all to make contact. Sends out innumerable opportunities for that to happen. One of them will hit home: maybe not in the way you were hit, but in her own way, his own special way. God does this work. We just pray, and wait with hope and trust.

SUNDAY, PROPER 21

Pss 66, 67 * 19, 46
2 Kings 17:1–18
Acts 9:36–43
Luke 5:1–11

When they had washed her, they laid her in a room upstairs.

ACTS 9:37

A tender last act of love toward the body of someone whose love has been a steady part of life: her women friends washed her body to prepare it for burial. They had no idea that someone would come and free Dorcas from the bonds of death. As far as they were concerned, this was good-bye forever.

I enjoyed making my mother's clothes. I also enjoyed buying them with her or for her. She wasn't always sure what looked well on her—I am never sure myself—and so we consulted frequently.

What dress should I choose for her burial? My sister-in-law and I looked in her closet. There were all her clothes, still smelling like her. I buried my face in their folds, and it was as if I were surrounded with her presence. But we had a choice to make. The burgundy jersey with shirring around the neckline. Such a comfortable dress, and she looked so nice in it. The brown plaid skirt and sweater she loved? No, it was spring. The party dress I had loved on her when I was little, which we had kept all those years? No, that would be silly: it was completely out of fashion now, and probably didn't even fit. In the end, we chose a blue knit suit.

She did not join in the discussion. She was silent. Didn't ask how she looked. She wasn't even there: her body waited at the funeral home for the ensemble we chose. She didn't know or care: the dead don't mind about such things any more. Dressing her one last time was something we did for ourselves, not for her. But it felt like it was for her.

Such times are not times in which common sense has much to do with anything. You stand on the edge of eternity with someone and choose an outfit to wear into it, as if it mattered what we wear. Silly. But you do it anyway, weaning yourself little by little from the beloved body, preparing to do without the voice, the eyes, the touch of the hand.Our early efforts in this regard are halting and foolish. Absence is new to us.

But we will have the rest of our lives to get used to it.

MONDAY IN PROPER 21

Pss 89:1–18 * 89:19–52
2 Kings 17:24–41
1 Corinthians 7:25–31
Matthew 6:25–34

So they worshiped the Lord, but also served their own gods...
2 KINGS 17:33

So now we know: this is why people were shocked when Jesus traveled among the Samaritans, when he talked to them. Why it mattered that the Good Samaritan *was* a Samaritan: nobody expected a Samaritan to be the good guy in a story. It was because the people of Samaria were immigrants from other countries, resettled in Israel by the king of Assyria, and they brought their local gods with them. When they were instructed about the God of Israel, they worshiped him, too, but also kept their old ones. They did both. And their descendants did the same.

Nothing upset the Israelites more than this syncretism, and Christians have inherited the angst. This is so even though we have borrowed freely from pre-Christian cultures for many things: for our stories about Mary, for our Christmas trees, for our wise men at the manger, for the very dating of our celebration of Christmas. Modern students of Christian mission remember these things, now, and are gentler with the indigenous faiths they find: the veneration of ancestors in African countries, for instance, is likely now to be recognized as resembling the communion of the saints enough to

221

make it no big deal. The Brazilian sea goddess Imanji has easily found a sister in Mary, Star of the Sea, and the Church in Brazil has a relaxed attitude toward a certain blending of the traditions. It was not always thus.

What is it in us that needs others to be wrong so that we can be sure of our rightness? Why do we think Christ can only do his work in cultures we recognize and approve, can only inhabit *our* stories about him? If it is through Christ that the world was created, why is it such a diverse world, unless its diversity is a good thing?

If God is as large as we say, there must be many things about God that we don't know yet. Can never know, while we live on this earth, since so many things of God are beyond the earthly. If God is free, no place on earth is beyond the divine reach, and we are probably not the gatekeepers of God's activity. Glorying in God's wisdom and humble about our own, we walk forth into the world curious, without assuming ahead of time that we know what we will find.

TUESDAY IN PROPER 21

Pss 97, 99, (100) * 94, (95)
2 Chronicles 29:1–3; 30:1 (2–9) 10–27
1 Corinthians 7:32–40
Matthew 7:1–12

I want you to be free from anxieties.
1 CORINTHIANS 7:32

What a good idea. I wouldn't mind being free from anxieties myself. Are my children all right? Is my husband all right? What will become of my grandchildren?

Worry in the night is an especially unwelcome guest: I add anxiety about poor performance the next day because of being tired to my list of frets: worrying about the effect of worrying.

At my feet, the kitten plays with a scrap of paper: pouncing on it as if it were alive, loving the rustle it makes, batting it into a corner and prying it out again, then dashing off with it in her mouth, bound for who knows where. Not a worry in the world, little Noodle.

In the wee hours, I receive news that our friends have finally had their first baby, after almost a week of labor. I imagine little Eli: wrapped up tight in his blanket, sleeping as they watch him breathe. Not a worry in the world. Doesn't know what one is yet.

On the website www.geraniumfarm.org, a bank of virtual candles: my webmaster has designed it so that you can type in a prayer intention and then click on a candle, and the candle will "light:" a flickering flame. This section of the website is called "Vigils": it's intended for late-night worriers, a place to take anxiety and, perhaps, find the grace to lay it there and just leave it. The rows of cyber-candles flicker on the screen: people's illnesses, the births of babies, the deaths of grandfathers. In the worried wee hours, I light a candle for Eli, and one for Rose. I ask for patience and wisdom. I want the candle to take my worry into its flame and burn it up. I remember that God came to Moses in a flame once, a flame that burned but did no injury.

Come to me in fire, then. Burn away my fear. I know that you will not hurt me.

WEDNESDAY IN PROPER 21

Pss 101, 109:1–4 (5–19) 20–30 * 119:121–144
2 Kings 18:9–25
1 Corinthians 8:1–13
Matthew 7:13–21

*"Beware of false prophets, who come to you in sheep's
clothing but inwardly are ravenous wolves."*

MATTHEW 7:15

Tartuffe is one of my very favorite plays: it is 350 years old and still making people laugh, so it's a hit by any measure. Even in New York, where competition for audience is stiff indeed, you'll fill seats with *Tartuffe*.

Orgon is a sincere but not overly bright nobleman with a pretty wife. Lately, as the play opens, he has become friendly with Tartuffe, a most religious man. More than friendly, really: he has come completely under Tartuffe's sway, viewing him as a prophet. All the nude statutes in Orgon's sumptuous baroque home are now modestly draped so nobody will be scandalized by the sight of a breast or an ankle. It doesn't take us long to see Tartuffe for what he is—a con man and a lecher—and the other characters in the book don't have much trouble figuring him out either. Only Orgon is fooled, and he is fooled enough to sign over all his property to the holy man, at the holy man's unctuous request. How Tartuffe is exposed is beautiful. I won't tell. If you haven't seen the play, you must.

We can forgive people's moral lapses of judgment—usually. We find it harder to forgive those who set themselves up as moral examples and misrepresent who they really are. Just now a senator who got himself elected braying about protecting The Family at every opportunity was denounced by his former wife for visiting sex clubs and pressuring her to do the same, and he had to abandon his suit for re-election. One or the other, please: be a libertine or be a guardian of traditional sexual morals, but don't tell me you can be both as long as nobody finds out. I'll forgive your mistakes, as I hope you forgive mine. Just don't set yourself up as a judge or an example. I promise I won't. I can't afford it.

THURSDAY IN PROPER 21

Pss 105:1–22 * 105:23–45
2 Kings 18:28–37
1 Corinthians 9:1–15
Matthew 7:22–29

*Or is it only Barnabas and I who have no right
to refrain from working for a living?*
1 CORINTHIANS 9:6

Read today's epistle again: do you detect just the tiniest bit of martyrdom in our dear friend Paul?

I thought so.

We have said before that he seems to have been a difficult man. Hypersensitive to criticism, Paul. That's one reason I like him, even if he did write a couple of dumb things about women and about husbands and wives, of which he had no personal experience. Paul's shabbier feelings are obvious, just as mine are. Paul is one of us.

Here is what is happening: Paul and Barnabas don't make their living preaching. They have day jobs. Paul is a tent-maker by trade.

The truth is, he would like it if things were otherwise. His envy of other apostles is palpable: some of them are supported financially by their communities. He would like it if the Corinthians would do the same for him. But he won't come out and say so. Instead, he says the crabby, martyred sorts of things I say when I don't think I'm getting the proper respect. Only in the last line do we pierce the self-serving sarcasm: "For I would rather die than have anyone deprive me of my ground for boasting."

Indeed. The lonely grandeur of the put-upon is hard to relinquish. We come to prefer the drama of our neediness to the satisfaction of our needs. Been there. I know just how he feels.

I really have never known people to be successfully shamed into loving other people. Perhaps they will yield to your whining in the short term, but that is not what will make them value you. What will make them value you is your being valuable, and then asserting your needs clearly and calmly. If Paul wants an honorarium, he should ask for one. If he doesn't ask, he shouldn't complain.

But they should know what I need! They should understand how I feel! How? By reading your mind?

It's scary to ask for what we need. I've been terrified of it all my life, which is why I understand Paul so well. Being that way has never gotten me anything I wanted. It has only fed my martyrdom complex, which—like some other parts of me—is already fat enough.

FRIDAY IN PROPER 21

Pss 102 * 107:1–32
2 Kings 19:1–20
1 Corinthians 9:16–27
Matthew 8:1–17

. . . children have come to the birth,
and there is no strength to bring them forth.
2 KINGS 19:3

Well, yes, there is. It just doesn't feel like it, when something that weighs eight or nine pounds seeks to emerge from an opening you hardly even knew you had. But the process of birth is a well-designed one: you can't go by that terrible *this just isn't going to work* feeling you get in the middle of it. It'll work.

The political process—including this ancient one, involving fear of attack by a formidable foe—is like childbirth. It often—

usually?—looks as though a favorable outcome is impossible. But things don't stay the same: eventually, each war ends, each crisis is resolved. Sometimes—usually?—it is a compromised resolution, full of holes, every bit as sinful as it is just. Once in a while it rises above the level of sordidness, and we are grateful and a little amazed. But it always comes to an end, and somehow we survive to fight another day.

And God stands ready with a supply of good, which will emerge from the greatest evil humankind can invent. Why the goodness of God must show forth against a canvas of evil is a mystery: it is expressed mythologically in the book of Genesis, in the tale about the sin of our first parents that cast us out of the happy land. Who knows why we couldn't stay? But we couldn't, and live now in our quilt of pain and joy.

Sometimes we think we just can't take it any more. Can go no further. Sometimes we come to the end of our rope. And there, at the end, is God again, as present as at the strong and hopeful beginning.

SATURDAY IN PROPER 21

Pss 107:33–43, 108:1–6 (7–13) * 33
2 Kings 19:21–36
1 Corinthians 10:1–13
Matthew 8:18–27

God is faithful, and he will not let you be tested beyond your strength, but with the testing he will also provide the way out so that you may be able to endure it.
1 CORINTHIANS 10:13

Interesting—this seems to suggest that our temptations themselves carry with them their own means of transformation into good things. That for which we long—even the illicit one—is just a broken restatement of an appropriate need, which could, and even should, be met another way not hurtful to us or to others. Our sexual misdeeds, our business scams, our feuds—is it possible that they all are unsuitable means toward something actually desirable and good?

First, we must find a way to tell ourselves and God what it is we really seek. Very few people wish to harm themselves or someone else: we all *think* we're trying to accomplish the good. What is it we want? Isn't it love, and a sense of worth? Isn't it freedom from want? Community? Aren't our deeds—even the foolish, wrongheaded ones—purposed to gain those things?

The celibate assailed with sexual temptation *does* need human touch in her life. The person who bites people's heads off *does* need a way to express her anger. The glutton *does* need to feel satisfied. Against these things, as Paul would put it, there is no law. But maybe there's another *path* to them, besides the twisted one they've been on with such disastrous results.

SUNDAY, PROPER 22

Pss 118 * 145
2 Kings 20:1–21
Acts 12:1–17
Luke 7:11–17

In those days Hezekiah became sick
and was at the point of death.
2 KINGS 20:1

A rich reading from Second Kings today, full of hints about ancient medicine, time telling, technology, and of foreboding about a seemingly innocent visit.

Half of the unguents in the arsenal of my half-hearted attempts to deal with aging skin contain fruit acids, and now here is Isaiah, recommending a poultice of boiled figs to cure the king's skin condition. I bet it worked. And there is a sundial in this passage—it showed the miraculous feat of running time backwards, as a sign that this healing would take place—just in case the king didn't trust the fruit poultice.

And then, some skullduggery. King Hezekiah is apparently too dim to wonder why the sons of the King of Babylon would choose to pay him a get-well call *now*, and unwisely shows them all his treasures. They must have left licking their chops. But he gets it, when Isaiah tells him the score, and even thinks it's not such a bad thing—after all, *he* won't be around to see it. The thought of his sons becoming eunuchs in someone else's palace appears not to trouble him at all.

Short-term security, for which we must pay heavily in the future. We, or our children. Do we love them enough to want to leave them a better world? A safer one? Or are we content to mortgage them to the hilt and despoil what is left of the environment—who cares, since we won't be around to deal with it? Could we put ourselves out just a little, refrain from consuming just a little, if we know that by doing so we would be preserving a good life for them? We could—but we don't.

Still, King Hezekiah, like us, was not all bad—he built a reservoir and a conduit for his city to have abundant water. Its remains are still there, an impressive feat of engineering. He could solve a problem when he had to.

So could we, I guess.

MONDAY IN PROPER 22

Pss 106:1–18 * 106:19–48
2 Kings 21:1–18
1 Corinthians 10:14–11:1
Matthew 8:28–34

When [Jesus] came to the other side, to the country of the Gadarenes, two demoniacs coming out of the tombs met him.
MATTHEW 8:28

There are a couple of odd things in this passage from Matthew. One is that Jesus seems to have a prior relationship with the demons who have possessed the two unfortunate Gadarenes: they know him. He even engages in a brief negotiation with them. They beg to be allowed to possess the herd of swine, and Jesus gives them leave. Why?

And then the people of the area don't react to the expulsion of the demons as one might expect them to. They aren't grateful. Not at all. They're scared. They want Jesus to leave.

I guess they thought that anyone who could order demons around like that must be one himself.

We think that, too. We think our only means of making our way in the world is to fold ourselves into its categories of power. The answer to our chronic anxiety about money must be more money. Unfulfilled at work? Work harder. Can't feel intimate with anyone? Have more sex.

But Jesus does not control the demons by *becoming* one. He does not give them a dose of their own medicine. The demons may be stronger than their human victims—or than their porcine ones— but Jesus is stronger still. And his strength is not like theirs: he brings life and deliverance, while they deal only in bondage and death. They can't walk free: they have to have someone to possess. Demons can't have life on their own. They must take someone else's.

Power is everywhere. Everyone has some. So how were they supposed to tell that Jesus was not a demon—the fact that he had power over demons didn't seem to clear things up. Maybe he was just a bigger kind of demon.

You assess the origin of power by the fruit of its action. No matter what it says it's doing—the demons are good liars—you watch what it actually does, and what happens as a result of what it does.

The power of God does not prefer itself. It pours itself out on behalf of the powerless, and all of us are powerless at one time or another. The demons are anxious for their lives, seeking to grab safety for themselves by increasing their hold on us. God is not anxious at all, and willingly spills his life out for us, seeking only our joy in his presence.

TUESDAY IN PROPER 22

Pss (120), 121, 122, 123 * 124, 125, 126 (127)
2 Kings 22:1–13
1 Corinthians 11:2, 17–22
Matthew 9:1–8

"I have found the book of the law in the house of the Lord."
2 KINGS 22:8

I'm not sure I really believe that somebody just happened to *find* the book of the law while they were repairing the temple. But maybe it did get lost. Remodeling is so awful, even now, and it was probably a lot worse then. And they'd been away for a while.

However it was, it's clear that this writer doesn't think the law was honored overmuch in the land of Israel. If the book of the law wasn't missing, it might as well have been, for all the attention anyone paid to it.

How do we handle the law? All our traditions from the past? We obey some of it, and let other parts of it slip into disuse. We cannot help but adjust it to new situations, because old law doesn't cover new situations. It must in some way be applied, re-explained. Interpreted. When we do that, some among us cry foul. And others want to know what's the big deal.

Everyone who reads scripture interprets it: whether it's story, poetry, or law. Nobody reads anything without interpreting it: that's what reading *is*. It's understandable that we don't all agree on matters of scriptural interpretation. We're each wearing a different pair of glasses.

The important thing is that we *do* read it. That we engage it. That what is there on the page is something with which we wrestle, on which we spend some time. Otherwise, we'll forget that we *come from somewhere*. We didn't invent ourselves in the twenty-first century. Or the twentieth. Or the fifteenth. Other centuries have given us birth and shaped us. Even if we no longer live in them, we ignore them at our peril. The goods and ills of one age may wear the clothes of another, but we can recognize them if we understand that we have met them before.

Perhaps the specifics of sexual mores, of dietary laws, of care for the poor all change from age to age. But that the whole of life is lived under the eye of a God who desires the good for us and from us has not changed. Where is that good today? Where the ill? And where, in the midst of it, are we who read?

WEDNESDAY IN PROPER 22

Pss 119:145–176 * 128, 129, 130
2 Kings 22:14–23:3
1 Corinthians 11:23–34
Matthew 9:9–17

For I received from the Lord what I also handed on to you, that the Lord Jesus on the night when he was betrayed took a loaf of bread, and when he had given thanks, he broke it and said, "This is my body that is for you. Do this in remembrance of me."

1 CORINTHIANS 11:23–24

The Words of Institution are old. Really old. Here they are in Paul's letter to the Corinthians, which is older than any of the four gospels. And even Paul did not originate them: *I received from the Lord what I also delivered to you,* he says. He *received* them. They were already old when Paul wrote them down. Already they were a liturgy: we know that because Matthew uses them again, word for word, thirty or more years after Paul wrote his letters to the Corinthians. Already people are saying these words, words we still say over a shared meal of bread and wine. Already, everybody knows them.

People in the sixteenth century argued a fair amount over the character of the Eucharist: was it a sacrifice or was it a memorial meal? Was Christ really present in it, as catholic teaching held, or was it a purely human event in memory of him, intended to put us in mind of his salvation?

The Anglican Words of Institution let us think our own thoughts about that: *The Body of Our Lord Jesus Christ, which was given for thee, preserve thy body and soul unto everlasting life. Take and eat this in remembrance that Christ died for thee, and be thankful.* If you think it's really the Body of Christ, it's there. If you think you're doing something with ordinary bread in memory of Jesus, that's there, too. One does not outweigh or exclude the other. They go together. How you come to terms with them in your own heart? That's up to you.

THURSDAY IN PROPER 22

Pss 131, 132, (133) * 134, 135
2 Kings 23:4–25
1 Corinthians 12:1–11
Matthew 9:18–26

*When Jesus came to the leader's house and saw the flute
players and the crowd making a commotion, he said,
"Go away; for the girl is not dead but sleeping."*
MATTHEW 9:23–24

Flute players and a noisy crowd: a Middle Eastern funeral. Here, a black hearse and a procession of cars with their headlights on, in broad daylight. In New Orleans, a slow, swinging brass band on the way out to the cemetery, a jubilant burst of Dixieland on the way back to town. In India, a silent procession of men, marching along the road, two by two, toward the funeral pyre. In Navajo land, silence, and a hasty dispatch of the corpse: the Navajo do not speak of death or of the dead, ever again: it might disturb their rest.

You can always tell a funeral if you're in your own country: the practices are always the same, ritual ways of behaving. Jesus heard the flutes and saw the crowd, and he knew what was happening right away. But he also knew that it was premature, even before he saw the little girl. She wasn't going to die. She was just asleep.

How we long for such a thing to happen to us! How it comes to us in our dreams: *she's not dead, after all! It was all a mistake! Oh, thank God!* And then we awaken. It was no mistake.

But it's not the last word. We wish for the miracles Jesus performed to be ours, and once in a while they are. But the victory over death they show forth is ours, too, each of us, without exception.

FRIDAY IN PROPER 22

Pss 140, 142 * 141, 143:1–11 (12)
2 Kings 23:36–24:17
1 Corinthians 12:12–26
Matthew 9:27–34

If one member suffers, all suffer together with it;
if one member is honored, all rejoice together with it.
1 CORINTHIANS 12:26

There is an ecology to the human body: none of its parts are isolated. Everything affects everything else.

Certainly there's an ecology to the human family. We affect each other, directly and indirectly. Everything we do. Everything we wear or eat or drive or burn or manufacture.

Of course, there's an ecology to the natural world, too. There would be even if there were no human beings in it. That's where we first learned what ecology is. Everything affects everything, whether we're in the equation or not.

And there is an ecology to the Body of Christ: we affect each other. This is why it is usually so difficult for us to be neutral in matters of religion, why anxious hostesses throughout the ages have begged their families not to talk about religion at the dinner table when guests are present, why people have stalked out of churches and entire denominations when there was disagreement, never to return. Faith matters to us. We worry when we are far apart in matters pertaining to it.

But sometimes we mistake healthy diversity for fatal disagreement. As if there were something wrong if we don't all think alike. But why would people think alike about something as important as faith? Why wouldn't we each be informed by the peculiarities of our own history and experience? And why should these peculiarities threaten us?

Here is an important biological truth: breeds that don't mix with other breeds become weak and unhealthy. There's definitely such a thing as being too purebred. Nature's way of keeping the creation strong is to mix it up. Regularly. Everywhere. That's how the creation works. Why should we imagine that the Body of Christ would be different?

Look to enhance and color the truth with which you begin. Look to add to it. Expect it to become lovelier and more textured as time goes on. Don't imagine that what you knew at twelve is all that you should ever allow yourself to know. That is not the case with any human knowing, and it is not the case with religious knowing. We're supposed to grow and change. It's supposed to be a struggle. That's not a sign that something's wrong. It's a sign that something's right.

SATURDAY IN PROPER 22

Pss 137:1–6 (7–9), 144 * 104
Jeremiah 35:1–19
1 Corinthians 12:27–13:3
Matthew 9:35–10:4

"The harvest is plentiful, but the laborers are few."
MATTHEW 9:37

When my father was a young man in the Dakota Territory, the schools shut down at this time of year so that everyone could help bring in the harvest. Boys could make a little money going from one farm to the next. They had to work fast: harvesting is a time-critical activity. You can't start too early or you're harvesting a worthless crop. Let it go too late and it's also worthless, overripe. Let it get wet and you can't store it until it dries. Let it get wet enough and it will rot right where it is and you'll never store it. Everyone in town is growing the same crop, more or less, and is bound by the same weather conditions, so everything comes in at once. Intense work from sunup to sundown for two weeks, three at the most. Everyone who can walk must work, whether in the field or in the enormous project of feeding everybody.

We think of all agrarian metaphors as serene and peaceful: sheep dotting the gentle landscape, shepherds playing their pipes and dozing off in the heat of the afternoon, farmers walking in a leisurely manner behind their cattle at the end of the day. But there's nothing leisurely about milking twenty cows twice a day by hand, not for the cows and not for the people. Your back hurts? Your daughter's getting married? The cows don't care. Twice a day, no matter what else is happening.

What we miss today in Jesus' statement about the harvest is the urgency. He's not just saying it's a big job. He's saying it's a big job that can't wait another minute. You don't have unlimited time to touch the lives you are called to touch in the course of your lifetime. The person before you now may never be before you again, and you may never have another chance with her. You may never see him again. If someone is going to experience Christ by experiencing you, you'd better start now. As if there's no tomorrow. There may not be.

SUNDAY, PROPER 23

Pss 146, 147 * 111, 112, 113
Jeremiah 36:1–10
Acts 14:8–18
Luke 7:36–50

When the crowds saw what Paul had done, they shouted in the Lycaonian language, "The gods have come down to us in human form!" Barnabas they called Zeus, and Paul they called Hermes, because he was the chief speaker. The priest of Zeus, whose temple was just outside the city, brought oxen and garlands to the gates; he and the crowds wanted to offer sacrifice.

ACTS 14:11–13

This is comic: imagine the oxen, garlanded with flowers, standing patiently at the gate of the city. All the priests. Torches. Dancing girls, probably, and musicians. All for two Jewish guys who don't believe in idols. It puts me in mind of a Bob Hope-Bing Crosby road movie in which the pair end up pretending to be desert sheiks or French Foreign Legionnaires.

Mistaken identity stories are always funny. Shakespeare loved them: *Two Gentlemen from Verona, As You Like It.* They're an old movie staple, too: *The Gay Divorcee, Some Like It Hot.* They've always been funny.

When people are mistaken for someone else in a play, we can see the differences between who they really are and who they've been taken for clearly. That's true here, too. Paul and Barnabas aren't Greek gods. Far from it. The opposite, in fact: they have come to say that there aren't a dozen or two dozen or a few hundred different gods, gods who act like people, who fight and argue with each other like people do, who come to earth and walk around and date mortal women. Of all people to be taken for Hermes the Messenger, Paul is the very last one I'd choose.

But we also see, in these old plays and movies, just how it is that the switch makes just enough sense that somebody falls for it. Jack Lemmon makes a pretty believable woman—or maybe it wasn't all that hard to fool Marilyn Monroe's ditzy blonde. Something in Paul and Barnabas made the people of Lystra search their own experience for something able to heal, as the two men healed, and they came up with their own gods. *They must be gods*, they thought. *That's got to be it.*

Paul and Barnabas aren't gods. But they bear the image of God within them. So do the Lystrans. So do we. So does everyone, even the one in whom it's so barnacled over that you can't see it any more. The image of God is in every person. Everyone. It's an image of possibility, a goodness written on the soul.

MONDAY IN PROPER 23

Pss 1, 2, 3 * 4, 7
Jeremiah 36:11–26
1 Corinthians 13:(1–3) 4–13
Matthew 10:5–15

Now the king was sitting in his winter apartment . . . and there was a fire burning in the brazier before him. As Jehudi read three or four columns, the king would cut them off with a penknife and throw them into the fire . . . until the entire scroll was consumed . . .
JEREMIAH 36:22–23

It was Mark Twain who said, "It is not what I don't understand in the Bible that troubles me. It's what I understand only too well." I guess that's what the king was afraid of: better to be able to claim not to know what God wanted than to know it perfectly well and get caught ignoring it. Why don't we just pretend we never got the memo? It'll be a lot easier.

This whole section of Jeremiah is about how far Israel had fallen away from the will of God—a common theme among all the prophets. The king didn't like such straight talk: he had prophets who worked for him, and they always told him nicer things. Jeremiah was a pain. The book he dictated was a pain and having people read it aloud was a pain.

You can ignore the will of God if you want to, but it will get its message across. There are so many ways of puzzling over what is best, so many approaches to truth and to courses of action: we're not going to be able to claim we never had the chance to find out what we're here for. Besides, people are going to talk. People will ask us about what we're doing. People will want the best from us in our dealings with them. We're not going to be able to say we didn't know.

Some New Yorkers just tear up parking tickets when they find them on their windshields. Later on, they may get a bill, but they ignore it. Some of them go on like that for years, until the time comes when their car gets towed and they go down to the pier to get it out. Nope. Not until you pay the $750 in parking tickets you've amassed. In cash. We'll just keep your car—and we'll charge you for storing it. You can't even get impounded for free in New York.

So there's no point in pretending we're not moral agents. It never works. We have ethics the way we have toenails: they are standard equipment on human beings. Throw away your parking ticket if you want to. Ignore your Bible and your conscience. They'll both be waiting for you at the end of the day.

TUESDAY IN PROPER 23

Pss 5, 6 * 10, 11
Jeremiah 36:27–37:2
1 Corinthians 14:1–12
Matthew 10:16–23

"Brother will betray brother to death, and a father his child, and children will rise against parents and have them put to death; and you will be hated by all because of my name. But the one who endures to the end will be saved."
MATTHEW 10:21–22

The family that prays together, stays together, say the billboards. The Knights of Columbus have used this phrase in their public service announcements for decades. What a hopeful thought: there's a way to ensure that we will never be fractured.

But what on earth does Jesus mean, then, with this grim prediction of turmoil and betrayal among family members? How horrible: a father betraying his children? Brother against brother?

At the time, it probably was literally true: some early Christians were persecuted by their families, who could not live with the new way of life and set of values, and some of them must certainly have been turned in by someone they trusted as much as a father, a brother. Some early saints were martyred by family members: my own namesake, St. Barbara, was imprisoned in a tower by her dad because she wouldn't marry a pagan, and then, when she broke out, he tortured her to death. Art concerning St. Barbara shows her with her tower, and she is often surrounded by lightning: her dad was struck by lightning as soon as he had finished killing her. *So there.* Thus, Barbara is the patron saint of artillery, or any kind of firearms or fireworks.

She seems also not to have really existed. She got fired from being a saint in 1969, when they went through and got rid of people who didn't really exist. That seems unkind: is it their fault they didn't exist? It is not. Anyway, they do now, if they didn't then: you can still buy candles dedicated to St. Barbara in the Latino neighborhoods of New York, and mariners from some countries still carry icons of her on board. Just in case of storms.

So she's a powerful figure of outrage at the betrayal of the normal bonds of love and protection that should bind families together. Her dad shouldn't have done that. God never demands that we injure each other—not strangers and certainly not family.

And yet—who can hurt us more than those we love? Who has the power? Whose unkind word cuts us more to the quick than someone we love? For whom would we be most likely to break the law, if we were to consider breaking it? For whose love do we long most of all, and who in the human family can restore us better by loving us?

WEDNESDAY IN PROPER 23

Pss 119:1–24 * 12, 13, 14
Jeremiah 37:3–21
1 Corinthians 14:13–25
Matthew 10:24–33

"Are not two sparrows sold for a penny? Yet none of them will fall to the ground unperceived by your Father."
MATTHEW 10:29

So ancient and so well known, and so comforting. If you don't read too carefully, you think it says that God keeps even little birds from harm, and surely protects us as well. More, even: *Are you not worth more than many sparrows?* Jesus asks. Of course we are.

But that's not quite what it says, is it? God doesn't keep the sparrow from falling. Eventually they all fall. Just as we do. It's not that we won't fall. Our blessing is that God will remain with us, right up to and through and even after our fall.

Early in life and early in faith, that doesn't feel like enough. Early in the life of faith, we think we've found a way around the sorrows of this world. I'll never be sad again, never be lonely, never have problems in my marriage or my job. I am in Christ now, and I will walk through life untouched by the things that touch . . . whom? People who aren't in Christ? Is that it? Are the people of God who follow Christ now immune from the sorrows of the world?

Well, no. We knew that.

But we continue to be surprised by our pain. How can I be depressed? I'm a *Christian*! Why am I angry? I just don't get it: I believe in God. How could I have gotten fired? I prayed and everything: what am I doing wrong?

Nope. The sparrow falls and the marriage falls apart. The sparrow falls and we become ill. The sparrow falls and we go to war. The sparrow falls and we declare bankruptcy.

The sparrow always falls. We always do. All of us sparrows.

Once we understand this—that the Christian life is not an end run around human life, not a way of beating the systems of this world through the power of the next one—we relax. We're still mortal. We still make mistakes. We still have troubles. But what we aren't, ever again, is alone. What we're not is deserted, no matter who we lose, and, sooner or later, we lose absolutely everybody but God.

Full of fear, the little bird plunges to the ground, powerless to prevent his own fall. Later, someone walks by his still little body, without even noticing. But it's okay, even if he never moves again. Bird heaven? Who knows? But all in Christ, all people and all planets, all living and all dead—all known and seen, all caught, safe, in the hand of God.

THURSDAY IN PROPER 23

Pss 18:1–20 * 18:21–50
Jeremiah 38:1–13
1 Corinthians 14:26–33a, 37–40
Matthew 10:34–42

*Then they drew Jeremiah up by the ropes
and pulled him out of the cistern.*

JEREMIAH 38:13

Not everybody needs to be a visionary. Take Ebed-melech, the Ethiopian eunuch, who saw the bad guys throw Jeremiah into a well. *He'll starve to death in there*, he tells the clueless king, and receives permission to take a couple of guys and pull Jeremiah out. And what does he do? He throws some old rags and clothing down into the well. Why on earth?

To pad the rope, so that it won't amputate Jeremiah's arms on the way up out of the mud. *Oh.* I never would have thought of that in a million years.

There are different gifts in the human family. Some are gifted with vision, the broad and long view of what will be or what might be. And some are implementers, the common-sense people, the ones who know what to do to get the job done. Put a visionary in charge of an implementation, if you want to see chaos. If you want it done right, find a no-nonsense implementer.

Many clergy are visionaries. They have an exciting sense of what might be, a desire to bring forth the fruit of the potential they see so clearly it is as if it were already there. Congregations must like them, because they continue to call them.

But if those visionaries don't understand that a vision alone is not enough to bring forth reality, the parish is in for some rough sledding. The best leaders know what they do well and what they don't, and make sure they surround themselves with folks who have skills they lack. And the very best ones listen to those folks, and allow themselves to be guided by them in their areas of strength.

So the most prophetic of priests accomplishes no good and probably does great harm if he or she can't listen to those whose pragmatic skills are essential to actually completing a task. If it hadn't been for Ebed-melech, a foreigner, a servant—and a eunuch, to boot—a powerless person compared to the king—Jeremiah might not have made it out of the well alive. And it wouldn't have mattered how good a preacher he was. No one would have heard him.

FRIDAY IN PROPER 23

Pss 16, 17 * 22
Jeremiah 38:14–28
1 Corinthians 15:1–11
Matthew 11:1–6

Then he appeared to more than five hundred brothers and sisters at one time, most of whom are still alive, although some have died.
1 CORINTHIANS 15:6

None of the four gospels record a post-resurrection appearance to five hundred people at one time, so Paul is on his own here. And he wasn't there himself: he was on the other side in those days, a sworn enemy of The Way. Or maybe he was just a kid then, a teenager, perhaps, since his letters date from twenty years after such an event would have occurred. So he must have heard about it from somebody. It's odd that such a large-scale appearance wouldn't have been remembered by someone else, in such a small and brief a world as Jerusalem in the fifty days following Jesus' resurrection. But Paul's assurance that it was so is all that we have to prove that it ever happened. So it's a good thing our faith isn't based on proof. We'd have been in trouble right from the beginning.

Although we think we'd have plenty of faith if we'd been lucky enough to witness these events, there were plenty of people around who saw them and didn't believe. The empty tomb didn't make everyone believe: some folks just thought it was a hoax. It seems that people who saw the Risen Christ didn't always know who he was until he had gone away.

Actually, we experience the Risen Christ in much the same way as they did—even now, two thousand years after the fact. It dawns on us. We don't get it at first. Don't want to, sometimes, or *do* want to but can't get beyond our utter intellectual bafflement about the whole thing; we don't feel the presence of God at all, or *do* feel it and can't quite name it as what it is—this goes on for decades, sometimes, in a person's life.

Paul, who hadn't known Jesus, had a dramatic conversion experience and spent the rest of his life trying to help others have one, too. Most of the people he helped didn't have dramatic ones like his: they had experiences more like ours. They had no evidence beyond the evidence we have, most of them, and sometimes their faith journey took them on a rocky road. Like the road we travel.

SATURDAY IN PROPER 23

Pss 20, 21:1–7 (8–14) * 110:1–5 (6–7), 116, 117
2 Kings 25:8–12, 22–26
1 Corinthians 15:12–29
Matthew 11:7–15

"Look, those who wear soft robes are in royal palaces."
MATTHEW 11:8

And Jesus did neither of those things. He wore rough clothes—a seamless robe that his mother probably made him—and he was homeless when he died. Before that, he had lived as an artisan's son, so his home can't have been anything too special. Probably well-built and well-fitted, though: Joseph was a carpenter.

Jesus is often thought to have been a carpenter, too, on the assumption that he apprenticed with his dad. Makes sense: most people did. Even today, in most countries in the world, the apple doesn't fall far from the tree. The radical upward mobility Americans expect, that children will far outstrip the parents in wealth and lifestyle, is relatively new, and it is confined to just a few places. In most of the world, you're what your parents were.

It mattered that the Son of God was of humble birth: even if the early Christian writers were at pains to demonstrate that he was of David's lineage, his kingdom was definitely not of this world. Most of us have this in common with Jesus. We're not very important, either. Nobody beyond our small circle of friends and family knows us.

Our modest circumstances discourage and frustrate us sometimes. We don't bend much of anything to our wills. Few people find it necessary to obey us, and so most of us give few orders. Surely Jesus knew that frustration as well: if we are to live in peace, it must train us to rely on God—or we will be furious all the time. We don't control much in life. Spiritual peace demands that we come to terms with that.

SUNDAY, PROPER 24

Pss 148, 149, 150 * 114, 115
Jeremiah 29:1, 4–14
Acts 16:6–15
Luke 10:1–12, 17–20

But seek the welfare of the city where I have sent
you into exile, and pray to the Lord on its behalf,
for in its welfare you will find your welfare.
JEREMIAH 29:7

The stern new creed of the immigrant: no matter where you came from, you're here now. The values here must be your values. Mostly, people are eager to embrace the new place, to learn the language, to get ahead. The Israelites did this in their captivity, even though they came in chains, and they did it well: lived in Babylon, learned Babylonian, set up shops and businesses, found husbands and wives for their children. They grew old there, and some died there. They adapted, and they were so successful that not all of them elected to return to Israel when it became possible for them to do so. A successful, if involuntary, relocation.

But there must be sadness in the heart, always: as the ship moves away from home and the people on it look back at a shoreline they may never see again. *I will keep my home in my heart always*, they tell themselves fiercely, but some of them suspect what all of them will learn in time: you can't go home again. You will never be the way you were. Your experience of living somewhere else for a long time will change you profoundly, and even if you make the long journey back home at last, it will not be the same.

This bit of advice from Jeremiah is so practical: pray for the city where I have sent you. Don't fight that upon which you must depend. Save your fight for saving the good, not for reflexively opposing the unfamiliar.

Surrender to the experience of the new: oddly, it will free you to treasure what you have left behind. Soak up what there is to learn: there is so much to learn. Accept, as soon as you can, the inevitability of change, so that your mind and memory are free to examine and cherish what is truly important in both your worlds, the new one and the old one.

MONDAY IN PROPER 24

Pss 25 * 9, 15
Jeremiah 44:1–14
1 Corinthians 15:30–41
Matthew 11:16–24

What you sow does not come to life unless it dies.
1 CORINTHIANS 15:36

Is it true that you can pull geraniums up and wrap them in newspaper and they'll grow again next year? Joan asks me on the phone. They are putting their beach house to bed for the winter, and don't know what to do with the plants.

Well, I've never heard that about geraniums, I say. Dahlias, yes. They come back if you do that. But still, why not give it a try? The geraniums are going to die anyway, if you leave them outside. So if you can't just pot them and bring them in to bloom in your window, I suppose you could try the newspaper thing. The worst thing that could happen is a dead geranium, which is what will happen anyhow if you leave them outside.

It's hard to abandon a plant to the winter. It's even hard to abandon the ones that expect it, the ones that *will* come back—hard to believe that they'll just go to sleep under the soil and begin again next year. I want them to remain as they were. That's the only thing that looks like plant life to me: green leaves and blossoms lifting their heads to the sun.

But there are other kinds of living besides the living we know. There is a life after this one—or, rather, in addition to this one. Beside this one, maybe. All around this one, maybe. Some *also-life*, of which this one is a part.

Begin to think about what death is and you run into confusion almost immediately. Where is it? What's it like? What are they like who live that life?

Someday we shall know. Or, perhaps, we know already—and don't *know* we know! When we long for the sight of someone who has died, long to hear that voice again, to see her sitting in her chair again, to hear him singing in the morning as he used to do, we feel that whatever the also-life is, it's not enough. We want the old one back.

No. We never get anything back from the past. It stays there. But it also has an existence in the mysterious future, and even in the contradictory present.

What are they like now? How are they raised? We do not know. But we wait for word.

TUESDAY IN PROPER 24

Pss 26, 28 * 36, 39
Lamentations 1:1–5 (6–9) 10–12
1 Corinthians 15:41–50
Matthew 11:25–30

"Come to me, all you that are weary and are carrying heavy
burdens, and I will give you rest. Take my yoke upon you, and learn
from me; for I am gentle and humble in heart, and you will find rest
for your souls. For my yoke is easy, and my burden is light."
MATTHEW 11:28–30

These gentle words are part of the lectionary specifically chosen for today. But they also are from part of the permanent selection of little readings for the tender office of Compline, the Church's quiet "good-night" to the faithful. You can choose among four different short passages, but I almost always light on this one.

Whatever your day has been, however difficult it may have been—come to me. However heavy your load, even if it's the heaviest you've ever borne—come to me. Take my yoke upon you, and I'll take yours. I can handle it. And mine is light: here, feel how light. That's because I have paid in full for all the sorrows of the world, yours included. I know just what you carry. Come to me, and I will give you rest.

We lie down in our beds, trying not to think too much about our worries. It is hard, though: they gallop through our minds like a team of horses. They seem bigger than we are, somehow. "Sleep on it," someone tells us, and that's good advice. But we can't. The thunder of hooves is relentless.

Unless. Unless. Unless we have spent a few years—or even just a few weeks—reading these sweet words every night. Dependable as a night-light, sweet as a kiss, they tuck us in at night. We grow accustomed to them. They plant themselves in our hearts and minds, and we come to believe them. And they calm us down: we hand the whole messy bundle of frets into the hands of Christ and turn out the light. And then we sleep.

WEDNESDAY IN PROPER 24

Pss 38 * 119:25–48
Lamentations 2:8–15
1 Corinthians 15:51–58
Matthew 12:1–14

*We will not all die, but we will all be changed, in a moment,
in the twinkling of an eye, at the last trumpet.*

1 CORINTHIANS 15:51–52

But we don't *want* to be changed. We want to stay the same. Paul intends these words to be comforting, perhaps, although you can never be sure with Paul: he is not an easy person. But most of us find them more than a little scary.

So how changed are they, those dear souls who have left us behind? Do they remember us? Is it really like a long church service where they are? Where are they, anyway?

We are told of the joy in which they live. This hurts our feelings a little, or maybe a lot: how can she be happy without me? How can he be happy, knowing that I am so sad? Maybe he didn't love me much, after all, if he doesn't even miss me.

The thing is, though, they're *not* without us. We're just without *them*. But the truth is that they are closer to us than ever before. Closer than you can be when you have a physical body. We are the ones who experience aloneness; they are not alone. They're with us, now. Right now, and always.

Well, he *said* it was a mystery.

But talk to some people you know who have experienced the death of someone without whom they thought they could not live. Choose people for whom the loss is not a fresh one: for a while, absence is all there is, and its anguish is mighty.

But later—later, many people report that they still feel close to their dead love, in a way that is more than memory. Still sad at the loss, still ambushed by tears sometimes. But for many bereaved people, now and then, there is an odd and mysterious sense of presence. Not every day. Not always enough to erase our sadness. Maybe what we wish we had. Not like it was before.

But not *nothing*, either. Stay tuned.

THURSDAY IN PROPER 24

Pss 37:1–18 * 37:19–42
Ezra 1:1–11
1 Corinthians 16:1–9
Matthew 12:15–21

But I will stay in Ephesus until Pentecost, for a wide door for effective work has opened to me, and there are many adversaries.
1 CORINTHIANS 16:8–9

Notice something here: Paul doesn't say that there's a wide door for effective work *in spite of* there being many adversaries. He says *and*. As if the presence of many adversaries was not surprising at all. As if he looked forward to the adversaries with relish: knowing what we know about Paul's argumentative nature, this is not hard to imagine. As if the presence of obstacles to good work were part of the plan.

I have long believed that life is a series of obstacles to be overcome. I even suspect that we die when we run out of them. Of boredom, possibly. Life's not supposed to be easy. To have an earthly existence is to struggle, and it is the very act of struggling that strengthens us as human beings. Without it, we grow flaccid and useless.

Think of someone you experience as a contented person. Is that person someone into whose life nothing difficult has ever come? I doubt it. We exercise the muscles of our souls by overcoming obstacles. We learn who is our help and how to lean on that help. We learn that an exception will not be made in our case, and that helps our humility enormously. And we learn what easy is, if we have known some hardship. Appreciate the good things in life all the more, if there is a certain, well, *contrast*.

Sometimes people think that the presence of obstacles is a sign that God opposes the course of action upon which we are embarked. That ease is a sign of God's will. I don't know how anybody could read the Bible and still think such a thing, but people do.

We're not magic. We live in a world in which life is beautiful but hard. We have the privilege of a sojourn here, and considerable freedom and equipment to make of it what we can. In the end, we won't surmount every obstacle. One of them is going to get us. But until it does, we're free to try.

FRIDAY IN PROPER 24

Pss 31 * 35
Ezra 3:1–13
1 Corinthians 16:10–24
Matthew 12:22–32

But many of the priests and Levites and heads of families, old people who had seen the first house on its foundations, wept with a loud voice when they saw this house, though many shouted aloud for joy, so that the people could not distinguish the sound of the joyful shout from the sound of the people's weeping, for the people shouted so loudly that the sound was heard far away.
EZRA 3:12–13

Some of those who remembered the way things used to be couldn't rejoice at the new beginning. All they could see was that it was different from what they had before.

Others remembered, too. But the memory sparked energy and joy.

A new thing will invite me into the future in hope. Whether or not I accept that invitation is up to me. My life can be a nostalgic song about a time to which I cannot return, or it can be an exhilarating hiking song, something that inspires me and everyone to whom I sing it to expect joy, and to set out on the road to it.

Notice how careful they have been, in these stories of rebuilding the ruined temple, to be faithful to the shape of the old one. They lay it out in the same way, to the cubit. Later, they will bring all the dishes they had before—whatever did they do with 2,000 silver bowls?—back home, and install them in the new place, in the same spot they would have occupied in the old one.

When the Italian monastery at Monte Casino was destroyed by Allied bombs during World War II, it was a body blow to the spiritual solar plexus of Italy. Monte Casino had been a holy place for centuries, a famous holy place. It was a destination of pilgrims.

After the war, the United States rebuilt Monte Casino. An exact replica, down to the way of manufacturing the bricks, faithful to the destroyed treasure to the last inch. It still stands, a faithful replica. But nobody goes to see it any more. It is not the same. It's not real. It's a replica.

It is not re-creating replicas of what we had that fills our souls again. It is recapturing the spirit, following it where it leads, wherever that maybe. Whatever it looks like.

SATURDAY IN PROPER 24

Pss 30, 32 * 42, 43
Ezra 4:7, 11–24
Philemon 1–25
Matthew 12:33–42

I, Paul, am writing this with my own hand . . .
PHILEMON 1:19

Paul dictated almost everything he wrote. He either traveled with a scribe or employed one when he arrived in a city, so he could keep up with his voluminous correspondence. Perhaps this was because his written Greek wasn't up to his command of the spoken language.

So this sentence must have stood out. It must have sprawled across the orderly landscape of the scribe's careful art and stuck out like a sore thumb. The ones who read the letter must have seen that it was in a different hand right away.

People say that handwritten notes will disappear soon. That so will actual physical presence: we'll just e-mail each other, or IM each other. All our written discourse will be in the bland Arial font of electronic communication, and nobody's will look any different from anybody else's. Maybe.

But nothing is as exciting as an actual letter in the mail. As actual, no-two-alike handwriting. A little <g> may signal a joke online, but how good a joke can it be that needs to be signaled in order to be understood as amusing? In a thousand ways, from the tremble of an elderly hand to the ironic glint of an eye, we need the physical reality of the communication we have with one another. It helps us gauge truth and meaning.

Paul was agitated and insistent. I can imagine his grip on the pen, the pressure on the parchment, and strong vertical lines, the darkness of the ink. You could tell he was in a swivet about something before you read the words: you could just *tell* by what they looked like.

We don't have the actual manuscript he wrote "with his own hand," not any more. All we have is this peevish line to let us know how important the release of Onesimus was to him, and how cautious he was in his expectation of success. It was a long shot. He put all the clout he had—and Paul had a lot of clout—on the line in this cause. *Go ahead*, this line says. *Do the wrong thing. I know you can if you want to. But I'm putting myself on the line for the right thing, so know that you'll be dealing with me if you do.*

SUNDAY, PROPER 25

Pss 63:1–8 (9–11), 98 * 103
Haggai 1:1–2:9
Acts 18:24–19:7
Luke 10:25–37

*He said to them, "Did you receive the Holy Spirit when
you became believers?" They replied, "No, we have
not even heard that there is a Holy Spirit."*

ACTS 19:2

I dial the number in my datebook, although I recognize neither it
nor the name I have written so clearly next to it. I haven't a clue who
she is or why I wrote down her number next to the 3:00 p.m. hour.

"Um, this is Barbara Crafton," I stammer. "I have a three o-clock
appointment next to your name in my date book, but I don't remember what I said I'd do at 3 o'clock. I'm so sorry. Could you call me
please? I do apologize for my terrible memory."

How embarrassing. I strain to bring it back, but it's no use. It's
gone. I might as well have written it in Sanskrit. I await the woman's
call. This happens all the time.

You need to learn how to apologize as you get older, because it
becomes increasingly necessary. Your energy fails you, or you forget
something you really should know. You can't stay up late any more,
and you find it harder to multi-task.

None of these things have to happen, it says in health books. You
can remain as high-powered as you ever were. Just take your vitamins
and exercise a lot. I take my vitamins and exercise a lot. But somehow
I haven't remained high-powered. I am distinctly less than I was.

But other people don't seem to mind. They seem to manage well
without me in the center of every project. They don't seem to need
a lot of advice from me. They don't really want my help.

But they do want *me*. They don't mind if I have to stop and rest,
or if I forget things. It turns out that the people who love you really

do love you for yourself, and not for what you can do for them or give them. When the time comes to slow down a little, it really is all right to do so.

MONDAY IN PROPER 25

Pss 41, 52 * 44
Zechariah 1:7–17
Revelation 1:4–20
Matthew 12:43–50

"Do not be afraid; I am the first and the last, and the living one.
I was dead, and see, I am alive forever and ever . . .
REVELATION 1:17–18

The cabbage begins to bubble in its water bath, its strong smell combining with the lovely smell of the sausage in its skillet. Suppertime. It makes me miss my little girls, all grown up now: cooking, filling the house with a delicious smell, calling them to come, hearing the treble notes of their voices as they made their way to the table.

I dial Corinna's number. Nobody home yet, but there is her voice on the answering machine. I listen to the message and the beep, then explain that I didn't really want anything, that I just called to say hello. I don't say I just called to hear her voice on the machine. Then I hang up.

I call Anna. She's not home, either, but I listen to her voice and leave the same message after the beep. I don't tell her the real reason for my call, either. Nobody needs to know.

Recorded sound makes time stand still. We can hear people talking when they're not with us. After they've died, even, we can still hear them. They sing their songs, new songs to them, old ones to us, as we listen decades later. Their voices soften the pain of their passing a little: they were just here, we feel. Their voices still hang in our air.

The ancients had no such thing. Their beloved voices were forever stilled in death. Absence was profoundly and sadly silent. We will never know how they sounded, how they really looked, what their daily lives were really like. They are far away from us now. We connect with them only in the pages of scripture.

But we bear witness to the same God they considered the beginning and the end. That God knows no absence or passage of time: *I was dead and see, I am alive forever.* I guess one day we'll hear them all for real.

TUESDAY IN PROPER 25

Pss 45 * 47, 48
Ezra 5:1–17
Revelation 4:1–11
Matthew 13:1–9

"A sower went out to sow."
MATTHEW 13:3

You can buy plants for your garden already in bloom: they stand in rows outside supermarkets, hardware stores, and, of course, nurseries. It costs money, though, to have someone else raise your plant to that point for you. For the romance, risk, and love of gardening, there is nothing like raising your plants from seeds.

Into the ground go the tiny black dots, no bigger than a speck of dust, the different colored beans, the clove-like seeds of flowers, the thin propeller-shaped marigold seeds: they don't really look like seeds at all.

Some of them you plant now: the bulbs are probably already in the ground in the north, ready for their long winter's sleep. Southerners may have theirs in the freezer down in the basement: bulbs need more cold than the south consistently offers. You can sow spinach and Swiss chard now, and kale, if your winters aren't absolutely bitter, and eat them for Christmas dinner.

Mostly what you're doing with seeds now, though, is thinking about what you will plant next spring, the seeds you will start indoors a few weeks after Christmas. The eternity we must wait for the coming of spring shrinks when you start seeds indoors: you see them break the surface of the soil in a week or two, see the first two tiny leaves open, and before you know it they're an inch tall, and then they have their permanent leaves and you thin them and it's April already and they can go in the ground.

The main thing about seeds is the uncertainty. They won't all grow; some won't make it. Jesus' hearers know all about this: they're all farmers in some way, whether for their own kitchens or to sell in the market. They plant seeds or they don't eat. But not all the seeds they plant grow.

God plants us. Many factors govern whether or not we will grow. Some of them—many of them—are within our power to change.

WEDNESDAY IN PROPER 25

Pss 119:49–72 * 49, (53)
Ezra 6:1–22
Revelation 5:1–10
Matthew 13:10–17

*With joy they celebrated the festival of unleavened bread
seven days; for the Lord had made them joyful, and had turned
the heart of the king of Assyria to them, so that he aided them
in the work on the house of God, the God of Israel.*
EZRA 6:22

Did you know that there's such a thing as the Christian Yellow Pages? Everything in your area, from swimming pool contractors to car repair shops, all Christian. So you can have all your needs met by other Christians, and neither you nor your money need ever touch the hand of someone outside the faith.

Frightening.

Can God work in people outside the Church? Are non-Christians unclean in some way? Are they, perhaps, damned, because they don't acknowledge Jesus or worship God as we do?

That cannot be.

And the king of Assyria is here to demonstrate that. A long and careful negotiation with him has resulted in his cooperation with something God wants to happen. God uses everything. Not just things of which we approve. God uses everybody. Not just us.

Few habits of religion have been more destructive than this clubbiness. We are prone to it. It has produced pogroms. It produced the Holocaust. It produced the Spanish Inquisition. I can't think of a single good thing to say about it.

Go to your Jewish psychotherapist, your Korean Buddhist greengrocer, your Hindu innkeeper, your Muslim cardiologist, and relax: there's just no Christian way to fix a transmission.

THURSDAY IN PROPER 25

Pss 50 * (59, 60) or 103
Nehemiah 1:1–11
Revelation 5:11–6:11
Matthew 13:18–23

As for what was sown among thorns, this is the one who hears the word, but the cares of the world and the lure of wealth choke the word, and it yields nothing.

MATTHEW 13:22

Most of us don't fall away on purpose, or become angry at God and just leave. Usually, it's something much less dramatic: we just get too busy. Life is full, and it takes over sometimes.

Good things, not just bad. Life is full of delights, and we become delighted with them. We have no trouble at all giving them all our time, these gifts of God. But they take us over, if we let them: we forget how we got them, who the giver was. We become intimate with them instead of with the God who showered us with them.

I have a particularly aggressive vine in the front garden. It reaches for the roses, rampages over the ground in all directions, twining itself around everything in its path. I would have ripped it out by now, except for one thing: I think it's pretty. Its leaves are nicely shaped, and it flowers, even at this time of year, are a delicate set of three or four little purple bells at the end of each stem. I have trained it on a homemade wooden tripod, hoping to contain it that way, that it will twine back upon itself, become bushy and beautiful. Quit threatening its neighbors.

But I must prune it every day in order to help it contain itself, even now, when the frost is all but here. Left to its own devices, it will not contain itself: I must apply the brakes. If I don't, it will choke everyone else in the garden.

I must keep the garden in mind. None of the gifts of God are sufficient in themselves to bear the weight of all our devotion. They must comprise a whole, and we must develop some kind of overview of what it will look like, and to whom it will look for its ongoing life.

FRIDAY IN PROPER 25

Pss 40, 54 * 51
Nehemiah 2:1–20
Revelation 6:12–7:4
Matthew 13:24–30

. . . I carried the wine and gave it to the king.
Now, I had never been sad in his presence before.
NEHEMIAH 2:1

Well, you don't show your feelings at work, do you? They don't want to know whether you're sad or not. Keep it to yourself.

We don't know what's going on in other people's worlds. They usually don't say anything: we don't know about their bedridden parents until the home health aide doesn't show up one day and they miss work to take her place. We don't know their hearts are breaking because of a teenager who seems determined to ruin her life. We don't know their marriages are in trouble, their husbands are dying, they're on the verge of bankruptcy. They look fine. They seem cheerful enough. They never said anything. We didn't know.

Then something happens and their human need shows, like a run in one of their stockings. Eventually, it affects their work. Sometimes people get fired then. You're not supposed to have human needs at work.

Now is the time when your humanity can show, too, in response to their need. You're not going to be able to cover their whole workload with your kindness, but you will honor and deepen your friendship by doing what you can. Maybe what you can do is absolutely nothing but lending a listening ear once in a while. Lend it willingly. You may get a run in one of your stockings someday.

SATURDAY IN PROPER 25

Pss 55 * 138, 139:1–17 (18–23)
Nehemiah 4:1–23
Revelation 7:(4–8) 9–17
Matthew 13:31–35

They will hunger no more, and thirst no more; the sun will not strike them, nor any scorching heat; for the Lamb at the center of the throne will be their shepherd, and he will guide them to springs of the water of life, and God will wipe away every tear from their eyes.
REVELATION 7:16–17

Deeply comforting, this funeral reading. When the choice is mine, I always choose it. It is also one of the Eucharistic readings for the Feast of All Saints.

I am tired this evening. I think of the coming holiday season and feel even more tired. This is not like me: I am usually excited by all the preparations. And then I read this, about the righteous dead, so safe from harm, of God caring so tenderly for them, comforting them, and I long to go there now.

Of course, you have to die to go there. So I guess I'll stay here, for now. Where the sun does strike us, and the rain, too, at this time of year. Right before the snow comes and belts us once—or several times—before winter is over.

When this ancient writer considered what heaven might be like, he thought about the weather: it must be very different there. So vulnerable to the heat in those days, they were—no air conditioning. But those who have lived in hot countries know that there are lots of things people do to cool off: ways of building houses, ways of dressing, ways of managing the times of day to best advantage. People vulnerable to the weather become very wise in its ways, and they are circumspect in the things they will and won't do in the face of it.

He must have had a picture in his mind: happy people setting forth on a walk any time they wanted to, not having to get where they were going before the blinding noonday sun drove them into the shade, not having to wait until dusk. People with enough water, fountains everywhere. Relaxed, clean, cool. And repaired, repaid for all the suffering they endured here: more suffering than just the hot weather. Everything made right. Everybody healed.

It's not hot here. It's cold. But it's hard, here, just the same. Someday—somewhere—it will not be.

SUNDAY, PROPER 26

Pss 24, 29 * 8, 84
Nehemiah 5:1–19
Acts 20:7–12
Luke 12:22–31

And can any of you by worrying add
a single hour to your span of life?
LUKE 12:25

Well, no, none of us can. Abundant evidence suggests that we shorten our lives by being anxious. And even if we don't shorten them, we certainly make them unpleasant. So it does no good and plenty of harm.

Why do we embrace anxiety, then? Why do so many of us insist on it, as if worrying about things somehow solved them? We won't let ourselves enjoy anything as long as the problem we brood over continues to exist, as if we hadn't the right to be happy until we solve it.

But problems go on for years sometimes: few of them are easily or quickly dispatched. Are we supposed to defer all our joy until we've gotten everything together? Or until the outside world somehow decides to leave us alone? Because neither of those things ever happens to the living: only the dead have no problems to solve.

Anxiety is actually a drug: it produces a chemical response in our bodies, a fight-or-flight hormonal flush useful to someone who is shortly going to have to climb a tree or run for his life, but not for someone whose only open course of action is to watch the market or wait for a crucial phone call. Anxiety belongs to a primitive state we no longer inhabit, and it is counterproductive to us now. It's vestigial.

Coach yourself. Acknowledge the reality of the anxiety, but acknowledge also that it is of no use. It is not part of the solution, not any more. Take ten deep breaths and say a prayer for peace and trust in God. Do this every time anxiety beckons you. If anxiety is a vestigial habit, maybe we can form a new one that will actually help us deal with modern life.

MONDAY IN PROPER 26

Pss 56, 57, (58) * 64, 65
Nehemiah 6:1–19
Revelation 10:1–11
Matthew 13:36–43

"Let anyone with ears listen!"
MATTHEW 13:43

When you're ready, you'll get it. Before then, you don't have ears to hear.

Remember when you were a teenager. Remember what your mother told you, or your father. Remember what your teacher told you. Remember how you said to yourself that they just didn't understand. Remember that you said that to them, too, come to think of it, and remember the frustrated-yet-somehow-sad look that came across their faces, a look that was enough like sympathy that it made you patronized and angry and you said something smart-alecky.

And then remember when you realized that what they were trying to tell you was true, that you were the one who didn't understand. That you were young.

Even people who aren't teenagers aren't always ready to hear. There is a season for certain information, and it can't be heard until its season has come. But people who aren't ready to hear things do file them away for future reference. They hear, all right, but they're not ready to allow what they hear to enter them. They can't, not until it's time. And the right time comes from within them, not from the clock or the calendar, and certainly not from the experience of other people.

If only it could be otherwise, those who love them say. If only she could hear me. That's what that odd look is about, that look of exasperation and sympathy combined. It makes them angry, that look.

But they do see. And they do hear.

TUESDAY IN PROPER 26

Pss 61, 62 * 68:1–20 (21–23) 24–36
Nehemiah 12:27–31a, 42b–47
Revelation 11:1–19
Matthew 13:44–52

*". . . the kingdom of heaven is like a merchant in search
of fine pearls; on finding one pearl of great value,
he went and sold all that he had and bought it."*

MATTHEW 13:45–46

At first, putting everything you have into your spiritual life doesn't seem possible; or if it is possible, it's something only the occasional saint does. Not normal people.

But something happens when you begin to pray regularly: you find yourself wanting to do it more. You like it. You look forward to it. You feel odd if you haven't done it—unlike yourself. You find yourself wanting more.

You have not become a fine person—at least, no finer than you were. You still have the piques and shortness of temper you always had. You look the same. The same sins plague you.

But you are changing. Your priorities are reordering themselves. It is a subtle process, for most of us, not a big bang. The Holy Spirit is taking over your life: not like an evil spirit in a horror movie, but kindly, encouragingly. You are still yourself. But you are also more.

Paradoxically, you may not notice this good thing happening until something bad happens to you. Until you lose something of value. Perhaps someone you thought you couldn't live without.

Does God ask us to give up everything we love? Not usually. But we do, in the end, *lose* everything we love: that is the nature of human life. Nothing is permanent here. We hold what we have for a season, and we are shocked, when it is over, at how brief a season it was.

WEDNESDAY IN PROPER 26

Pss 72 * 119:73–96
Nehemiah 13:4–22
Revelation 12:1–12
Matthew 13:53–58

So I remonstrated with the officials and said,
"Why is the house of God forsaken?"
NEHEMIAH 13:11

Don't let the detail-heavy narrative of the book of Nehemiah bore you into not noticing what is happening. They are rebuilding their community after a disaster. They are reviving their faith. They are returning to something they left behind. They are repenting: they believe that God allowed the Babylonians to take them into captivity because they had fallen away, and so they want to get back home. Home to Jerusalem, certainly, but also home to the observance that their faith requires. We may not make grain offerings, or tithes of wine and oil, but we do know what it is to want to come back home to God.

Perhaps you never left. But perhaps you did, for awhile, for some good reason or for no reason you could put your finger on. And then you walked past a church one Sunday morning when people were going in, or walked into one on your lunch break, and something in your heart gave a little lurch and you wanted to come back.

Maybe you left because something made you angry or hurt your feelings. The Church is much better at those things than it should be. Or maybe your life took you somewhere you knew to be unworthy of you, and you felt you could not return. Or you were puzzled about its teaching and stayed away because you could not understand.

Welcome home. Now you know that nobody really understands, not everything, and that nobody is worthy—at least, no more worthy than anybody else. That there are cranky people everywhere, including in churches, and you're going to meet some of them, and you mustn't let them get under your skin.

And things don't always go well. Nehemiah leaves town for a few months and returns to find that all hell has broken loose: they've rented out the sacristy to somebody's cousin, and broken their Sabbath observance so thoroughly they don't even remember that there is one.

But they come back. You can always come back. You can always start again. Someone like Nehemiah arises and leads you back. Maybe Nehemiah arises within your own spirit and makes you long to be faithful.

THURSDAY IN PROPER 26

Pss (70), 71 * 74
Ezra 7:(1–10) 11–26
Revelation 14:1–13
Matthew 14:1–12

"Blessed are the dead . . ." says the Spirit,
"they will rest from their labors . . ."
REVELATION 14:13

I say this line a lot: every priest does. It's one of the anthems we say as we walk into the church behind the casket of someone who has been brought there for the burial office. Solemn, that walk—unaccompanied by music, often, just the lone human voice speaking the ancient words, a collection of biblical sayings about rest and welcome into the life that lies beyond this life. It is sad, because it is so different from most processions into church, which are accompanied by music. But its very solemnity is oddly comforting: it is ancient, this sadness. Everybody dies. We are doing something that has been done many, many times before, something that will be done for us someday.

Sometimes the procession is different. Sometimes it's the congregation singing a hymn, instead, one selected by the deceased, perhaps, when he was still alive. The music brings him closer to us, and in that very closeness we feel, abruptly, the pain of the new separation. He is not here, not enjoying the music he picked out. He would have loved this, we say bravely to each other. He has the best seat in the house, we say. But we wish, now, that he didn't leave the best seat, that he was sitting beside us, that we could see him, that it was like it was before.

The service carries us through our sadness. It doesn't try to sugar-coat it or distract us from it. But it is firm about the main message: the life we have lost from among us was not the only life belonging to the one who has died. She has a new life. It's a life we will also have. It is our bodies that are separated—our spirits remain joined in love, as they have always been. This is indeed a good-bye, a wrenching one. But it is not final.

The more friends and family you have on the other side, the more you come to believe this. That's because we want to, of course. But it's also because the long days of bereavement teach us things we didn't know before, things we couldn't have known. The communion of saints is real throughout our lives. We just don't notice it until we need to.

FRIDAY IN PROPER 26

Pss 69:1–23 (24–30) 31–38 * 73
Ezra 7:27–28; 8:21–36
Revelation 15:1–8
Matthew 14:13–21

Now when Jesus heard this [John's death], he withdrew
from there in a boat to a deserted place by himself.
MATTHEW 14:13

What are you doing? my daughter asks in the afternoon. I am recovering from yet another angioplasty, and she calls frequently to check up on my behavior.

Well, I'm listening to Jonathan Schwartz and writing some essays.

Writing isn't resting, she says.

Well, listening to Jonathan Schwartz is.

You're supposed to be taking a nap.

I know I've had this conversation before. Oh, yes, I remember now: it was with her, when she was four. Only we seem to have switched roles.

I'm supposed to be learning how to manage my stress and take care of myself, and I am trying. I'm supposed to take a deep breath, all the way from down in my abdomen, every time I see one of the cats. We have four of them at the moment, so I'm a little afraid of hyperventilating, but What's-Her-Name doesn't hang around much, so I guess I'll be all right. I'm supposed to rest.

Jesus' work was more important than any of my work, and he found time to rest. He seems to have made a special point of it: he got tired of the press of the crowd around him, tired after his preaching, just like me. So I shouldn't feel guilty about taking some time for myself, I guess. None of us should.

Time to think. Time to be sad, if that's what we need: Jesus had just lost one of his best friends, and right then he needed to be alone, not to try to prove to anyone how strong he was by soldiering on. Time to weigh things we don't have time to think about during the busy days. Time, maybe, just to sleep, or listen to music. Or maybe just time to breathe.

SATURDAY IN PROPER 26

Pss 75, 76 * 23, 27
Ezra 9:1–15
Revelation 17:1–14
Matthew 14:22–36

. . . they sent word throughout the region and brought all who were sick to him, and begged him that they might touch even the fringe of his cloak; and all who touched it were healed.

MATTHEW 14:35–36

I have seen a cloth-of-gold ball gown worn by Catherine the Great. I have seen the boots of her forebear, Peter the Great; he was an enormous man, and you could bathe a baby in one of those immense boots. I have seen Franklin Delano Roosevelt's inauguration suit, cape, and top hat, Teddy Roosevelt's monocle, and several of Jane Austen's dresses. I have seen a pair of Charlotte Bronte's tiny white kid gloves. I used to own a set of bongo drums that had once belonged to Bobby Vinton.

These objects, worn by—or at least touched by—famous people of the past, seem to retain something of them in their fabric. Those aren't just any bongo drums: Bobby Vinton played them and sang, and thousands of people applauded, and it was wonderful. Catherine the Great danced the night away in that dress, and then—if what we are told about her proclivities is correct—probably disappeared into her boudoir with somebody who probably had no business seeing what was underneath it.

Pieces of the saints' bodies, fragments of the true cross, the Shroud of Turin: we know that God is spirit, and yet somehow we cannot bring ourselves to regard these objects once used by holy people with neutrality. *He touched them. This was part of her. Perhaps it will heal me.*

We live in our bodies, while we are here. They are not just objects. When we die, someone will treat them tenderly, preparing them for burial or cremation. The things we owned, too, will be special to someone just because they were ours. Foolish? Maybe. Any healing power they have is power with which we invest them. But healing is a strange thing, and we do not control it. To come close to the love of God as it was lived on earth long ago is a potent spiritual experience. Who is to say how potent?

SUNDAY, PROPER 27

Pss 93, 96 * 34
Ezra 10:1–17
Acts 24:10–21
Luke 14:12–24

But this I admit to you, that according to the Way, which they call a sect, I worship the God of our ancestors, believing everything laid down according to the law or written in the prophets. I have a hope in God—a hope that they themselves also accept—that there will be a resurrection of both the righteous and the unrighteous.

ACTS 24:14–15

So being a Christian was, for Paul, another way of being a Jew. At least at first. They called it that—"The Way." A path to follow.

Certainly, you can live without a rule of life. You can just let it happen to you: fall into and out of things and people as they happen along. You needn't have a goal at all. You need never ask yourself where things come from or if they have any meaning beyond their appearance. Until somebody stops you, I suppose you can live without any formal ethical posture at all: just do what you want to do when you want to do it.

Initially this would be an easy life, with a certain charm. I would have a hard time with the lack of meaning after a while, though: there would be nothing in my life bigger than I was. It would be like being a large baby. I would be, entirely, a creature of the moment.

It was important to Paul that his examiners know that he and his followers were rooted in something. That they came from somewhere and had a structure recognizable to the community in which Paul had been raised. Something they could describe to others. How do you live your life? What do you believe? He wanted to be able to answer that question in terms people would understand.

And you? What do you do? What do you think? What puzzles you? For what would you give your life, if it ever came to that? And, short of giving your life for it, how do you show forth your devotion to that prize?

MONDAY IN PROPER 27

Pss 80 * 77, (79)
Nehemiah 9:1–15 (16–25)
Revelation 18:1–8
Matthew 15:1–20

Then the disciples approached and said to him, "Do you know that the Pharisees took offense when they heard what you said?"
MATTHEW 15:12

I can imagine that this rather frightened some of the disciples. The Pharisees were the legal sticklers of ancient Israel, the most observant of the observant. They knew the law and they knew when it was being infringed, however slightly, and they didn't mind saying so. It's painful and a little frightening to know that you're coloring outside the lines when everyone else isn't.

Because Jesus was definitely coloring outside the lines. That the law was for the benefit of people, should be tempered with common sense and compassion—not everyone thought that. That God could and did reveal further aspects of the divine personality and the divine truth than were revealed in the Hebrews scriptures— very few people thought that. The intimacy of Jesus' relationship with God was scandalous: who did he think he was, anyway?

They must have been torn, those first followers of Christ. To go against the order from which you have come is a special kind of risk to take. It is a leaving of home, a rejection of your upbringing, even if you're at great pains to show that it is not a rejection at all, that you have nothing but respect for your old world. The fact is, you didn't stay. You're doing something different from what your family did. The fact is, the old order didn't meet your needs and you could not find your moral self in it any more. You had to leave it behind. As necessary as it may be, we can never do this without discomfort.

So the presence of personal discomfort is not, by itself, a sign that you are on the wrong course. It is a sign that you have ventured beyond the boundaries of the world you used to live in. All growth carries us into a new world, at least a little distance—or maybe miles and miles.

TUESDAY IN PROPER 27

Pss 78:1–39 * 78:40–72
Nehemiah 9:26–38
Revelation 18:9–20
Matthew 15:21–28

And all shipmasters and seafarers, sailors and all whose trade is on the sea, stood far off and cried out as they saw the smoke of her burning, "What city was like the great city?"
REVELATION 18:17–18

Approaching the New York harbor after the attack on the World Trade Center was terrible: the cloud of smoke and debris hung in the air for what seemed like forever, obscuring the sight of everything in Lower Manhattan: a weird grayish winter in the early fall. People who couldn't come any closer than 14th Street hung on the police barricades and peered into the low clouds of smoke, willing themselves to see something, anything.

Later, they stood behind the same barricades when they could get close: across Broadway, gazing down Fulton Street beside St. Paul's at the charred walls, still leaning crazily on each other, at the posters still hanging improbably on the wall of what was left of the Borders store at Seven World Trade. They stood there, some of them weeping: secretaries who had worked in the buildings, people who came down from uptown to see, people from out of town. Some people refused to come down there. They just couldn't bear to see it. Some people still haven't.

The sky is clear now. The site is cleaned up, and the new Path station is operating. Ground has been broken for the new Freedom Tower. But approach it from the sea—or from the air—and the sight is still terrible: you don't know where you are. You can't orient yourself. Your eyes sweep the skyline for something upon which to fasten until they came to the Empire State Building, and that's forty blocks uptown. Come up out of a subway station below the Village and you are similarly disoriented. *Now, where am I?* you ask yourself, missing the twin towers that told you which direction was downtown. You figure it out from looking at the nearest Avenue sign, but a faint feeling of remembered fear in the pit of your stomach lingers.

It won't be the same, of course. Nothing ever is. There was nothing like it.

WEDNESDAY IN PROPER 27

Pss 119:97–120 * 81, 82
Nehemiah 7:73b–8:3, 5–18
Revelation 18:21–24
Matthew 15:29–39

*"Go your way, eat the fat and drink sweet wine and send
portions of them to those for whom nothing is prepared,
for this day is holy to our Lord; and do not be grieved,
for the joy of the Lord is your strength."*

NEHEMIAH 8:10

The first day of the rest of your life is a holy day. Even if every day up until that day has been a mistake. To make a new beginning after years, or even a lifetime, of wrong is cause for rejoicing.

Notice that the people are invited to rejoice and celebrate before they have proved that they can live according to the law! They haven't demonstrated it yet. They're celebrating before they begin.

I don't deserve to treat myself well until I've lost some weight, the young woman tells me. She is beautiful, not as heavy as she thinks she is, funny and kind to everyone. *I'll get some new things when I've lost a lot. I don't deserve it now.* Her weight loss never succeeds, though: her harsh attitude toward herself is self-defeating. Her withholding of love from herself wilts her soul, and it faints under the burden of her self-disapproval.

Why don't you try doing it differently this time? I ask her. *Give yourself some treats: maybe a magazine you've been wanting to read, or a nice bath, or call a friend you've been wanting to talk to and have a good chat. Something nice.*

She shakes her head. *I need to be firm with myself until I've seen some results.*

Firm, huh? No. Begin to live the life of joy to which God calls you the minute God calls you to it. The call is the beginning. Celebrate it!

THURSDAY IN PROPER 27

Pss (83) or 23, 27 * 85, 86
1 Maccabees 1:1–28
Revelation 19:1–10
Matthew 16:1–12

So they built a gymnasium in Jerusalem, according
to Gentile custom, and removed the marks of
circumcision, and abandoned the holy covenant.

1 MACCABEES 1:14–15

We are distant, now, from the outrage of this act. Well, why not a gym? we think. It's good to be active in sports.

But a gymnasium in the Hellenistic world was an impossible place for a Jew to be. To begin with, games were played in the nude. In order to fit in with their Gentile friends, young Jewish men who began to frequent the new gym took steps to remove the marks of their circumcision: I do not know how they went about this, and don't believe I want to know. Nor do I want to know what the reaction was at home. We forget just how earthy a heritage we have.

And the pantheon of Greek gods was involved in the gymnasium. Games were dedicated to them. You sacrificed to them at the games. The atmosphere may not have been very reverent, but the gods were there. From a Jewish point of view, there was not a good thing about the gym except for an improvement in cardiovascular health, and nobody knew about that in those days.

Everything in the story of the Maccabees is about membership in the tribe. Fidelity to the tribe's tradition. The worst thing any Jew could think of was being alone, outside the community of fidelity to God according to the tradition they knew. Separateness was the highest value for behavior they knew. It protected them from contamination.

Is that the way we are? Do we think that the most important thing about us is who we are not? How separate should we be?

Should we be frightened of the world and avoid it at all costs? Or should we plunge into it and lose our identity entirely? This is thin ice indeed, and religious people walk on it every day.

The Jews of the first century were afraid of some things they needn't have feared. We embrace some things we'd be better off leaving alone.

FRIDAY IN PROPER 27

Pss 88 * 91, 92
1 Maccabees 1:41–63
Revelation 19:11–16
Matthew 16:13–20

"Who do people say that the Son of Man is?"
MATTHEW 16:13

It is as if Jesus is asking two questions, not two versions of the same one. This "Son of Man"—who is he? So then, who do you think *I* am? Do you consider me a magical figure who will sweep the whole earth into its cataclysmic end? Is that what my words and my miracles have meant to you?

Not that such a conclusion is unreasonable. Jesus is clearly not an ordinary person. But flesh and blood doesn't reveal him: he doesn't qualify as the Christ because of the number of his miracles, or even because they are more spectacular than anyone else's. Maybe the miracles aren't really as much about this world as they are about the next. Maybe it's not about the end of this world that we should be concerned. Maybe Jesus is here to show us the kingdom of God.

Sometimes there's an article in the news about an asteroid heading straight for our planet, like in the movies. About the odds that one will slam into us and blow us all to smithereens. People in Jesus' time saw the coming of the kingdom of God a little like that: sudden and destructive of everything but a chosen few.

Maybe it is like an asteroid, but a divine one: maybe it has struck us already, maybe we're already in it and don't know it. Maybe we sparkle with asteroid dust and can't even see it. Maybe we didn't recognize who Jesus was because he was quieter than we expected our Messiah to be. Didn't know what hit us, as they say.

The kingdom of God is within you, Jesus has said. In some sense it *already is*, even though we look around our sorry world and don't see much that resembles it. The Jesus who asked his friends to name him was not transformed in any way. He didn't glow, the way he would on the Mount of Transfiguration—that came later. He looked just like he always looked. And he didn't do something new and different: he was consistent with what he had been before.

So it must have been they who changed. It must have been their perception that found the truth about him, after months and years of being together on the road and not understanding who he was.

And as for what it would mean, to be who he was—they still weren't ready for that.

SATURDAY IN PROPER 27

Pss 87, 90 * 136
1 Maccabees 2:1–28
Revelation 20:1–6
Matthew 16:21–28

When Mattathias saw it, he burned with zeal and his heart was stirred. He gave vent to righteous anger; he ran and killed him on the altar.

1 MACCABEES 2:24

A familiar ring to this beginning of the book of Maccabees: a leader is born out of an act of violence. Like Moses, who slew an Egyptian overseer, Mattathias cannot go back. He has sealed his future in blood.

And he seals his sons' futures, also. Blood never stops demanding more blood, apparently. We are so many centuries distant from this ancient act of religious zeal that we do not recognize it, at first, for what it is: if Mattathias were to do today what he did on that day so long ago, we would call him a terrorist.

What are we to think of old tales like this in our sacred texts? Generations have been inspired by them. Murders and suicides, combinations of both, in the name of God. In the distant past, they are compelling. But they have refused to remain in the distant past.

There are many ways to be inspired by scripture. I read of a healing and want to be a conduit of healing to others. I read of a murder and think that it's a terrible waste, an ancient example of an evil that continues among us to this day. That the ancient chroniclers of these deeds admire them doesn't mean that I must admire them.

The writers of scripture were doing what we still do: recording their stories and struggling to make sense of them. That they left us the accounts of their struggles is a great gift, more than worth the trouble we must take to enter into a dialogue with them, one respectful, in equal measure, of them and of ourselves.

SUNDAY, PROPER 28

Pss 66, 67 *19, 46
1 Maccabees 2:29–43, 49–50
Acts 28:14b–23
Luke 16:1–13

"But we would like to hear from you what you think, for with regard to this sect we know that everywhere it is spoken against."
ACTS 28:22

It was a sect of Judaism, at first—and not a popular one. Orthodoxy resists change, whether in an AA meeting or an academic classroom or in a political party or in the Church. Those in charge got where they were under a certain set of beliefs, and it's hard for them to imagine that what has worked so well for them might not be true for everyone, in all places at all times. If something else might be right, then I might be wrong: it can't possibly be that two different things can be true. Truth is one thing, not two.

Well, probably not. God is more complex than human beings, not less so. History reveals and reveals itself, like the peeling away of the thin layers of an onion. The picture of reality that each human being has is a little different, colored and formed by what has happened to him or her through life. We don't all see the same thing, even if we're all looking at the same thing. We need to allow for that, or we'll be at each other's throats all the time.

It can't be true that the faith needed to grow and change in Paul's time but doesn't need to grow and change now. That first-century Judaism needed to adjust to new things, but we don't. God is alive and moving in history, and we are all alive, too, making the world a pretty busy place.

People try to avoid dealing with the world's changes—try to live in golden ages they imagine to have existed in the past, try to be people from other eras. We can't do that. History moves forward and we move forward with it, making some hard decisions as we go, and we are never absolutely sure of our rightness as we go along. Because faith isn't a way out of the world; it's a way to live a holy life within it.

MONDAY IN PROPER 28

Pss 89:1–18 * 89:19–52
1 Maccabees 3:1–24
Revelation 20:7–15
Matthew 17:1–13

". . . but I tell you that Elijah has already come, and they did not recognize him, but they did to him whatever they pleased."
MATTHEW 17:12

He means John the Baptist: Jesus is referring to the Jewish belief that the prophet Elijah will return just before the messiah comes. The folk belief persists to this day: at the family's Passover Seder, a cup of wine is set out for Elijah, and somehow—to the amazement of the younger children in the family—he always finishes it by the end of the meal.

Was Jesus really so explicit about who he was, or is this just the enthusiasm of the gospel writer, putting something in Jesus' mouth that he thought Jesus ought to have said? We can't know. And I'm not sure it matters much: do we need to think that Jesus had it all worked out in his mind beforehand, in order for him to have been the long-awaited Son of God? And to be our own blessed Savior?

We can have opinions about the things that happened or didn't happen in Jesus' life, but we do not have *knowledge*: we weren't there. And we don't need knowledge about those things, although we learn a great deal from reading the stories about him, written by people who probably were also not there, but wanted very much for others to know what they knew. What we need is to be in relationship with Jesus now, with the Jesus we have received from scripture and tradition and the one we discover in prayer and meditation. We need to ponder how it is that they are the same person, and how it is that we continue to live in his living presence. If it doesn't feel living to us, we need to pray for our own awakening, and be open-minded about the possibility of one, and we need especially not to insist on understanding everything about him before we will enter into a relationship with him. We don't know everything there is to know about the person we marry: there are many unknowns between the bride and groom. They embark together on a journey of discovery and mystery.

So it is between Christ and us.

TUESDAY IN PROPER 28

Pss 97, 99, (100) *94, (95)
1 Maccabees 3:25–41
Revelation 21:1–8
Matthew 17:14–21

"See, I am making all things new."
REVELATION 21:5

In all the elaborate and strange goings-on that puzzle us so in the Revelation to John—all the battles and beasts, the evil painted women, the fierce angels, all the warfare and conflict—this from the one who sits upon the throne is comforting: all this strife has an end. It's not going to be endless fighting against endless streams of evil. We can begin again. The slate can be wiped clean, all the scars of our suffering and error.

These ancient verses are about the end of the world, with a hefty dose of first-century politics—politics we no longer remember—thrown in. But, in between the politics and the many-eyed beasts, they are also words of hope for us: the decades of life that have stretched from the beginning of your life until now need not sum you up, no matter how spattered with the mud of compromise and failure they may be. No matter who you are and what you've done, there is room for you, and healing. God can wipe it all clean, and there is nobody for whom that is not true. It is never too late for you to surrender and be changed.

We love stories about people being changed, starting out mean and ending up full of love: Scrooge, the Grinch, Heidi's grumpy old Grandfather. They give us hope for ourselves: maybe I, too, can still become who I long to be. Maybe there's still time.

There *is* time: there's right now. That burden you have carried for years? You can just set it down. This very day.

WEDNESDAY IN PROPER 28

Pss 101, 109:1–4 (5–19) 20–30 * 119:121–144
1 Maccabees 3:42–60
Revelation 21:9–21
Matthew 17:22–27

*". . . go to the lake and cast a hook; take the first fish that
comes up; and when you open its mouth, you will find
a coin; take that and give it to them for you and me."*
MATTHEW 17:27

I don't know about this one, John says. *A fish with a coin in its mouth? It's like a magic trick. Isn't that a little crass?*

And it is. One of those stories of Jesus that arises from someone in the community a little less sophisticated than, say, the writer of the gospel according to John, whose hymn about the Word is so stately and so mysterious. Some of the gospels that didn't make the cut were full of things like this, weird stories long on sensation and short on edification. Someone must have found them compelling, but not enough people did: they remained on the cutting room floor of the early Church, and we no longer read them.

This variety is not so much about Jesus as it is about us. We bring who we are to the reading of these texts, as they brought who they were to the writing of them, and who we are varies widely. A test: think about the Jesus story you liked most when you were a child, and the one you find most moving now. Are they the same one?

Does the same thing attract you now that drew you when you were ten? Probably not. We don't just vary from person to person in the things we bring to faith. We vary from ourselves to ourselves, over the course of a lifetime.

And that's why we have more than one gospel and more than one story. It's why the stories we have of Jesus don't quite fit together, some of them, and why there seem to be some pieces missing. There *are* pieces missing. What we have is the record of people making sense of the story, each in his or her own way. And writing it down. And leaving it for us to find. So we can make sense of the story.

THURSDAY IN PROPER 28

Pss 105:1–22 * 105:23–45
1 Maccabees 4:1–25
Revelation 21:22–22:5
Matthew 18:1–9

*I saw no temple in the city, for its temple is
the Lord God the Almighty and the lamb.*
REVELATION 21:22

No temple. There was a time, not so long before these words were written, when such a thing would have spelled incomprehensible tragedy. Unthinkable. No temple meant no daily sacrifices, no sacrifices for the birth of a child, no guilt offerings to make things right again. No way to reach God. You could only offer sacrifice in the temple. If the temple was gone—then what? How?

Of course, the temple *was* gone by the time John was writing. He didn't have to imagine a world without a temple: he lived there. It wasn't coming back, either, not any time soon. Two thousand years later, it still hasn't come back. Its remaining wall is the Wailing Wall in Jerusalem; people go there to pray, and stick their prayers on rolled-up pieces of paper in between the stones. That's all that's left.

No need for a temple in the kingdom of God, of course. You don't have to reach God there. You're already *in Christ*, as Paul says, as close to the divine self as you are to your own self. Closer.

The earliest Christians were Jews, too. People who grew up with the temple. People who stood in disbelief as it was destroyed, who couldn't believe their ears when they heard. Quickly, they had to find a way to explain to themselves what had happened. Quickly, they had to find a way to be faithful and *portable* at the same time. They had lost their special place to go: this was a tragedy. But now, they began to see, they could go anywhere and still be who they were. And that turned out to be a great strength: none of the other Near Eastern religions of the day have survived—only the Jews.

Like a modern Jew, a Christian is not tied to any city. To any building. A church doesn't need a building at all: all it needs is people and a Bible and some bread and wine. In the end, there will be no need for a structure that brings us closer to One in whom we will be completely alive. The church is like the scaffolding of a building: necessary before the building is complete, but you tear it down once the building is finished and can stand on its own.

FRIDAY IN PROPER 28

Pss 102 * 107:1–32
1 Maccabees 4:36–59
Revelation 22:6–13
Matthew 18:10–20

"Take care that you do not despise one of these little ones..."
MATTHEW 18:10

Kids always take it on the chin, my friend says. We are talking about an especially ugly divorce, in which the father lavishes money and presents on the children of his new wife and fights his old one about child support. He doesn't visit. His little boy has begun talking about wanting to die.

It's true: kids take it on the chin. They didn't cause the divorce, didn't want it, and yet it is their childhood that is disrupted by it. They don't have a father they can trust: this will have enormous implications for their own choices of friends, of mates. For their image of who God is.

The way we treat the weakest among us reveals who we really are. We kowtow to the strong, hoping they will reward us with some favor, hoping they at least won't step on us. We respond to strength of force out of self-interest. But it is compassion that makes us respond to weakness. We gain nothing material from being fair and kind to the weak, and so that is where our ethical obligation lies.

God has implanted this moral knowledge in us: the father's behavior is very unusual in a parent, so much so that we're all shocked by it. He's not acting like a dad acts, and everybody can see it. It's not normal. God made it normal for us to replace our customary power arrangements with love where our children are concerned, and we almost always do that. Because it is the way God has made us.

That dad didn't take care of his own kids. We are programmed to do that and called to do much more: called to be sure everyone can care for his or her children, called to make the world safe, called to make it as nourishing a place as it can be. For Jesus, this was no oh-by-the-way detail. It was central. *Care for the weak. The strong can take care of themselves.*

SATURDAY IN PROPER 28

Pss 107:33–43, 108:1–6 (7–13) * 33
Isaiah 65:17–25
Revelation 22:14–21
Matthew 18:21–35

*"Lord, if another member of the church sins against me,
how often should I forgive? As many as seven times?"*
MATTHEW 18:21

Our hearts sink when we read the answer to this. *I do not say to you seven times, but seventy times seven.*

We don't do this. We have a hard time forgiving once, let alone 490 times.

But here are some quick thoughts that might help us think of forgiveness in a new way. I present them in the context of ideas you may always have had about what forgiveness is.

You may always have thought that we should forgive and forget. But forgiving is not at all the same thing as forgetting. History has happened. It cannot be undone.

You may always have thought that there are some people who are too guilty to be forgiven. But forgiveness is only *for* the guilty. The innocent have no need of forgiveness. As hard as it may be for us to accept, the possibility of forgiveness is not related to the seriousness of the crime. As a matter of fact, forgiveness isn't nearly as much about the perpetrator as it is about you.

You may always have thought that forgiveness means restoration to the way things were. Things are never the way they were. Restoration of presence, in particular, may not be possible in some situations; in some situations, such as many instances of domestic abuse, it's not even safe. In some situations, the possibility of forgiveness actually depends on a safe distance.

You may always have thought that forgiveness means there will be no punishment for a crime. But actions have consequences.

That someone is forgiven does not mean he will not have to pay for his crime.

You may always have thought the forgiveness is a quality you must somehow come up with, in order to be pleasing to God. This may have distressed you more than any of the above: how on earth am I going to forgive, when I am so angry I can't stand even to think of my adversary? But forgiveness is not ours to create. It is a gift from God. Can't bring yourself to forgive? Of course you can't. It's too hard. Maybe it's time to ask God for the forgiving spirit you cannot muster on your own.

SUNDAY, PROPER 29

Pss 118 * 145
Isaiah 19:19–25
Romans 15:5–13
Luke 19:11–27

On that day Israel will be the third with Egypt and Assyria . . .
ISAIAH 19:24

An astonishing ancient vision of something we have yet to see— unity in the Middle East. Even then, it was the stuff of dreams and prophecy.

Then, unity could only be imagined in the form of religious uniformity. They would all be in harmony, Isaiah thought, because they would all be worshipping our God. That will not be the case in modern times. Can there be peace if we allow the differences between faith and cultures that now exist? Or must we always retreat into ghettos of people who are like us in order to have peace?

And who says that worshipping the same God brings about unity? Episcopalians worship the same God, and we argue all the time. The Jews have a saying: two Jews, three opinions. The history of religious faith is the history of faction. Maybe it could be otherwise, but the truth is that it never has been.

Often, of course, the fighting is only tangentially about religion. Faith seems to be the lightning rod that attracts the energy of a conflict that was already afoot. Who would maintain that the terrible decades of fighting in Northern Ireland were really theological battles about Catholicism and Protestantism? They were about turf and power, colonialism, economic oppression, much more than they were about faith. Religion provides a means of naming, a claim of dignity, the baptism of a position within the conflict. Religion can carry the perverse human delight in excluding people, ascribing the same delight to God.

Maybe religion can do all that. But I'm not sure *faith* can.

A person of faith is connected to God. A person of faith reaches beyond the narrow boundaries of his own vision or upbringing to touch something much more universal.

A person of faith is secure in her faith. She doesn't need to browbeat others with it.

MONDAY IN PROPER 29

Pss 106:1–18 * 106:19–48
Joel 3:1–2, 9–17
1 Peter 1:1–12
Matthew 19:1–12

"So they are no longer two, but one flesh."
MATTHEW 19:6

I'll meet you at 5 o'clock, I tell the bride. *It'll take about five minutes.* Here is what happened: the wedding was about a month ago. Maybe six weeks. It was lovely: the couple knows lots of artists and actors, and all kinds of creative things happened in the ceremony. One thing didn't happen though: nobody remembered to bring the marriage license.

That's okay, I said. *Call me when you get back and we'll sign the papers.* But I guess they got busy. And so now they've gotten a new license, since the old one expired. So I will hear their vows again in St. Clement's chapel. No harm done, unless somebody small got his or her start on the honeymoon, somebody to whom they'll have to offer an explanation in twenty years or so. Even if that did happen, though, I'm sure he or she will understand. Everybody knows that first babies can arrive at any time.

I'm an agent for the state when I do a wedding. The state never wants to know who I've baptized or buried. But I send a signed statement that I officiated and two other people witnessed the exchange of marriage vows back to the registrar of vital statistics. So nobody can say they're not married.

But the fact is, nobody could say they weren't married even if I didn't send the paper. They could prove they were married in a court of law: they could bring in two people who attended the ceremony and could say what they saw. All that's required for people to be married is two other people who can testify that they saw the exchange of vows. The license is evidentiary shorthand for that testimony. You don't have to search for two old friends who were there, if you ever want to prove it really happened. You can just produce your license.

So I don't really marry people. They marry themselves. Their friends watch and witness. I send in the papers. All the rest—the counseling, the readings, the music—is church stuff and personal stuff, not legal stuff. And for us, these things are the most important things. The state couldn't care less about them.

But we do. That's why they forgot the license: the wedding was so authoritative, it didn't seem to need further authentication.

TUESDAY IN PROPER 29

Pss (120), 121, 122, 123 * 124, 125, 126, (127)
Nahum 1:1–13
1 Peter 1:13–25
Matthew 19:13–22

"Let the little children come to me, and do not stop them;
for it is to such as these that the kingdom of heaven belongs."
MATTHEW 19:14

I light scented candles and spray the bed curtains with lavender water. I turn on the radio and turn down the bed. Rosie comes in from her shower with her head wrapped in a towel, unaware of how exquisite she is. She is wearing a housecoat of mine as a nightgown. I tuck the covers in around her and stroke her back a little.

It is so nice have them spend the night. To have young people in the house again. To spoil them. We spent the early part of the evening exclaiming over cookbooks: Thanksgiving is coming.

Let's make this pumpkin flan, I told her, *and not make a normal pumpkin pie at all.*

Okay, she said, and put a bookmark beside the pumpkin flan recipe. The pictures of gorgeous desserts jockeyed for position, and we settled on four of them. There should be many dessert choices at Thanksgiving dinner, I have always felt.

I pat her shoulder one more time and leave the room; Rosie is already half asleep. I will leave in the morning before she awakens. I must be at a church in another state by nine. No leisurely breakfast waffles prepared by Q: instead, an adolescent sleep into the late morning, and her mother will come for her to take her home.

As busy as I am, I hope the memory of baking together, of spending the night here, the feel of the sheets and the smell of lavender will last as long in Rosie's mind as my own memories of my grandma have lasted in mine. My grandmother was busy, too, but my experience of her was that she was all mine, always available, always eager to be with me. Was that true?

She was able to make me feel that it was.

WEDNESDAY IN PROPER 29

Pss 119:145–176 * 128, 129, 130
Obadiah 15–21
1 Peter 2:1–10
Matthew 19:23–30

Once you were not a people, but now you are God's people; once you had not received mercy, but now you have received mercy.
1 PETER 2:10

"Not my people" and "Not receive mercy" are not just expressions: they are code words. Any Jew reading this letter would have recognized them right away: the prophet Hosea named his two children "Not My People" and "Not Receive Mercy." He did this as signs of Israel's impending doom. Let's hope the kids had cute nicknames.

The judgment of God is stern: law is law, and good is good, and there's a difference between good and bad. By and large, we haven't done very well in following it. We make more messes than we straighten out. Scripture tells us the same thing the headlines tell us, the same thing we hear on the evening news: we need some serious help. We have lost whatever worthiness we came in with, and can't seem to summon more with which to approach our God and each other. From age to age, we just keep repeating our mistakes.

It's over, this letter says. Our estrangement from God is over now, ended by Christ's saving life and death and rising. Where we were powerless to change, we are now empowered for goodness and love. We may still choose not to live in that power—people do. But it is available to each of us. Community is possible. Love can reign. Things do not have to be as they are, not if we don't want them to be.

THURSDAY IN PROPER 29

Pss 131, 132, (133) * 134, 135
Zephaniah 3:1–13
1 Peter 2:11–25
Matthew 20:1–16

It has listened to no voice; it has accepted no correction.
ZEPHANIAH 3:2

Israel seems to be acting like a teenager. The same thing that animates a two-year-old resurfaces at about fifteen: we need to learn how to be independent, and we need to do it in a hurry, before we are turned loose on the world. Usually, we do not do it gracefully: Don't talk to me! Leave me alone! I don't have to!

They manage to ignore their manifest dependence on you for everything in life: you shelter, clothe, feed, and educate them—they hate that. They want to be independent, and half the time they imagine that they really are. Then something brings them back down to earth. How humiliating. They're not on their own, not at all. They're still kids.

Sometimes it looks to you as if they're just not going to make it, and you despair of them. They're going to be thirty years old and still slamming doors and stomping out of rooms. I suppose some of them will. But almost all of them become loving, responsible adults eventually, pretty much what you hoped they would be, even if they swore they couldn't care less about what you thought was important.

They can't stand you, but they need you. They hate you, but they also love you: they wouldn't hate you so much if they didn't. You are the one they run to when they're hurt, and then they turn around and tell you they just can't talk to you.

We are like them with our God, refusing to acknowledge our dependence, rebelling at our weakness, denying it. They grow out of it. We will, too: if not on this side of glory, on the other.

FRIDAY IN PROPER 29

Pss 140, 142 * 141, 143:1–11 (12)
Isaiah 24:14–23
1 Peter 3:13–4:6
Matthew 20:17–28

*Then the mother of the sons of Zebedee came to him with her
sons, and kneeling before him, she asked a favor of him.*
MATTHEW 20:20

Mostly, it doesn't work if you ask for a request to be granted without first saying what it is. It didn't work this time, either; Jesus wanted to know what the mother wanted. And what she wanted was predictable: good jobs for her two sons.

We shouldn't interfere in our adult children's lives. We don't really know what's going on in them, even if we think we do. Becoming a higher-up in the Jesus organization would mean that, according to most measures, you'd be heading downward in the world's idea of success, not upward: toward a life of trial and hardship, ending in a death like the one Jesus would shortly face. Probably not what Mom had in mind.

A fair number of people hope that being a Christian will have a direct effect on their prosperity. It makes some sense, at first: I'm in touch with God, and I follow Jesus, and I live the best life I know how to live. Why shouldn't I expect all these good things I do to get me some of the good things in life? It's certain that bad behavior bears bad fruit, so what's wrong with expecting a little success?

Nothing wrong with it. It's just that the life of faith doesn't guarantee it. We don't believe in Christ in order to win the lottery: the lottery is a game of chance, and remains one after our conversion. The life of faith isn't an end run around the sorrows and dangers of the world. Many things this side of heaven are beyond our control, and we do not choose them. Becoming a Christian won't change that.

But it changes us. Re-orients our values, so that the world's categories of success are not nearly as important to us as they once were. We have our eyes on things that will last, and nothing here will last. We want the same worldly things everyone else wants, but we are not completely invested in having them. They come and they go. God alone remains forever.

SATURDAY IN PROPER 29

Pss 137:1–6 (7–9), 144 * 104
Micah 7:11–20
1 Peter 4:7–19
Matthew 20:29–34

But let none of you suffer as a murderer, or a thief,
a criminal, or even as a mischief-maker. Yet if any of you
suffers as a Christian, do not consider it a disgrace,
but glorify God because you bear his name.
1 PETER 4:15–16

Right inconveniences wrong all the time, and the evil has plenty of representation here on the earth. You can get yourself killed doing the right thing.

The writer of 1 Peter knows this, of course. He is writing to comfort people who are surprised and alarmed at their persecution as Christians. I guess what they're really asking is, "Is it worth it, if what happens is that you die like a common criminal anyhow?"

Thousands of people in the early Church and even more in our own day have been able to answer yes to that question. We imagine that the early Christians sought out martyrdom as a badge of honor, like modern-day suicide bombers. They didn't; they hid from authorities, and tried to escape, as any sane person would. But when escape was impossible, they stood for who they were in Christ and died for it.

I suppose their friends and families wished they hadn't, with all their hearts. Perhaps they begged them not to. We probably would have. It is against the backdrop of this pain that the writer seeks to comfort those who have had to watch someone dear die a terrible death: he reminds us of the meaning of what is happening to this little community, of what happened to Jesus of Nazareth, of what awaits us all in another place. That life must still go on, that moral decisions must still be made, that the world cannot stop, even though such terrible things are happening.

The veneer of civilization is thinner than we imagine: it cracks quickly in time of war and turmoil. It's every man for himself. Just because your world is ending, he says, is no reason to throw everything overboard. We still must live together, and we still must live in such a way that the world will see us and want to live as we live.

And enough found the courage to live that way that we, their spiritual heirs, are still here.